CHANGE YOUR AURA,
CHANGE YOUR LIFE

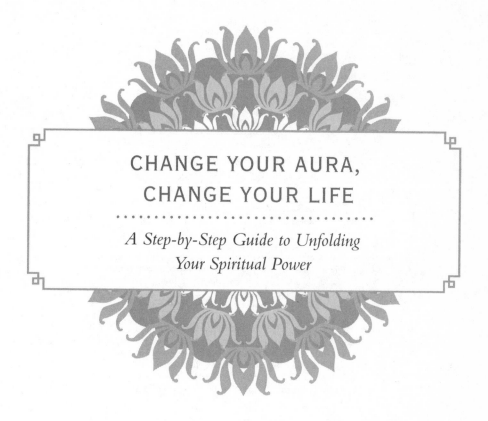

CHANGE YOUR AURA, CHANGE YOUR LIFE

A Step-by-Step Guide to Unfolding
Your Spiritual Power

BARBARA Y. MARTIN AND DIMITRI MORAITIS

A TarcherPerigee Book

tarcherperigee

An imprint of Penguin Random House LLC
375 Hudson Street
New York, New York 10014

First published by Spiritual Arts Institute 2003
This revised edition published by TarcherPerigee 2016

Most TarcherPerigee books are available at special quantity discounts for bulk purchase
for sales promotions, premiums, fund-raising, and educational needs. Special books or
book excerpts also can be created to fit specific needs. For details, write:
SpecialMarkets@penguinrandomhouse.com.

Library of Congress Cataloging-in-Publication Data
Names: Martin, Barbara Y., author. | Moraitis, Dimitri, author.
Title: Change your aura, change your life : a step-by-step guide to unfolding
your spiritual power / Barbara Y. Martin and Dimitri Moraitis.
Description: Revised Tarcher-Penguin edition. | New York : Tarcher-Penguin,
2016. | Includes index.
Identifiers: LCCN 2015045262 | ISBN 9781101983065
Subjects: LCSH: Aura. | Color—Psychic aspects.
Classification: LCC BF1389.A8 M37 2016 | DDC 133.8/92—dc23

Printed in the United States of America
1   3   5   7   9   10   8   6   4   2

Book design by Lauren Kolm

This book is lovingly dedicated to all students
of metaphysics searching for the truth.

CONTENTS

ILLUSTRATIONS

Illustrations in italics appear in the color insert.

ACKNOWLEDGMENTS

· ·

*T*he Penguin edition of *Change Your Aura, Change Your Life* represents the third incarnation of this work, the first edition inaugurating the writing collaboration of the authors. The manuscript was built on decades of notes and materials Barbara had gathered on the aura from her countless clairvoyant experiences. With each version of this book, information was added, and there was a refinement in the presentation of the many spiritual principles and exercises. We offer our gratitude to all who creatively contributed to these earlier versions.

Our profound gratitude goes to Ariste Reno for spurring us on and supporting us to initiate the process of writing this new edition. We thank all the students of Spiritual Arts Institute who practice these Divine Light principles, many now becoming certified healers and teachers in these auric techniques. Very special thanks to Megumi Yamada, Neil and Anna Mintz, Joel Morris, Minna Yu, Ray and Jane Barger, Matthew and Janine Hannibal, Juliana Nahas, Bill Perry, Ruth Green, Jim Dydo, Teresa Quinlin, Stephanie Ortiz, A.J. Le Shay, John and Carolyn Harrison, Rakesh Garg, Jan Dunham, Trisha Kelly, Melinda Noble, and Patricia Bowman for their support. Our gratitude to Barbara's family: Vasilli, Ria, Ken, and Amanda. And to the Moraitis family: George, Philip, Ann Marie, Ellen, Anne, and Julia, and in memory of Dimitri's mother, Christine.

Our agent, Simon Warwick-Smith, has been a strong support, effectively helping us build our publishing presence over the years for which we are grateful. Our thanks go to Joel Fotinos and Andrew Yackira at Penguin/Tarcher for taking on this project. This is our third book together, and they have been a wonderful publishing partner. Andrew shepherded the book's publication, and we deeply appreciate his skill and care to honor the work yet bring a freshness to reach out to new audiences.

ACKNOWLEDGMENTS

Our thanks go to the production and marketing staff at Penguin for their talent and professionalism. Our thanks to Nita Ybarra for her wonderful cover design, revising the original cover she did for us years ago and making it once again original and inviting. Our gratitude goes to Jeffrey Bedrick who did the color and black-and-white illustrations. It was a big job to bring to life on the intricate world of the aura. He was particularly effective at capturing the luminous quality of the aura.

PREFACE TO THE NEW EDITION

. . . .

Since the initial publication of this book, interest in the aura and spiritual energy has greatly increased. Energy healing and meditating with Divine Light has become a centerpiece of many spiritual practices. There is so much to say on the aura. One book can hardly cover it all. Yet, the growing recognition of the importance of the aura represents a milestone in understanding human nature and the spiritual forces at work in our consciousness.

In this updated edition, we have refreshed the manuscript to better reflect the wisdom gained from many years of teaching this material. The goal is to make working with the aura and spiritual energy as clear, accessible, and practical as possible. Metaphysics is an art and a discipline. The more you incorporate these meditations into your lifestyle, the greater the benefits.

We have included new material offering greater insights into the human energy field. A new chapter has been added on the aura as it relates to your spiritual evolution. Also included is a new chapter on the effect the color you wear in your clothing has on your auric field—a topic many have been asking about. There are also new things added, including understanding the inner aura, introducing children to the auric power, and sending Divine Light to others.

We hope this book inspires you to delve even deeper into your spiritual nature and the miraculous spiritual power that supports everything you do.

Light and love,
Barbara and Dimitri

*I*t has been an honor to contribute to the writing of *Change Your Aura, Change Your Life*. I have known Barbara for many years and the changes that have come over me as a result of working with the aura and spiritual energy have been miraculous. In my case, it was not so much a matter of my overcoming a trauma or personal tragedy. As a matter of fact, I came from a well-adjusted home life. I grew up with loving parents and a brother who's my best friend. What I did have was an inexhaustible desire to tap into the spiritual side of my life. That desire has been realized to a greater degree than I had ever imagined possible through my association with Barbara and this work.

At the time we started working together, Barbara had very little organized information covering these marvelous teachings. She had been teaching for many years, but most of the instructions were given orally. For those who have been with or studied great souls, this mystery becomes understandable. It often becomes the duty of the people around such an inspired teacher to organize and distribute the teachings presented. It remains the teacher's job to maintain the spiritual connection necessary to be effective and accurate. So in addition to my becoming her student, we became writing partners, which eventually led to our collaborating on *Change Your Aura, Change Your Life*.

In all the time I've known Barbara, her teachings have remained entirely consistent and reliable. I've never once had reason to question the integrity of these instructions. I've been a witness to many healings and transformations received by others, demonstrating all the more the validity and usefulness of spiritual energy.

No book can replace the direct experience of working with the aura and Divine Light. Yet I hope with all my heart that *Change Your Aura, Change Your Life* makes that magnificent journey to enlightenment a little brighter and more understandable for you, as it has for me.

Dimitri Moraitis

A miraculous spiritual force operates in the midst of us. Although invisible to physical sensing, it is vividly alive and active. It is a part of us and we are a part of it. This force is known as the human energy field—the aura. In the following pages, we'll explore what the auric field is and how to improve it by working with spiritual energy. This book is designed to be a hands-on training manual in how you may work with the aura to improve the quality of your life. It introduces a powerful meditation tool for accessing an unlimited source of spiritual power that is simple and easy to follow.

The depth of activity that goes on within each of us, unseen by the physical eyes, is truly amazing. For anyone who has studied this subject, it becomes clear that there is far more to the unseen part of life than there is to the seen. It is my hope that this book will give you a greater knowledge of yourself, who you really are, and your unlimited potential as a spiritual being.

Every spiritual process described here has been experienced through my own direct clairvoyant observations. I was born with the gift of spiritual sight. From early childhood, I could see auras, and I had countless other spiritual visions as well. These experiences have always seemed normal. As a matter of fact, when I was very young, I assumed that everyone saw what I did. It was a rude awakening when I found out that they didn't.

Clairvoyance (from the French, for "clear seeing") is the ability to observe the normally invisible spiritual processes of life. I was about three years old when my spiritual sight opened to the beautiful world of auras. I began by seeing them around people and things. Though I had little comprehension of what I was seeing, I remember watching the auras around my parents and siblings and noticing how the colors would change according to their moods and actions. I remember taking trips into the country and seeing the auras around trees and flowers and thinking how beautiful life is. And how God must be everywhere.

I had an experience when I was about four years old that taught me an important lesson about my abilities. My father was a Greek Orthodox priest who had wonderful engineering skills as well. The archdiocese would send him to various towns to build a church and then build up a congregation. He did this in many places around the country, always with great success. As a result, our family constantly moved, which wasn't always easy on us. I had three brothers and two sisters. Living on a priest's salary was quite a feat in those days, especially considering that we moved so often. How my mother was able to keep us happy and well cared for could be a book in itself—she did a wonderful job.

One day, we all went to the dedication of a new church. It was a major event, and our family was a big part of it. The archbishop had come from the Archdiocese of New York. There were thousands of people. The archbishop stood very regal, resplendent in his tiara and cross before the altar. Beside him, to his right and left, were two bishops who were officiating with him. I studied the aura of the archbishop and found his energy field to be menacing. Instead of brilliant, uplifting colors, he had dark, grotesque colors emanating from him. However, the bishop to his right, who was lower in rank, had a very beautiful aura with striking pearl luster colors.

In the Greek Orthodox faith, it is customary to kiss the hand of the officiating archbishop, priest, or bishop. When it was our turn to go down the aisle and kiss the hand of the archbishop, I refused. My mother insisted. In front of the whole congregation, I screamed, "No, he's a monster! He eats children!" Needless to say, my mother took me out and gave me a good spanking.

So I learned that this gift could be a curse as well as a blessing. Who wants to see ugly energies around someone—especially a family member or loved one? I learned to keep quiet about what I saw and to shut off these gifts when I needed to, so I wouldn't be overwhelmed.

In my teens, I learned that it was possible not only to observe the aura, but to change and improve it. I also became aware that I was not alone in this process, that

I was being helped by beings from the spirit world. From childhood, I could see them, but as I grew older, they were making their presence much more known to me.

In my twenties, I embarked on a training program with these celestial beings, who instructed me in many facets of the spiritual world. This training eventually led to my becoming a teacher of metaphysics, including most of the principles imparted in this book. I also had an important spiritual teacher in the physical world who taught me and helped prepare me for the rigors of teaching.

When it came time for me to begin my professional work, I hesitated. I was working at an insurance company at the time, a single mother supporting two children, and this spiritual work seemed like a risky venture, even though I knew its value. I also knew how much responsibility was involved in being a spiritual teacher and wasn't sure I was up to the task. However, I was prompted—in the most unusual of ways—by many who saw that I had something to offer. By the time I was in my early thirties, I had given up my job and begun teaching metaphysics full-time. I've been teaching ever since.

I wish to emphasize that the exercises in this book are by no means a replacement for trained professional guidance. Sometimes your own spiritual efforts will not be enough to remedy a condition, and you will need experienced outside help. Certainly, if you are experiencing serious physical or psychological disorders, you should consult a doctor, counselor, or experienced spiritual healer to complement any spiritual work of your own.

A note about the illustrations: While I have made every effort to show the aura as accurately as possible, a certain amount of interpretation is inevitable. In addition, it's almost impossible to see the whole aura, in toto, at the same time. When I'm reading a person's aura, I focus on one part before going on to the next. In these auric illustrations, I have tried to show specific qualities of the aura as well as the human aura as a whole. Most of these renderings are cross sections of the auras described. In actuality, the aura is very much three-dimensional and has movement.

I wish to thank the many friends, family members, colleagues, and students who have been so patiently supportive during the writing of this book. It has been many years in the making. I would like to acknowledge my coauthor, Dimitri Moraitis, for his tireless work. Dimitri has been a dedicated student and friend for many years and has developed a thorough understanding of the knowledge presented here. I drew on a great deal of past knowledge as well as fresh inspiration for the material in this book. It became Dimitri's job to distill the information in an organized, literary form. The shape this book has taken is largely due to his creative contribution.

I hope this book will inspire you to new spiritual heights. I have been teaching for many years, and it has been fulfilling to see how working with the light has helped people to grow and express more of their true potential. Someone once said that it's wonderful to build bridges or magnificent buildings, but that the greatest feat of all is to be builders of men. I couldn't agree more.

Barbara Y. Martin

Part I

HOW THE AURA

REFLECTS YOUR LIFE

CHAPTER I

Your Spiritual Bank Account

. . . .

*I*magine a bank account in your name with unlimited cash reserves awaiting your use. First you'd say it was impossible, but if you saw the account and were actually able to make a cash advance, things would change, wouldn't they? Right now, you have the ability to tap an unlimited, spiritual reservoir of energy that can help you in every aspect of your life. Think of it as your spiritual bank account. Need more love in your life? Bring in the energy that is the embodiment of love. Looking for new inspiration? Call on the energy that inspires new ideas. How about more prosperity? Draw in the very power that manifests wealth. This spiritual account of living light is far more valuable than any cash account could ever be, and nothing is asked of you other than to use it.

This gift from God is one of the essential keys to developing a better life. By tapping into this spiritual account, you can greatly quicken your personal and spiritual progress. You can produce what you want faster, solve personal problems more effectively, and be able to help others to a greater degree.

This divine power can be perceived as a brilliant, iridescent light, with colors far more splendid than anything found in the physical spectrum. Spiritual light has its own source and purpose, which is very different from the light we see with our physical eyes. I have seen the Divine Light help mend relationships; pull people out of suicidal depressions; heal physical, mental, and sexual abuse; create harmonious marriages; help overcome addictions and perversions; get people out of financial disasters; and take them to spiritual heights they never dreamed possible. The more these people dedicated themselves, the more the light could work for them. Some of these transformations were instantaneous, others took time, but all were realized.

Throughout the centuries, spiritual light has been depicted in scriptural writings, literature, and art. In Genesis, one of the first acts of God was to bring forth light. In the New Testament, the dove of peace blesses humanity by beaming rays of light from its mouth. The light of Christ temporarily blinded Saul while he was on the road to Damascus. Countless pictures show angels and archangels beaming light to suffering souls to heal and restore them. Most benedictions show the recipient anointed with light. People who have reported near-death experiences almost always acknowledge the presence of a magnificent light. Divine Light is the backdrop to almost every heavenly scenario and the centerpiece of every religion.

If you've studied metaphysics, you're familiar with the white light. People use it in specific situations such as for protection or to illuminate a condition. The image is very strong: light dispelling darkness. The white light is definitely part of your spiritual reservoir. In addition, there is a vast array of other spiritual energies at your disposal for personal and spiritual development. Just as physical light can be divided into its spectral colors, spiritual light reaches you in rays of various colors—with each ray serving a different spiritual purpose.

How does your aura fit into all this? First, your aura is energy. Everything you feel, think, and do radiates a spiritual energy that comes through in various colors and hues. This essence is the aura. It is through the miracle of the aura that the Divine Light expresses itself in you. Your aura, then, is an individual expression of the Divine Light in action. Just as the spiritual reservoir is your divine bank account, your aura is a spiritual bank statement that registers and keeps a record of how you're using that spiritual energy. When you draw in spiritual energy, you first draw that energy into your auric field before putting it to use in your life. So, by making a change in your aura, there will automatically be a corresponding change in your life. Change your aura, you change your life. That's one of the spiritual laws.

Spiritual energy may be defined as *the Divine Light that propels the life force of God to all creation.* In other words, there has to be a power that sends the love of God, the peace of God, the wisdom of God, and all the attributes of God to each of us.

Spiritual energy is the conduit of consciousness. Without this energetic conduit, we would have no means of receiving anything from God. Take time to contemplate this, as it is the key to effectively working with spiritual energy.

Spiritual light is part of the divine radiations that emanate from the very heart and mind of God. It is this energy that sustains all life and is the power behind all activities, physical and spiritual. From its purest state, light flows from the highest spheres and planes of creation down into various gradations, to fulfill many applications. If you need more love, the light will bring to you a flow of Divine Love. If you need prosperity, Divine Light will be imbued with a different quality and bring you the consciousness of wealth.

As Divine Light flows from this celestial source into your aura, it generates the spiritual power necessary to create whatever it is you are focusing your attention on. To give you an example, when my eldest brother, Philip, was young, he wished to become an opera singer. He had an incredible voice, and everyone felt he was destined for greatness. When he started out, he had little training or money. His voice teacher gave him complimentary lessons because he saw his potential. In my brother's aura, I could see the spiritual power connected to creative talent—a bright electric blue light. I also saw a deeper royal blue energy, which showed his determination to succeed at his art. These colors were the beginnings of what would become the fulfillment of his spiritual purpose.

As I watched his aura through the years of training and struggle, his auric colors gradually brightened as his talent and skill increased. At one point, I began seeing a sparkling turquoise in the energy coming into his aura, indicative of prosperity. This energy was showing itself even though it had not yet materialized in his life. It was then that I knew good things were around the corner for him. His aura had all the earmarks of success, and sure enough, he soon became very successful in his field.

You have the ability to change and improve yourself. It doesn't matter where you are or what you've done with your life. You are here for a purpose and have been given the spiritual tools to succeed at that purpose. By working on yourself you attract the spiritual energies that improve your life. We all go through the experiences of learning and growing. Behind this activity we're gaining in spiritual power, which is the key to manifesting the fruits of our efforts.

YOUR SPIRITUAL BOOSTER SHOT

The most important act you can perform is to earn Divine Light. It's the key to all activities in life. You earn spiritual power by your every constructive thought, word, deed, and feeling. Every positive thing you do, however small, recognized or unrecognized, adds to you. The more light you earn, the brighter your aura becomes and the higher in consciousness you climb. That's why it's so important to conduct yourself in a spiritual manner and treat others kindly.

You may ask, "Why not just be a good person? Why not simply do the best you can and let God do the rest? Why go through this very focused process of working with the aura and divine energy?" Of course, doing and being good is an essential part of spiritual growth. It's the hallmark of an evolving soul. But just being good in itself doesn't complete the whole spiritual picture. You need to combine a loving nature with effective spiritual tools to be successful in your personal and spiritual growth. There will be many times when you will get stuck somewhere in life's pursuits and could benefit greatly by tapping into your spiritual reservoir. How many times have you been aware of a problem or a fault and felt motivated to correct that fault, but no matter what you do, it just doesn't seem to happen? How can that change come about if the power to make it happen isn't there?

Let me give you a few examples of how working with spiritual energy helps accelerate change. I had a student who asked me if I could help her sister. Her sister was a clothes designer, and I went to see her at a small studio she had in Hollywood. When I walked in, I saw an attractive, kind-looking woman, but one who also appeared to be bedraggled and confused. Her hair was disheveled and she had circles under her eyes from lack of sleep. Despite being such a brilliant designer, she was wearing a shabby coat and clothes that looked like they came from a thrift store. Clearly something dramatic had happened, and she needed help desperately. She told me she had hardly eaten in days, so the first thing we did was go to a restaurant to get some food in her.

She quickly told me her story. It turned out that her husband, who was also her business partner, had up and left her, taking all the money they had. They owned a small design studio that was doing well, yet somehow he absconded with all the funds, which left her penniless. She was trying to stay in business, but without funds of her own, she'd lost accounts and her business was quickly collapsing. She'd even lost her home. When I met her, she was sleeping in her studio and using the pattern table as a makeshift bed! She was confused, angry, bewildered, and frustrated. She couldn't understand how her husband, who'd helped pay her way through design school and start the business, would take advantage of her in such a callous and cruel way.

When I first met her, I could see that this was a very talented person. She had electric blue and powder blue in her aura, indicative of talent and inspiration. There was gold and white light above her head, indicating that she had spiritual potential. At the same time, she had allowed the experience she was going through to muddy many aspects of her aura, and it was very disoriented. There was a lot of gray, showing fear and worry. There was also a scratchy tan-colored energy, showing lethargy. The traumatic experience had put her in a mental fog. Although she was trying, she didn't know how to get out of her predicament. There was anger toward her husband, which came through in vitiated red. There were also dark brown, dark green, and little black energies around the emotional aspects of her aura. These colors were reflecting her dark feelings and desire for revenge.

Happily, she was *very* willing to work with the Divine Light and took to the light right away. She worked with spiritual energy daily, and diligently used many energies to get the job done. To her amazement, she started feeling the effects of the light right away, and almost immediately she began to regain the hope and optimism she needed to get her life going again. She used the purifying rays to cut loose the dark thoughts and emotions that were building inside her. She used the dynamic energies to rekindle her self-confidence, as the whole experience had left her self-esteem very low. She worked with the balancing energies to bring her life back into harmony and spiritual rhythm once again. There was a great deal of forgiveness work done with the love ray, as well as working with the reenergizing energies to build up her vitality and spiritual power.

Within three months, her diligence paid off. Her aura had dramatically improved. It was much brighter and more luminous. The grays and muddy disoriented colors were gone. Her vengeful feelings toward her husband were gone, too, and she forgave him. The muddled energies that had been clouding her thinking vanished, and now her mental body was sharp and clear, with lemon yellow and silver. Emerald green was also strong in her aura, showing that her life was much more balanced, her thinking much clearer. Perhaps best of all, she was expressing her loving nature once again, which showed up as a deep rose pink light. Her whole demeanor improved, and she was a better person than ever before.

This change in her aura was reflected markedly in her life. She found a place to live with a studio where she could do her designing. Although the business she had started was gone, she enrolled in school to expand her expertise and soon found a job in a manufacturing company as a designer. She had landed on her feet and was thriving! And she's been doing well ever since. Another wonderful blessing was that the two of us became great friends. This is the power of spiritual energy.

In another situation, I counseled a compulsive spender. He was married, with four children, and making good money as an accountant. Yet, he was in deep financial waters because of his overspending. He would buy himself cars, yachts, or whatever popped into his head, until all his funds were depleted. Then he hadn't even enough money to care for his family and was always strapped for cash. His wife was so stressed by his behavior that she eventually left him. His kids were just as angry. He knew he was causing great pain, but in the grip of a raging compulsion, he felt powerless to resist.

He went to several psychiatrists, seeking help. In therapy, he discovered that his problems stemmed from childhood experiences with his parents. Pathologically frugal, they would deny him toys and other things that he wanted. Whenever he desired something, they would usually refuse him. As a result, he'd always felt deprived and emotionally insecure. Now an adult, making good money, he felt an intense urge to overcompensate by buying all the things he wanted—buy them outright, buy them *now*. Yet, not even his newfound insight could stop him from compulsively spending.

When I first met him, he was up-front about his problems. He was a good man and really wanted to fix things and save his marriage. To his great advantage, he was open to working with Divine Light. His aura showed that the negative energy he was creating hadn't had time to really settle in, but that he obviously had several areas to work on. He had lemon yellow and silver energies radiating from the mental part of his aura reflecting his strong, good mind. It was, however, clouded by some gray energies mixed with mustard yellow, showing depression and disorientation. There was also a gray cloud of worry above his head, born of preoccupation with his condition.

Despite some worry vibrations around him, the bright orange in his aura showed him to be an optimistic person. Dazzling blue energy in the emotional part of his aura declared his passion for life. He was always out there, trying to make the big score.

His obsessive desire for material things showed up in his aura as a bright red energy. The fact that this energy was bright revealed that there was nothing inherently wrong with his wanting these things. His problem centered on the way he was going about getting the things he wanted. However, he also had cocoa brown, signifying that he could be petty—which accounted for his lack of attention in family matters.

In the upper part of his aura, just beyond the shell, he had some bloblike thought forms. A dark green and black thought form on his right side showed envy, as well as hatred of others who had more money or things than he did. A thought form on the left was a vitiated red energy. This showed his aggressive approach to being one step ahead of the next guy, no matter what.

Fortunately, he'd become disciplined from his accounting training and was able to dedicate himself to his transformational work. First, he worked on cutting loose the anger he had toward his parents. Using the white light, he transmuted old memories and the frustrations he felt from never getting the things he wanted as a boy. He worked with blue-white fire to build up new life force, and deep rose pink to forgive his parents for what they had done. He gradually began to see that it was his parents' right and free choice to give or not to give him things. They had their own reasons, and he couldn't blame them for that. He also worked with the orange-red flame to cut loose the thought forms of compulsive spending that he had created as a result of his anger. He brought in a lot of gold and silver light to illuminate the immaturity of his actions and to build logic and discipline into his spending habits.

Finally, he worked with the emerald green ray to help regulate and stabilize his thinking habits.

Once he started to get a handle on himself, he began to use the deep rose pink light on his family, so they would forgive him. He prayed for his wife to come back to him. Once she saw that he really *had* changed his ways, she forgave him and went back, as she was still very much in love with him. The whole process took about a year, but he saved his marriage. His aura had greatly brightened. He still had the silver and lemon yellow in his mental center, but gone were the lethargic and depressing energies, as well as the destructive thought forms that were encroaching on his aura. He had a lot of rose pink light, showing the high degree of love he had developed. He was expressing a beautiful royal blue energy, demonstrating the deep loyalty he now had for his family. No longer would he put his own desires and ambitions ahead of his family's needs. A brilliant emerald green light expressed the balance and harmony he was now feeling. He stopped spending on himself and used his money for his family's needs instead. With his spending habits now under control and his accounting skills to help him, he was able to get out of debt.

Could these people have worked things out on their own, without tapping their spiritual bank account? Of course they could, but it would have been a slow, grueling process, with the likelihood of setbacks before they could get on their feet again. The point is why go through unnecessary struggle or setbacks when God gives you the ability to access spiritual energy that will definitely facilitate growth?

Life gives you all the time you need to achieve the great goal of improving yourself. Yet, once you're awakened to the greater possibilities of life, you're much more motivated to pursue your spiritual unfoldment. By calling on spiritual energy, you can make changes in your life faster and more effectively, your chances of sustained success far greater than if you went at it on your own.

HOW TO USE THIS BOOK

In the following pages are many examples of how to work with the light in very practical situations. Yet, to gain the greatest benefit from using this book, I want you to think of your light work not only as an opportunity for help in the everyday challenges of life, but as an opportunity to come closer to God. That is the ultimate purpose of the light work. By using Divine Light to help you in the challenges of life, you are actually drawing closer to God in all the divine infinite variety, closer to God's love, God's peace, God's joy, God's wisdom, and so on.

It goes without saying that you draw on this spiritual light only for constructive purposes. Divine Light is not a genie or magic wand designed to service your every whim, but a tool in your spiritual arsenal. It's an opportunity to invite God to come closer into your life. If you use the light beneficently, for the good of all, access to your spiritual reservoir is naturally strengthened and increased. If you misuse the light persistently or maliciously, you won't be able to draw on the reservoir as before until you're back on the right track.

The spiritual light facilitates change by giving you the power to step into a greater spiritual awareness of life. That is the secret of spiritual light. As you draw more power into your aura, you're expanding your spiritual awareness. Light and consciousness walk hand in hand. The more light you have, the higher in consciousness you can climb. And as your consciousness heightens, change is inevitable.

For example, a nurse who attended one of my classes was skeptical of the light. She was dedicated to helping people, but thought some of these metaphysical ideas were a little far-fetched. One night, as she waited in a bar with her friends for dinner, two men nearby began arguing at the top of their lungs. The argument soon turned into a fight. She had learned about healing relationships with the love ray in class that week, so she decided to test its power. As the men argued, she silently asked that they receive the deep rose pink ray of spiritual love. To her great surprise, the fighting stopped within minutes. The men looked at each other, wondering why they were fighting at all. It turned out they were good friends who had gotten a little drunk and were arguing over nothing. They ended up hugging and buying each other drinks.

The woman was dumbfounded. She came to class the next week and related her extraordinary experience. Her skeptical mind could easily have dismissed the whole thing as coincidence, but she knew better. She said she'd never doubt the power of the light again.

How did the Divine Light stop these men from fighting? It didn't. The light helped these men receive a spiritual quickening of love, so they could see for themselves what they were doing. Once quickened, they chose for themselves to stop fighting. The fact that they were already good friends made it easier to receive the light. And although the nurse was not a firm believer, the fact that she was willing to give the light a fair chance made her an effective emissary.

Drawing in Divine Light brings more divine awareness of whatever you're working on. If you're calling on the light to increase prosperity, you're actually drawing in more divine consciousness of prosperity to create conditions of abundance and supply. Or if you're calling on the light to receive peace, you're expanding your awareness of divine peace, which will create a more peaceful condition around you; and so on. Under the umbrella of the spiritual light, all your earthly interactions and situations are opportunities by which you can grow and develop. Daily life becomes a sacred experience. And as you grow, you begin to see the light of life all around you: in the face of a friend or family member; in a moment of adversity or in the ecstasy of inspiration; in the homeless person you greet on your way to work every day; in all your fortunes and misfortunes.

SEEING THE AURA

One of the biggest questions I am asked is "Does the light work for me if I can't see it?" Of course it does! Divine Light works for you always. Actually, you're drawing in the light already but probably don't realize it. Without this spiritual energy, you couldn't exist. You depend on its steady flow of nourishment to keep yourself spiritually and physically alive. This power is drawn unconsciously, similar to the way your subconscious mind controls and regulates many of your bodily functions.

When you first begin your light work, you may not see the energy in activity. That's normal and to be expected. You don't need to see Divine Light any more than you need to see your heart to know it's beating. Most people start by feeling the light as a rush of energy, a physical vibration, or heat. Regardless of how you perceive it, Divine Light is going to start working for you immediately. As you grow with it, you'll become more attuned, and the light will become your greatest ally. The majority of people do not see energies, but they see the effects of spiritual energy in their lives, and that's the key. The sooner you start working with the light, the sooner you'll see the results.

This is not a book on seeing auras. No book can do that. If there were a simple way to be clairvoyant, that would be wonderful. We'd all have the spiritual sight. In fact, to see the aura as described in this book takes years of development. In my own case, even though I was born clairvoyant, it was many years later, and after much training, that I became a *trained* clairvoyant and could harness these spiritual gifts. Clairvoyance is a by-product of your spiritual evolution. Eventually, at the right time, your spiritual vision will open, as everyone is potentially clairvoyant. Working with spiritual energy is immensely helpful in building the bridge to clairvoyance.

THE METAPHYSICAL TRADITION

The study of the aura and spiritual energy may appear new, but it is actually part of an ancient heritage. This ancient study is called metaphysics.

Metaphysics is the study of the spiritual root of physical life. It comes from the ancient Greek, meaning "that which comes after the physical." In this way, metaphysics shares similar goals with other noble studies such as philosophy, general spirituality, theology, mysticism, theosophy, and ontology. Traditionally, there are two branches of metaphysics—theoretical and practical. Theoretical metaphysics is mainly an intellectual study and is not the subject of this book. Practical metaphysics bases its knowledge and understanding on direct spiritual observations and experience. In its purest form, higher metaphysics is a sacred art, practiced by trained mystics who can see beyond the physical veil of life. The study of spiritual energy and the aura falls into the realm of practical metaphysics. All metaphysical references in this book refer to this practical, higher application.

There are various schools of metaphysics. The background I was trained in is a mystical tradition known as the Kingdom of Light Teachings. Although its roots can be found in the Judeo-Christian tradition, these teachings are nondenominational, universal principles designed for anyone wishing to delve into a greater understanding of the Divine Light and metaphysics.

DEFINITION OF TERMS

I would like to clarify a few basic terms we'll be using throughout this book.

THE ENLIGHTENED AND UNENLIGHTENED CONSCIOUSNESS

The enlightened consciousness is one that is expressing the divine awareness. The unenlightened consciousness does not have this spiritual awareness.

POSITIVE AND NEGATIVE ENERGY

In metaphysical terms, positive energy is spiritual energy charged with divine essence. It is constructive and operates at a very high frequency. All references to Divine Light, spiritual energy, power rays, and so forth, refer to this constructive, positive energy. Negative energy is positive energy corrupted through misuse. As a result, its frequency has been greatly reduced and it has a draining and destructive effect on the aura.

SPIRITUAL EVOLUTION AND DEVOLUTION

Evolution in metaphysics means the building up and unfolding of our soul qualities. Devolution means the tearing down and stagnation of the soul life. The evolution of the soul is generally not a vertical line upward. There are highs and lows, upward and downward motion, as the soul evolves and devolves in its growing process until it becomes strongly dedicated to the spiritual life.

DIVINE—SPIRITUAL

The word "divine" pertains directly to the world of God, our original source. The light we speak of in this book is an abbreviated term for Divine Light and refers to the spiritual emanations as they flow from the God source. The word "spiritual" has its root in the Latin word *spiritus* (breath, air, breath of life), but in metaphysical terminology it is actually a more generic term. It refers to all realms that are non-physical. In other words, negative energy is technically still spiritual energy because it is not of physical origin, yet because it is corrupted, it's definitely not divine energy. But unless stated otherwise, we'll use the word "spiritual" interchangeably with the word "divine" to mean the higher, pure world of God.

CHAPTER II

Anatomy of the Aura

· ·

One afternoon when I was three years old, I was playing with a favorite red ball in our family living room. I was bouncing the ball around in all directions, when it knocked against a piece of furniture and rolled into the kitchen. I ran after it. My mother was at the sink washing dishes. She was alone and happily singing to herself. I grabbed the ball and looked up to see if she had caught me. She hadn't seen me at all. Suddenly, as I looked at my mother, I could see a glow of light all around her. In this glow were all kinds of bubbly pink and lavender colors moving around. I was startled, yet fascinated. What was this? For a moment, I thought I was dreaming. I remembered having seen bits of color around people before, but this was so unmistakable, so real. There was no question about it—I was seeing the aura. At the time, I didn't even know what it was called, but the aura has been a part of my life ever since.

In this chapter, I would like to explore the fascinating world of the aura. For all the years that I have been working with the energy field, I still find it captivating. It teaches so much about ourselves and how we are all part of an incredible spiritual process. The auric field gives us tremendous insight into who we are as spiritual beings. The aura is crucial to our spiritual growth because it is where we make changes in our lives first. To create any condition, we must first have the spiritual energy present. The aura is where we generate that spiritual power. By understanding how our aura works, we gain a much better grasp of how to make effective and lasting improvements.

As the anatomy of the aura is explained in this chapter, try to get a sense of what your own aura looks like. You do not have to see it to gain an understanding of it. By learning about its various components and how they operate, you can ascertain where you are in your energy field even without seeing it. This evaluation of your auric strengths and weaknesses will give you a much better idea of where in your aura to focus the light.

The aura may be defined as an invisible (to the physical eye) vibratory essence that surrounds all living things. Humans, animals, plants, and all objects in nature give forth a vapor or cloud, indicative of their real constitution. Inanimate objects also have an aura or auric emanations. A person's state of mind, physical health, emotional nature, and spiritual makeup all radiate energy, which together constitute the aura.

The aura is a blueprint of our active soul qualities. It's not the actual soul but the expression of the soul. As we attract spiritual energy through our various thoughts and activities, those energies register in the auric field. Our talents, strengths, and weaknesses are all laid out in our auras. There's no guesswork. In physical life, we can hide our true character from others if we choose to. In the aura, there can be no concealment or deception: our true character is clearly visible. If we have done terrible things, those deeds register in our aura. If we have done wonderful things, those wonderful energies will also appear. As a result, the aura is completely consistent and reliable in displaying our qualities and spiritual makeup.

Does everyone have an aura? The answer is emphatically *yes*. Every single person on this Earth has an auric field, regardless of who he or she is. The aura is common to everyone. The only time an aura diminishes in power is when a person is ready to make their transition from this Earth life. In this case, the aura does not dissipate; rather, along with the soul, it withdraws its power from the physical plane of existence and returns to its spiritual origin. Other than this, the aura is always active and visible.

You don't have to actually see the aura to know its operation and power. Most of us can feel the aura, because the aura vibrates. People say, "Oh, I don't like that person's vibe." Why? Although you may not see an aura, you intuitively react to its energy field. As a result, a person with a rarefied aura will feel uncomfortable around someone with a dark aura and much happier around a person who has a similarly bright aura. Likewise, a person with a very dark energy field will feel more at home with someone of like vibration than with someone whose aura is very bright. The old adage "Like attracts like" holds very true with the aura.

Most striking about the aura are its dynamic colors. Your thoughts and feelings all radiate colors indicating the quality of thought or feeling being expressed. These colors, to the untrained clairvoyant eye, first appear to be random, but they're not. Each color is there for a specific reason and as a result of a particular way you have attracted and used the Divine Light. As you change your mental and emotional states as well as your actions, your aura changes accordingly. This change can sometimes be dramatic. Parts of the aura can be tranquil as water one moment, then impulsive as flames the next moment. Other parts change much more gradually over a long period of time as our character changes. This dynamic quality is our saving grace. We're never stuck with an aura the way it is.

SHAPE OF THE AURA

The aura is not something amorphous or vague: it has definite form. For the most part, the shape remains constant throughout our lives. Other emanations within the aura can fluctuate, giving the appearance of contraction and expansion, but the basic shape remains the same. This "shell" is the basic framework in which the other aspects of the aura reside. It might at first seem strange that the human aura would be contained in such a defined shape or shell. Yet as we look at nature we find incredible shapes and exquisite designs. Metaphysics has dedicated a science to the understanding of sacred geometry.

Within the basic auric shape are bands or zones of various colors. They look like compartments filling the shape. There are nine of these zones. The physical body appears contained within this shell and its compartments. These zones are stationary and their colors change very slowly. It can take a lifetime to bring these colors into their fully illuminated state. Generally, the upper compartments will have brighter colors, showing the enlightened energies the person has developed, while the lower compartments will be darker, indicating undeveloped states of consciousness that the person is trying to bring up into a more enlightened state.

The Rounded Shape

This is not a perfect round. There is a slight oval at the top and bottom, but it's mostly round. (See Illustration 2.1A.) The top is approximately six inches above the head and extends a little beyond arm's length. The outer rim is usually silver or gold but can change according to the needs of the individual. The rounded aura shows a soul in the process of gradual spiritual growth.

The Squared Shape

The square-shaped aura is actually slightly larger than the rounded aura and literally looks like the person is in a cube. (See Illustration 2.1B.) The physical body is slightly off center within the shell, with more room at the bottom than at the top. The square-shaped aura can show a devolving state of consciousness. We are not born with an auric shape like this. Over time and with repeated misuse, our auras can change from the rounded shape into this squared shape. The square-shaped aura can also represent the primitive aura. Souls who are still in the infancy of their spiritual unfoldment will have a square-shaped aura. In this situation the aura is not devolved at all. The square indicates the foundation energy helping the soul build its spiritual power. In this scenario, other bright energies help differentiate this type of soul from the devolved aura, which would have much darker, menacing energies.

The Pointed Oval Shape

The pointed-oval-shaped aura is pointed at both top and bottom. (See Illustration 2.1C.) It's about as wide as the rounded aura but reaches up about twenty-four inches above the head and below the feet. The pointed oval shape is the mark of a spiritual master. The circumference is usually gold for protection. A person with this shape of aura is either very near to or has reached his or her enlightened self.

DIVISIONS OF THE AURA

Many people think of the aura as splashes of colors and symbols when, in fact, the aura is a vast, intricate manifestation, just as we are. Nowhere can this intricacy be more clearly seen than in the auric divisions. The divisions may be seen in and

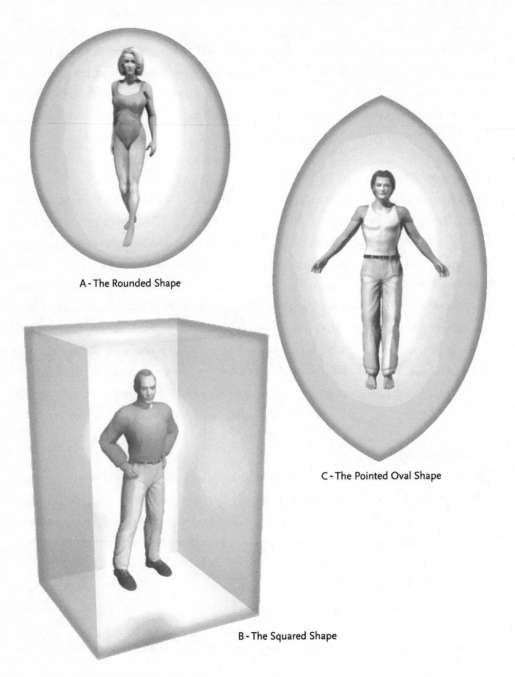

A - The Rounded Shape

C - The Pointed Oval Shape

B - The Squared Shape

ILLUSTRATION 2.1-*The Three Auric Shapes*

around the auric shell. They cover a broad spectrum of your nature, and together comprise the sum total of your character traits. By improving the qualities of these divisions, you can vastly improve the corresponding quality of your life.

Health Division

The health division takes in the entire physical makeup, including all organs, glands, tissues, and one's general condition.

This division has health lines, or striations, that move out from the physical body to the perimeter of the auric shell on both the right and the left side. (See color Illustration 2.2A.) These health lines help supply the physical body with the spiritual energy it needs to function properly. When a person is in excellent health, these striations come through in very strong silvery white energies that shimmer. They are exceptionally beautiful to see in this condition and immediately demonstrate that one is in radiant health. When a person falls ill, the health lines start to lose some of their luster and change to a dull metal gray. If someone is very ill, the lines become dull and droop closer to the body, depending on the severity of the illness. And when a person is approaching death, the health lines will droop very close to the body and continue to deteriorate to a dark metal-gray energy. In this condition, the person is ready to depart from the physical body.

In addition to health lines, the physical body itself radiates an aura of about two inches along its contours. You will see reds and oranges when the body is robust and strong. The miracle of the aura does not stop there. Each organ in the body has its own aura! Healthy organs usually have a rosy hue, while sick organs will have a dull gray aura around them.

Mental Division

This division, which also goes by the term "mental body," deals with your thinking. Thoughts are among the easiest of areas to disturb in the aura, and therefore one of the most important areas to keep alert and clear. The mental division is one of the primary areas of the aura on which to begin work. The energies of the mental division may be seen moving in and around the head. (See color Illustration 2.2B.) There are many energies connected to the mental division and these can vary with the individual. Yet there are some energies that are basic to a healthy mental division. Often there is a gold band, giving power and strength to the mental body, above the head. A glow of lemon yellow light around the upper part of the head like a halo indicates the intellectual capacity of the individual. This is common to every aura. In the average person, this energy will radiate a few inches from the head, but with a mental giant or a genius it can extend quite a bit farther. Just above the head, silver diamond points of light indicate intelligence.

In the center of the forehead is the mental energy center. This center is part of the mental division and it radiates an energy corresponding to the quality of a person's thoughts. Most of us move back and forth from enlightened to unenlightened thoughts, with the two sometimes bumping into each other. Many times, we don't even know when we're in the unenlightened state. We sense the confusion or disorientation but don't identify it as unenlightened thinking. We generally know when we are in the enlightened state because there is such bliss involved.

Emotional Division

This division is located in and around the abdominal area and extends to the outermost part of the aura. (See color Illustration 2.2C.) The emotional division is the total makeup of your emotional nature—good, bad, or indifferent. If you are angry, dark red energies will shoot out like firecrackers and can extend quite far if the outburst is very intense. If you are in love, beautiful fuchsias and pinks will radiate. The feeling nature is an intense, powerful influence in the aura. Too often, we act out of our feeling nature without allowing our mind levels to direct our lives. We all know how feelings can color the mind. The emotional division acts as an anchor for the aura, balancing the whole auric field. Someone who is a master of his or her emotions will have very bright, radiant oranges, pinks, greens, or blues in this division. These energies will move out quite a bit farther than the mental radiations. The emotional center is in the middle of this division.

With someone who's very destructive emotionally, there can be dark browns and greens and even black, showing intense hatred. The energies in a volatile emotional condition move contrary to their natural flow. Notice the expressions "sick to my stomach" and "gut-wrenching." The emotional "gauge" lies within the solar plexus.

For most people the emotional division is a mixed bag, including both positive and negative emotions. Someone may have the love flow, which brings in the pinks, but may be very jealous, which would move in dirty, avocado green energy. Like the mental division, it's critical to keep this division as clean and clear as possible, so you don't dissipate your spiritual power.

Magnetic Division

This division is very interesting because it shows the creative talents and abilities of an individual. Its center of energy may be seen on the left side of the chest, a little above the heart. (See color Illustration 2.2D.) It is round in shape, similar to the energy centers. It's about two inches in diameter and peacock blue in color. From this blue point, rays of light shoot out when the division is active.

The magnetic division reveals to what degree a person has developed talents and abilities. If bright electric blues and oranges are radiating from this point, it means the person is actively using his or her abilities. For example, if a person is an excellent pianist and actively playing, the energy coming out of the magnetic division will be bright and radiant. On the other hand, if that person has neglected the piano, the energies will become dull. The talent is there, but inactive. One must use his or her particular gifts—otherwise, the energy will fade.

Geniuses have a very pronounced magnetic division because they are using their gifts to a high degree. The talent and abilities expressed can be in any area, including music, literature, art, medicine, engineering, physics, computer science—you name it.

Color Division

Interpenetrating the other divisions, the color division reveals character traits of an individual. About eight inches thick, it forms an oval shape that extends from about eighteen inches to two feet all the way around the person. (See color Illustration 2.2E.) The colors in this division move in small pinpoints of light that resemble heat rising from a sidewalk on a hot day. These points of light are so thick you can barely see through this division when really focusing on it. In the color division of an enlightened aura, these points of light sparkle in a rainbow of pearl luster colors, making the whole aura iridescent and creating a euphoric effect. As we work on bettering ourselves, this division brightens.

This division reveals the importance of building character. Every time you strengthen a facet of your nature or better yourself in some way, you brighten this division. Even if you are not receiving acknowledgment from others, your goodness shows in your aura and becomes part of your life expression.

Spiritual Division

The spiritual division reveals the spiritual advancement of an individual. This division is seen about two feet above the head in arcing bands of light. (See color Illustration 2.2F.) There are seven of these bands. They are about a half-inch thick, fanning out in various pearl luster colors and creating the effect of a rainbow. We all have these spiritual bands to varying degrees of intensity. They are the accumulation of spiritual light we have earned in our evolution. The brighter these bands of light, the more we have advanced spiritually. The colors can move into pale pinks, lemon yellows, and light greens. In a very advanced individual, a pronounced indigo shows up in one of these bands. It's a beautiful sight to behold and one of my favorite aspects of the aura to watch.

THE INNER AURA

In addition to the spiritual aura, there is another aspect to the energy field—an inner aura. This inner aura is also known as the "soul aura." The soul aura is a very sacred part of you. It is deeply involved in your evolution and helps you to reach your highest spiritual potential. It reflects some of the deepest part of the soul energy.

While the "outer" aura explored in this book gives you the power to create and interact with the world, your inner aura gives your soul the power to evolve. The inner or soul aura surrounds the body and radiates about a foot in all directions. This aura is intense to see and reflects the life lessons the soul comes to Earth to learn.

You are born with a certain configuration of this inner auric power. This configuration gives you the power to master the lessons of your incarnated life. When you come to Earth, you have many things to learn. However, one overriding lesson dominates many of the various soul experiences. It may be your soul lesson to learn patience or to be more dynamic or to express your creative gifts more fully, to be more tolerant, and so on. This basic lesson will be a running theme in your life. For example, if your basic lesson is patience, this inner aura might be emerald green, giving you the power to be patient. If you are meant to learn determination and devotion, your inner aura might be a beautiful royal blue. A pink inner aura indicates the key lesson to learn is love. A white inner aura shows someone who's meant to express purity in life and not settle for less. As your soul learns this essential lesson, the inner aura brightens until the lesson is learned and the soul has absorbed the spiritual power. If you do not learn your life lesson, then this inner aura weakens.

THOUGHT FORMS

Thought forms are concentrated pockets of energy produced as a direct result of concentrated thinking, feeling, words, and actions. When you think about something intensely, for example, your aura will attract and radiate an energy that corresponds to the quality of that thought. If you consistently think that thought over and over again, you will create a thought form of energy. For example, if you think about someone you love, your loving thoughts could produce a deep rose pink energy. If these thoughts persist, this loving energy will produce an actual thought form of love. That form will take the particular quality of the love expressed. I've seen love thought forms take the shape of pink bubbles or pink and gold winglike forms. They're beautiful to see. The wonderful thing about these created forms is when they're on the positive side, they become like good friends. Enlightened forms enhance and beautify our aura.

Thought forms are seen floating in and around the aura. Sometimes they are static and other times they have a life of their own. The shapes can vary from vague, amorphous, cloudlike forms to distinct, recognizable forms. The quality of the form is dependent on the way the form was generated. For example, take a student who's trying to decide what college to go to. The student feels intense focus on finding the right school but confusion and indecision as to which school to go to. The intense focus would create a light yellowish thought form, but because the focus has no clear direction, the shape would be a simple roundish light somewhat resembling an apple. It would have color and form but no detail. On the other hand, a focused thought can create a very definite form. I once saw a quill-like form, a beautiful pointed and feathered gold and turquoise thought form, around the head of a friend of mine. He was determined to make this certain investment which he knew would make him money. He was so determined and clear about what he wanted, he produced this attractive form. These forms are not unusual. I've literally seen musical notes around well-studied musicians.

What you have to watch out for are thought forms created as a result of destructive thinking, feeling, and acting. You can create some grotesque and devitalizing energies in your aura this way, which can act like unruly children. For example, a strong outburst of anger, such as seen in the illustrations in chapter 3, can create dark red energies like firecrackers all over the aura. These emotional forms can take two weeks to clear out of the aura, and that's just one single outburst! If a person were in a continuous state of rage, he or she would be creating and building up some very unhealthy forms faster than the aura could release them. Compounding the problem, one unenlightened form tends to create another. If I'm angry a great deal, this could turn into a hatred that could create a black cloudlike thought form around the head.

UNDERSTANDING THE ENERGY CENTERS (CHAKRAS)

Now we come to one of the most important aspects of the aura, especially as it relates to working with spiritual energy. These are the energy centers, or chakras.

In the aura, there is a linking up of spiritual power through energy centers. Many people use the Sanskrit word for the energy centers: *chakra*, meaning "wheel of light" or "wheel of force." Actually, the centers are *spheres* of light, sparking out rays of various colors. The centers look like miniature suns, varying in size from about two and a half to three inches in diameter, with a pearl nucleus of light in the center. Their color is basically gold, but each one has its own dominant color particular to its individual purpose and character. They can also appear to be multicolored because of the energies that move in and out of them.

These energy centers are vital in the process of spiritual transformation because they are where you will be making changes in your aura first. When you draw light into your aura, the first place the light makes contact is in these energy centers. If the aura is the first place you make changes in your life, the chakras are the first place you make changes in your aura. In working with the Divine Light, you will become intimately acquainted with the operation of these points.

Each center is responsible for a different aspect of your consciousness, activity, and spiritual expression. They are given when you are born and they stay throughout your life. The reason you have these points is to receive and transmit energy, and you're constantly doing one or the other. These centers are focal points of the tremendous power moving in and out of you.

When these centers are in alignment, they will spin in a *clockwise* motion (as seen by an outsider facing you). (See Illustration 5.2 in chapter 5.) If one or more of the centers is spinning in a *counterclockwise* direction, then there is disharmony, which can throw off the balance of the other centers and diminish the power and accuracy of the energy being received and transmitted.

In understanding the chakra system, it's important to be aware that each human soul embodies more than one set of chakras. These various chakra systems correspond to different auric manifestations. In this book, we are focusing on the master chakra system of the spiritual aura that controls the others. The Tibetan and Indian schools of metaphysics, which have long directed great attention to the chakras, often emphasize another chakra system connected to the etheric aspects of the aura. These etheric chakras have their own functions in the consciousness, including helping the spiritual aspirant understand the inner life of his or her being. By placing attention on these etheric centers, the soul can discover aspects of its inner nature that would be otherwise inaccessible. Such contemplative states may lead to moments of heightened awareness. There are stories of yogis entering blissful states by contemplating the beauty of the opened crown chakra, for example.

The chakras are essential in your spiritual evolution as it is through these chakras that you forge your spiritual mettle. They are indispensable in your light work and have an immediate effect on your life. Improving the flow of light through these centers will facilitate swift improvements in your outer world.

The number, basic appearance, and location of these centers are the same for everyone. Some of the earliest illustrations of these centers, which again came from the East, focused on seven main centers lined up in a straight line from the base of the spine to the top of the head; all had either a flower- or a disklike appearance. This was a somewhat symbolic representation of the etheric chakra system and not intended to be taken literally. It was the way early spiritual writers chose to teach the principles of the chakras. I have tried to illustrate these centers exactly the way I see them, without symbolic embellishment. (See Illustration 2.3.)

The Crown Chakra—the Spirit Self

Most books on chakras will point to the top of the head as the location of this center, but in the spiritual aura chakra system, this point is actually about six inches *above* the head. The crown chakra reveals how awakened a soul is in its spirit self. For most people, the crown chakra is closed. The majority of us haven't yet reached that state of consciousness of being spiritually awake. When this center is closed, it is oval shaped, like the bud of a flower that hasn't opened, and pure white. It does not rotate or radiate energy. There's nothing wrong with the center being in this state. You can be fully active in life. It just means that you haven't started awakening to your spirit self yet.

As a soul begins to evolve and awaken spiritually, the crown chakra, or the "thousand-petal lotus," as it is also called, begins to unfold. Petals of Divine Light begin to slowly and gracefully unfold, and the center becomes glorious to behold. Its petals shoot out about eighteen to twenty inches upward and outward, very much like a lotus blossom. The predominant colors are white and gold. In this condition, it resembles a crown sitting on the upper part of the aura, and it makes an unmistakable statement as to where you are in your spiritual development.

It takes time and effort to open this center: no matter how you may meditate or pray, this point cannot open until you have *earned* that power and vibration. When you improve yourself and work with the light, the crown chakra will unfold gradually. One interesting note: when the soul passes on from this world through the process we call death, it leaves through the crown chakra.

The Mental Center—the Conscious Mind

The mental center is the nucleus of your conscious thinking self. This energy point, located in the center of the forehead, is esoterically called the Trinity Chalice. The center is gold in color and about three inches in diameter. Within this center is a triangle of a lighter golden hue with a beautiful point of white light in the center. The center spins quickly because of all the activity going on, but the triangle remains stationary.

The mental center is a hub of intense activity. It's constantly receiving and transmitting thoughts, and these thoughts are extremely potent. This energy point sends power to the other energy centers, especially the emotional center. When thoughts are in the enlightened flows, the connection between emotion and thinking and the subconscious levels will be working successfully. When the thinking level is very high, silvery sparkles move out of the mental center. This is indicative of a quick, intelligent, and aware mind. There is usually a pronounced amount of lemon yellow as well.

As the crown chakra is above the head, the mental center is the highest point of light within the body, which makes it the gateway to higher or lower levels of consciousness. The mental center is the director of your conscious mind. The mind is the navigator of the soul. Through the mental center you receive inspiration from the higher mind and express those ideas through the power of your intellectual self. Please note: the mental center is not the same thing as the "third eye"—these are different facets of your consciousness, just as your brain is different from your eyes.

The Throat Center—the Power of Your Words

Esoterically known as the Eternal Ego, the throat center is located, appropriately, in the middle of the throat. It, too, is a golden sphere about three inches in diameter, slightly smaller than the mental center, with a magnificent royal blue diamond-shaped nucleus.

Through this center, you project the power of your word. Your words radiate tremendous spiritual power. You may think you're just making sounds, but behind those sounds is potent spiritual power. This is why you must be very careful about

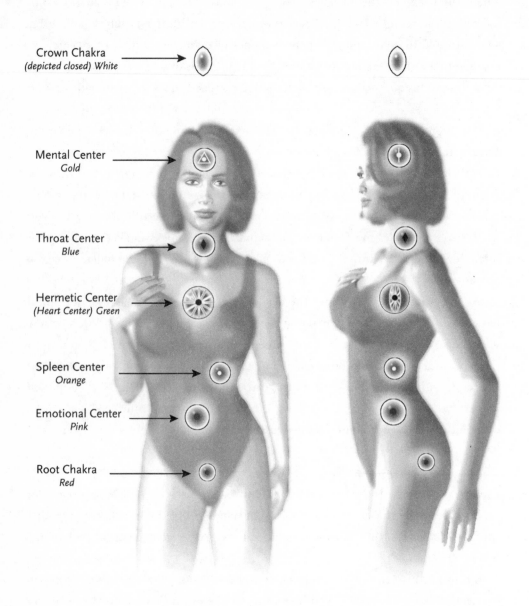

Crown Chakra
(depicted closed) White

Mental Center
Gold

Throat Center
Blue

Hermetic Center
(Heart Center) Green

Spleen Center
Orange

Emotional Center
Pink

Root Chakra
Red

ILLUSTRATION 2.3-*The Energy Centers (Chakras)*

the words you speak and to choose your words thoughtfully. Aim to say the right word at the right time.

The spiritual energy that radiates out of this center moves in one of two ways: spiritual tone or harsh sound. When you speak in spiritual tone, it means there is divine power in the words you speak. These uplifting tones can move out in vibrant royal blue energy and other shades of blue emanating from the diamond nucleus. These energies can stream out about a foot and a half in all directions. Great singers like Caruso, or inspired orators such as Emerson, will have this blue moving out from their throat center.

When you speak hurtful or destructive words, the spiritual energy moves out in harsh sound. This means there is little or no spiritual vitality in the words spoken. The energy can move out in broken and jagged rays. The colors will vary according to the type of destructive words spoken but they are unenlightened, dirty colors. I've seen avocado green energy of deceit emanating from someone who was trying to cheat another person of money. The deceitful energy moved out in a snakelike form from the throat chakra, illustrating how intense destructive words can be. It is important to bring more purity, love, and idealism to the spoken word.

The Hermetic Center (Heart Center)—the Nucleus of Your Personal Affairs

This center is in the middle of the chest and is commonly known as the heart center. In this book, we will use the term "Hermetic center," following the traditions of mystical teachings. This center is gold with a brilliant emerald green point in the middle. It's the largest center in the body.

The Hermetic center deals with your personal world affairs—how you energetically interact with the outer world. This includes persons, places, things, and situations. That's quite a bit! In the aura, there are twelve avenues to your human earthly affairs and within the Hermetic center there are twelve related power rays. These rays resemble spokes on a wheel. Seven of these avenues pertain to your day-to-day affairs and are called the seven solar rays. They are represented by the colors green, blue, turquoise, gold, white, pink, and red. Then there are five mystical rays that are related to five mystical avenues of your spiritual expression. They are of heavenly colors not found in the physical spectrum and to the clairvoyant eye appear white.

This center reflects the things that are happening in your life and activities you are initiating. It also expresses your true motivation for the things you are doing. For example, if you are ambitious and strive to be your best and highest self, there will be a brilliant bright orange energy emanating from this center. You need to have ambition and drive to accomplish your goals and aspirations. But if you are ruthlessly ambitious, where you pursue your goal no matter what the cost to other souls, the energy emanating from the Hermetic center will degrade to a dirty burnt orange energy, indicating the selfish motives. On the other hand, if you are afraid to take a chance to reach your goals and do not try at all, then the energy can move to a gray color, revealing worry and apprehension.

It is important to protect this center from undue pressures of the world. It can feel overburdened when you take too much to heart and try to carry all the world's woes. Strive to be "in the world, but not of the world." Involve yourself and be keenly aware of what is happening, but refuse to claim its troubles as your own.

The Hermetic center is known as the "seat of the soul." This is because when the soul incarnates in physical life, its nucleus of expression is the Hermetic center. Within the Hermetic center there is a sacred energy point that is a connecting link to the soul. This contact point is known as the "holy of holies." It can be seen within the emerald green nucleus and looks like a golden white point of light. This inner point of light is your doorway to the inner realm. Since this center is the seat of the soul, it keenly responds to how the soul feels. Joy, exhilaration, love, sadness, weariness, anxiety, frustration, disappointment, depression—these all affect the Hermetic center. As a result of this connection, your life experiences register more deeply in the heart center than perhaps anywhere else.

The Emotional Center—Your Feeling Nature

Located just above the navel, this center is esoterically known as the Spiritual Heart. It is the second-largest center in the body, after the Hermetic center, and it is gold with a beautiful deep rose pink nucleus. It rotates at moderate speed.

This center deals with your emotions. In the aura, emotions are the engine that gives life to your thoughts. A thought with emotion behind it is very potent and will propel the soul to action. This is a crucial chakra for sending Divine Light to, to keep the emotional nature uplifted and in a positive, constructive place. Unfortunately, this chakra is usually the weakest part of a person's aura. Many people don't know how to effectively express their emotional life. They too often let emotions get the better of them. This is why it's so important to develop a healthy emotional life so the feeling and thinking blend well together in high positive flows. If you are in a good place emotionally, there will be beautiful streams of pinks, oranges, and reds emanating from the pink nucleus.

The Spleen Center—the Vitalizing Chakra

This point is not a center in the same way the others are, but rather a very important focal point of energy. The spleen center is about two and a half inches in diameter and is located on the left side of the body, concurrent to where the physical spleen is. It's orange in color with a golden nucleus of light, and it spins in a clockwise direction at a slower speed than the Hermetic center.

The spleen center is a distributor of energy. One of its big jobs is to receive and distribute the sun's energy throughout the physical body, especially the bloodstream. It's also a storage place for solar rays, so that when we need energy, it can be called upon. Some metaphysical schools refer to this chakra as a second sun because of its life-giving properties. This point is responsible for helping to keep the physical body vital and full of stamina. It also brings in harmony and joy. When it's in a healthy state, red, orange, and gold light shoot out from the nucleus of this center. Lots of sunshine will benefit the spleen center.

The Root Chakra—Your Creative Drive

The root chakra is located at the base of the spine toward the tailbone and is actually easier to see from the side or the back. It's gold in color with a carnation red nucleus of light. This point does not rotate but remains stationary. Its flow of energy is different from that of the other centers. This chakra has three important functions. One function is to deal with experiences of the past. These are memories that are still being carried in the consciousness and need to be worked out. The root chakra holds the excrement, or the refuse, of our unenlightened thoughts and deeds. In this way, the root chakra is the means through which the unenlightened atoms are released from the aura. The root chakra periodically needs cleansing as it can become congested if you have been hanging on to disturbing energies. Once cleared, the root chakra is a powerful ally.

Another job the root chakra does is harness a spiritual power appropriately called the root chakra energy. This energy appears bright red when healthy. The root chakra energy stimulates your creative drive. As children of the Divine, we are all inherently creative. It's part of the nature of life itself. This root chakra energy is not the actual talent you may have (which is expressed through different aspects of the aura, such as the magnetic division), but it amplifies the urge, the drive to create.

A natural flow of this root energy is for sexual expression. This energy is part of the creative expression of sexual intimacy between couples. It is an essential power in the holy act of conceiving children. Yet this power can be used in other ways as well. It can be redirected to move into creative acts, such as designing inventions or artistic creations. The root chakra energy can be redirected to move into purely spiritual endeavors, such as in the unfoldment of your divine nature. This is where the spiritual expression "going down into lower Egypt" or "coming up out of lower Egypt" comes from. The root chakra plays an important role in building up the spiritual drive needed to ascend from your lower nature to your higher, divine nature.

Unfortunately, this root chakra energy can be misused and corrupted. The bright red can turn to a dirty maroon red, indicating an overly indulgent, lustful nature. If someone really perverts the sexual energy, the root chakra energy can move downward instead of upward, in a dark maroon red, indicating the energy is moving in a devolving momentum and is degrading rather than enhancing the aura.

The root chakra works with another well-known energy called kundalini. Kundalini is a spiraling, serpentlike energy rising upward along the spine. Kundalini is a spiritual power already within us. The purpose of this energy is to strengthen and energize the spiritual centers. This energy slowly awakens in the consciousness as a soul evolves. It is famously connected to the process of spiritual enlightenment and for this reason it holds a special allure for the spiritual aspirant.

As part of your spiritual growth, the kundalini opens slowly and naturally without any conscious effort. The soul is slowly earning the vital power of the kundalini.

This way, the person is able to handle the kundalini energy and its unfolding becomes a beautiful, sublime experience.

Some metaphysical schools teach opening the kundalini by conscious effort. This training was intended for the advanced spiritual student and was not intended as an exercise for casual or everyday use. Kundalini is a spiritual fire. Like any fire, physical or spiritual, when used correctly it can be of great benefit. Yet when mishandled, it can be the cause of great distress. In my own training and experience, I have found tampering with the kundalini directly to be unnecessary and potentially dangerous. I have counseled people who were severely traumatized because they managed to open the kundalini to a certain degree prematurely. They were seeking instant spiritual illumination but found out the hard way that that's not the way it works. And this is not necessary. The beauty is, the kundalini opens in its own time and rhythm, without conscious intervention, as you work with the Divine Light.

ENERGY CENTER RADIATIONS

Flowing out of your energy centers are various types of emanations. These radiations show the variety of activities within each center. In developing the aura, your main purpose is to elevate and enlighten the quality of these radiations. There are many types of energy radiations, but there are four foundational types of energy center radiations.

Active Emanations

Active emanations look like rays of sunlight radiating from the nucleus of the chakra point. Generally, they are seen as straight rays of light, but they can take a great variety of forms, as you will see in many of the illustrations throughout this book. The colors can run the gamut, from the highest white to the blackest black, and everything in between. These rays fluctuate the most of the four principal chakra emanation types. They can be like a snapshot of where a person is in his or her consciousness at any given time. Remember, some aspects of the aura change slowly over time. Other aspects of the aura can change quickly as your thoughts, words, actions, and emotions change. Active emanations can change quickly. These are often the most expressive indicators of a person's immediate state of consciousness.

Stabilizers

Stabilizers help keep the flow of energy moving steadily. They move out in three to four straight rays and are gold in color. (See color Illustration 2.4A.) They stay the same color regardless of what's happening to the individual. Because there is so much power moving in and out of the centers, it is essential to keep the points steady to keep the consciousness steady.

Fanning Rays

Fanning rays are among the chakras' most beautiful emanations. They shoot out from the nucleus to either side in a solid color of light. (See color Illustration 2.4B.) The extent of their radiation depends on the development of the person and they begin to appear in the aura after a person has reached seven years of age.

Fanning rays are seen in the mental, Hermetic, and emotional centers. They show the *tendency* of expression. Whereas active emanations can change quickly depending on what you are doing at any given time, fanning rays will stay the same color unless the whole direction of energy changes. For example, say a person has a pink fanning ray radiating from the emotional center, demonstrating a loving nature. This person can still have days when he or she feels irritable and out of sorts. This doesn't necessarily mean that the emotional fanning ray will change color, because the thrust of the person is still to be loving. But if that person were to become irritable on a regular basis, then the fanning ray would change color.

Spiral Rays

Spiral rays spin with the movement of the center and reflect the spiritual progress of the individual. (See color Illustration 2.4C.) At birth, these radiations are white and gold in color. After seven years of age, they begin to develop, and they continue to develop throughout life.

EXPLORING THE MIXED, DEVOLVED, AND ENLIGHTENED AURAS

Let us now put together all aspects of the aura that we've been exploring and look at the energy field as a whole. Of course, there are as many variations in auras as there are people, but in my experience, auras fall into three broad categories. Also please note that even with clairvoyant sight, you do not see all of the auric anatomy at one time, as it would be too confusing. A trained clairvoyant learns to spiritually focus on specific aspects of the aura at one time, almost like tuning into a specific radio station and not the others. Yet for the sake of these illustrations we are putting together a composite of the auric power.

The Mixed Aura

The majority of humans have mixed auras. Even souls that are higher on the spiritual ladder will have the mixed aura until they near the spiritual pinnacle. The mixed aura has a rounded shape and has both positive and negative energies active at the same time. (See color Illustration 2.5.)

A soul with this type of aura is in the process of evolving and is going through the normal human condition in all its vicissitudes. And isn't this the human conundrum, the good and the not so good living side by side? The soul with a mixed aura might be that of a fine artist who has a drinking problem, or someone who is very smart and inventive but also selfish and mean, or a person who is fundamentally good, yet weak-willed and gullible. Variations are endless. The good news with the mixed aura is that it holds more enlightened than unenlightened energies. Over time, it becomes the job of the soul with the mixed aura to use the enlightened parts of that aura to transform the unenlightened parts until all are in Divine Light.

In the illustration here, the soul is on an upward swing and has many redeeming qualities. The light green band of light to her left shows she's growing spiritually. This band of green is often around people who have awakened to the spiritual life and are learning spiritual truths. The gold pyramid above her head shows she is searching for truth. The pink bubbles of light to the right show she is in love with someone. But the energy is not very strong, which usually means the love is one-sided and the other person is not returning her affections.

This soul also has creative energies. The winged forms above her head show inspired enlightened thoughts; the light blue formation to the left shows creative vibrations. However, its position indicates that she has not yet expressed this creative power. Vitality is apparent in the red energy coming from her hands, and good health is shown by the bright health lines moving out from either side of her body. Emanations of blue coming from her throat center tell us that she speaks positively; purple waves of light at her feet show she has overcome some tragedy or adversity. Her color division is clear with bright colors, and her spiritual division is fairly bright—she has developed spiritual powers somewhere in her evolution.

At the same time, this soul has plenty to work out of. Most prominent is the dark green cloud formation to her right, showing that this person is actively expressing jealousy. The gray compartment in the lower part of her aura shows she's overcoming a lot of fear from earlier in her life. The brown compartment harbors pettiness, suggesting that she can be mean at times, but is working out of this as well.

From this stage of spiritual development, we eventually realize the enlightened state. However, if we refuse to express our higher nature and choose to walk away from the light, we can fall into the next auric expression—the devolved aura.

The Devolved Aura

This square-shaped aura reflects a soul that has consistently misused its spiritual powers. As a result, many of the energies have been corrupted. (See color Illustration 2.6.) Such an aura has become square-shaped because, by its persistent refusal to connect with its higher nature, it has retarded its evolution and reverted back to a more primitive, instinctual state of consciousness. The dark energies have restricted and choked the spiritual flow to the point where little Divine Light can get through. During the sixties, the expression "He's a square" was often used. Ironically, someone really *can* be a square! In contrast with the mixed aura, the challenge with the devolved aura is the person has created more unenlightened energy than enlightened energy in the aura. The things he is doing takes him further away from his spiritual source rather than toward it. We are not born with an aura like this. As the auric power is degraded over time, we devolve to this spiritual level. This soul has a long climb back into the light, not only because of all the work needed to redeem it, but also because living in the dark propels it on to ever darker thoughts and deeds. The person with such a soul could be a tyrant or mass murderer, but doesn't have to be. I have seen this aura around what you would call "normal" people who hold no conspicuous positions in life.

I would like to note here that the square-shaped aura can indicate a young, primitive human soul in the early stages of its evolution. However, in contrast to the devolved aura, the energies of the primitive aura are brighter and much better balanced. The physical form is centered and the cube-shaped aura acts as a foundation energy to build spiritual power. It's a very different scenario from when the squared shape is the result of a spiritual devolution.

The devolved aura seen in the illustration is very muddled; the lower half is especially disorganized. The black compartment holds sustained hatred, which he has tried to control. It may also indicate that he has been involved in murder.

The dark green and brown compartments on the lower left indicate a conniving, cheating nature, compounded by cruelty. His emotions are all mixed up. There's a lot of anger, shown by the blotchy energy to his left at the emotional division. The health lines are turning gray and beginning to droop at the bottom, which means that his misdeeds are leading to physical illness. The head area has a brownish yellow energy, showing pettiness and a lethargic quality to his thinking. The dark green shooting from his forehead shows he is planning some sort of deception. The black thought forms around his aura show hatred toward someone that has recently been expressed. The dark, dirtied blue compartment across his head area shows he's constantly moody and brooding over his life. The sparkles of his color division are much smaller than in the color division of the mixed aura, and many of the points of light are dulled and dirtied. Notice, too, that the energies radiating from his centers are filled with darker colors and do not reach as far as with the mixed aura. This shows he's in an active state of depression. His spiritual division remains unaffected, but he has no access to those powers until he turns his life around.

Despite his condition, there are some bright colors in this aura. A lemon yellow energy compartment above his head shows intelligence and a strong mind when it isn't clouded by wrongdoings. Red and orange compartments across his torso show he is energetic and motivated. These areas of energy and motivation are often the most redeeming qualities in the devolved aura. The purple compartment on the lower left side of his aura shows he can be calm when necessary. Bright green and gold rays shoot out from the center of his chest, indicating he is active in world affairs, and probably successful. And isn't that often the case? Very destructive people can be quite successful in the work world and financial arena even though they are far from living life correctly. This often confuses people around them into believing that their actions are meritorious.

Fortunately, a soul in such a devolved state is something of a rarity. I have seen maybe a hundred devolved auras in my life, but that's a hundred too many. A soul like this is certainly not past redemption, but it has a lot of work ahead to turn things around.

The Enlightened Aura

In sharp contrast to the devolved aura is the enlightened aura. The enlightened aura is the ideal we all aspire to. In building your ideal image of the things you most want in life, this is the auric image to visualize in your heart and mind.

The evolved aura has the beautiful pointed oval shape. (See color Illustration 2.7.) There is an outer gold aura that can radiate an additional two feet, creating a feeling of great expansion. All components of this aura are in full operation, well developed, and organized. Its colors are in the high pearl luster ranges and are moving in beautiful flows and striations. The compartments of the auric shell are clear, definite, and well organized. Notice the gold in the upper compartment, showing the high spiritual state of this soul. In addition to the pointed shape, a striking feature of the enlightened aura is a lack of dark colors. This doesn't mean the person with this type of aura is perfect. Unenlightened energies can and do show up, and a person with this type of aura is still developing and strengthening his or her character. But it does mean this soul has reached a magnificent level of spiritual maturity and perfection. Every soul, no matter how developed, is in a continual process of spiritually evolving. Enlightenment is a process that unfolds in many degrees. Yet without question, a soul like this has reached a pinnacle of human achievement, one we all aspire to. The illustration here can only hint at the beauty of such an auric field.

A halo of lemon yellow light filled with diamond points shows the keen intelligence this person has. There are triangles inside each main spiritual center, signifying that the centers are working at optimal power. Notice the expanse of radiations coming from these centers: they reach almost to the edge of the auric shell. These beautiful flows show he has control over his mental and emotional nature and is living his life in ways that only add more light to his aura. The crown chakra, above the head, is fully opened, displaying the glorious thousand-petal lotus flower shape that reveals the soul's state of enlightenment. This soul is fully awakened in its spiritual nature and is fully aware of its purpose on Earth.

Enlightened thought forms are all around this aura. The white stars to his left show purity of thought. This person's mind is completely focused on God. This man has spent untold time refining and developing his divine attributes. The beautiful formation to his right shows he is in pursuit of a spiritual mission, a higher purpose. This soul, if not already a master of life, is very close to that level. The purple at his feet expresses the tremendous peace and spiritual stability this soul has attained. The color division is similar to that of the rounded aura, but the colors are now primarily gold and purple. The bands of light above his head are very bright and vibrant. This person is a blessing to be around and creates good wherever it goes. From here, the aura can expand even further, for perfection is never static: we grow "from grace to grace."

I have seen such an aura maybe a handful of times in my life, yet it is the destiny of all of us to have such an aura.

TYPES OF AURAS

Within these three auric types are infinite possibilities of auric emanations. Depending on character, development, desires, and talents, each aura is going to take on its own quality. For example, around a schoolteacher would be a prominent lemon yellow energy because of all the concentrated study involved. Silver would also be seen because intelligence is part of the profession.

The aura of athletes would show more red and orange energies because they are active physically. Someone who works more in the creative aspect of things, such as music or art, is going to run a little of the gamut of spiritual energies. Actors express a lot of the emotional aspects of their nature and that will come through strongly in the solar plexus area of the aura. The hues will vary depending on whether they are doing comedy or drama. Powder blue light will often be seen with creative people. The aura of a newborn baby is wonderful to see. It usually has a lot of green and violet in it. A fascinating characteristic about a baby's aura is that it has no dark energies in it. It's as if they are given a clean slate to make good in the world.

In the case of a leader, such as the president of a country, a variety of energies will be pronounced. If he or she is a strong leader, this person will have a lot of emerald green and gold in the aura. These colors show a balanced individual combined with inner strength. The gold with the lemon yellow will also show that this individual is decisive. Communication is an important part of the job, so there will be silver energies. If this leader is a more evolved soul, various degrees of pure white light will be seen coming through this individual. Royal blue will be seen with leaders if they are loyal to their people. If the individual is clever but conniving, making deals for his or her personal benefit and not caring what effect those decisions will have on the people he or she represents, that would generate dark light, such as cocoa brown and avocado green.

A doctor will have a lot of blue, related to healing, and purple and orange, for motivation, if he or she is dedicated. A good surgeon will be bringing in some artistic energies as well as gold energy for inner strength. On the other hand, a doctor who does not fit the profession will have energies that are less pronounced in their degree and hues. There may be gray in such an aura, showing depression. Such a person doesn't really want to be doctoring but may have chosen it because of the money.

A thief is going to have very mixed colors and darker hues. Stealing obviously diminishes the aura. Because this person plans and plots, he or she will have some silver and lemon yellow, but these colors will be mixed with the lower shades. This person will also have some gold in order to have the strength to carry out his or her ideas. As time goes by, if this person continues to steal, the aura gets darker. With the brutal criminals, you see a lot of inky black and cocoa brown energies. The situation is different with someone who has a good soul but, due to whatever the circumstances and influences, enters into the world of crime. His aura will not be nearly as dark as that of a hard-core criminal who has been doing it for a good portion of his life.

AURAS OF ANIMALS

Although this book is focused on the human aura, everything in nature has an aura. To help put the human aura in perspective, let's look at some of the other types of auras.

Animals, most definitely, have auras. They're not going to have as large an aura as humans, but they have strong auras just the same. Also, their auras are nowhere near the complexity of the human's. They have no auric shell, no divisions as the human does. Their aura has two basic components: there is the aura around the entire body and there is a point of white light in their forehead that also radiates energy.

The aura around the body of the animal radiates evenly in three to five colors depending on the development of the animal. A cat will have an aura that reaches out about a foot in all directions. The colors will often be pink, red, and yellow. A dog will have a slightly larger aura, extending maybe a foot and a half. Blue, red, and pink are often seen in a dog's aura especially if it's a loyal dog. The aura around a horse will be even larger, extending maybe three feet in all directions. Horses are usually spiritually well-developed animals, often with green, yellow, red, pink, blue, and violet spiritual colors. All animals have a white point of light at the forehead. This is the seat of their intelligence and spiritual life. The energy almost always seen here is silver, showing they are expressing that intelligence. The interesting thing about animals is they often live life closer to their potential and nature than humans do. Perhaps they can do this because life is simpler for them. The other fascinating thing about animals is they are natural clairvoyants. They can often see auras around each other and people!

Like a human, soul qualities apply to animals as well. Animals are very definitely on an evolutionary path. An animal's aura can change depending on its feelings and mood. They can express anger, fear, sadness, and joy in their auras like humans do. To see a dog with a very bright pink shows that it's a loving dog. If it's angry, little firecracker energies of red light will shoot out in all directions. A very dull gray in the aura of a dog would show that this animal is sick.

Dolphins have very beautiful auras. They have a lot of intelligence and are very loving and compassionate. Light pinks and yellows can be seen in these animals. A snake is on the lower order. A monkey's aura is a very energetic aura, a lot of reds and oranges. An aggressive animal such as a tiger or lion has a lot of dynamic power. On the other hand, an elephant has a lot of compassion so it, too, has pink. The lovable cocker spaniel will have a lot of pink, too. Animals, by the way, respond very strongly to love. If you want to lift an animal up, give it love. They also respond very well to the spiritual light.

AURAS OF PLANTS AND MINERALS

Plants move on a whole different spectrum from the animal and the human. There is consciousness with plants, but it's obviously on a much more basic level. A plant's growth process is focused strongly around adapting to its environment. And we have seen countless examples of how ingenious nature is in its adaptability.

The aura of the plant has usually two or three colors in it. Naturally enough, green is very predominant in most plants' auras. However, a variety of energies exist here, too. The aura of an oak tree is red and pink and radiates about two feet around the contours of the tree. The pine tree has pink and green radiations. Pink around a tree or plant indicates the plant is content and likes where it is. Fruit trees are interesting because they have two different auras—the aura of the fruit itself and the aura of the tree. An orange tree has red and pink coming from the fruit and green and pink emanating from the tree itself. If a tree is very healthy, you might even see a little gold. If the tree is not so healthy, there will again be gray.

Ferns have a lively aura also, with pink and green shoots of energy. The aura of a carrot is pretty small with orange emanations. Vegetables and fruit when they are cut don't have as much of an aura as when they're still on the tree or vine. Many times, when I am in a market, I will buy fruits or vegetables by the vibrancy of their aura.

Flowering plants usually have more of an aura. The rose, a very spiritual flower, has pink hues around it, especially when it's healthy. It doesn't matter what the color of the flower itself is. Plants, too, respond to love. A loved and nurtured plant will grow better than a neglected one. Directing energy to a plant or tree helps it to grow better.

From the plant kingdom we now enter the mineral kingdom. This is a fascinating area because objects considered inanimate are actually quite alive. Everything is alive and teeming with energy. The difference is that minerals have an even slower vibration than the plants. Their aura will extend just a little and appear in one or two colors. If we were observing a horseshoe, for instance, its aura would be emanating a bluish white energy out about a half inch. It would not have as large an aura as a piece of wood because it is not as alive as the wood is. Gems and crystals are very interesting minerals. People feel good wearing gems, but there is a reason behind that. Their auras follow true to their color. An amethyst crystal will have a purple hue; an emerald, a green hue; and so on. Of all the gems, the diamond has the greatest radiations. It usually radiates a silver energy and sometimes a variety of colors three times the distance of the other gems. These crystals and gems have healing properties of various kinds that can be beneficial when working with the aura. We are rekindling the esoteric meaning and healing power of stones and gems.

CHAPTER III

The Colors You Are

. . . .

*W*hen I started seeing auras, one of my first reactions was to wonder what a particular color meant. Bright, beautifully colored auras attracted me and dark, disturbing auras repelled me. Beyond that, I couldn't understand why one person would have certain colors around him, while someone else would have very different colors. I tried early on to find some information or material about what I was seeing, but there were no teachers I could turn to for help. And since no one else was seeing these spiritual colors, I had no way of putting my experiences into perspective. All that changed when I was eleven years old and enrolled in a private drama school run by a woman named Dorothy LaMoss.

Dorothy headed one of the best theater stock companies in the Midwest. She had also gained a reputation on Broadway and in Hollywood. She was an eccentric woman. On the outside, she had an appearance of austerity, but once you got to know her, she had a good sense of humor and could be quite charming. We got along well together. She knew her craft and was a demanding teacher who produced results.

One day after I had been with her for about six months, she asked me to come on a Saturday to see her. I arrived that Saturday, wondering what she wanted from me. At the time, we were rehearsing a play, and I thought she was going to drop me. When I got there, she started asking me questions that had nothing to do with the play. She asked how I perceived things. I told her I saw things just like anyone else. Then she asked if I could see colors around people. *That* got my attention.

"Why do you ask me that?" I asked.

"Because you can see the aura," she said.

When she said the word "aura," I jumped.

"Is that what it's called?!" It was the first time I had heard the term.

"Yes," she said. "And I would like to pass on to you what my grandmother and mother have taught me. I am a hermetic scientist. I would like to teach you what I know and give you a better understanding of your gifts."

Thus began my first encounter with real knowledge of the aura. Every Saturday, I would study with Dorothy in private. She had several ancient books on hermetic science, covering many aspects of metaphysical work. The books were hundreds of years old and were based on writings that were much older. I spent many hours at her home, copying reams of information from the hermetic teachings. Dorothy had diagrams and drawings that showed the various types of auras. Charts included auric colors in all their shades and hues. These were broken down very clearly, and the meanings of those colors were given in detail. It was an illuminating time I shall always remember. Even today, with interest in the aura and metaphysics blossoming, I have yet to see the same depth of information I was given by Dorothy and those sacred texts. It became the basis of my spiritual teaching years later and is one of the reasons I am writing this book.

Spiritual energies in the aura range from the beautiful, high, pearl luster colors of the advanced soul to the inky blacks, dull metal grays, and dirty maroons of the undeveloped individual. Most people fall into the middle range, with both higher and lower energies moving in their aura. When the soul is ready to progress to the next level of development, the shade becomes lighter and is frequently mistaken for white.

The auric emanations seen around a highly developed person are more real and vivid than colors perceived in the physical world. Blues and greens, as beautiful as they are in the colors of sky or leaves, are even more vivid and powerful in the spiritual dimension. The opposite is also true. The energies seen around a devolved aura can be grotesque and hideous. In addition to the unappealing colors, there's a feeling and vibration accompanying the colors that does not exist in the physical realm. Luminous colors are uplifting and scintillating, while colors of the lower vibrations actually take on depressing and often chilling qualities.

Spiritual colors fall into two categories: enlightened and unenlightened. Enlightened colors are spiritual energies imbued with their divine essence and being expressed in the aura as they were intended to be. Unenlightened colors are spiritual energies that have been corrupted. They started as divine energy but through misuse lost their spiritual vitality and degraded to the unenlightened status.

As you review these energy color definitions, reflect on how they pertain to you. Again, you don't need to see Divine Light to recognize its operation in you. By knowing the meaning of the various energy colors, you can determine what energy you have in your aura. For example, if you're a loving person, you can bet there's deep rose pink light of spiritual love in your aura. If you find you're getting angry a great deal, chances are you're expressing vitiated red in your aura that you'll need to work out of.

ENLIGHTENED COLORS

Enlightened colors are spiritual energies that we have attracted and earned as a result of our positive thoughts, actions, and deeds. They express the spiritually attuned part of our nature. These energies have retained their divine essence and purpose and are actively working to realize our spiritual potential. It's also with these positive energies that we are helped to transmute the darker parts of our aura. (See color Illustration 3.1.)

White

Along with gold, white in an aura is considered one of the highest colors. It means purity. It symbolizes the light of God bringing illumination to humanity. Many spiritual attributes are connected with the white light. This energy in the aura indicates a spiritual, often visionary, soul. Revelation is connected with white light. A great deal of gentleness comes with this color as well. Pearl white represents kindness and a forgiving quality. Oyster white, which has almost a very light yellow in it, means the soul is steadfast and trying hard to learn lessons. Crystal white, the purest form of white, shows that the soul has acquired complete mastery; it represents the blending of strength, courage, vitality, determination, and perseverance.

Gold

Gold is the energy of wisdom, illumination, self-confidence, faith, inner strength, and courage. It is a very strong protective energy. If you have gold in your aura, you have the power, the will, to master the lower self. You have the confidence of knowing who and what you are. You know what you can accomplish and do. You move and act decisively. Gold brings in strong dynamic powers that can cut you loose from feeling futile, frustrated, and inadequate.

Pink

Pink is the color of love, especially the deep rose pink. Pink is a universal color expressing joy, comfort, compassion, human and divine love, and beauty. It comes through in many shades from the high pearl luster to the fuchsia and rose red pinks. Crimson shows a natural, unpretentious, loving nature. A pearl luster pink, which is a lighter shade than the deep rose pink, shows a soul's pure, selfless love for God. This pink is absolutely devoid of jealousy and selfishness.

Silver

Silver is the energy of spiritual intelligence. Silver in the aura shows a person with keen powers of perception and a quick, alert mind. This person will not let others do the thinking for him or her. I often see silver sparkles or diamond points of light moving around a person's head when he or she is in tune with this power. The brain and cells of the body have silver radiating from them, as well as from the health lines, in a healthy, active individual.

Blue

This color is often seen around a person who is in pursuit of spiritual truth, and this is more or less a royal blue. This individual, as a rule, will overcome all obstacles in the search for truth. Bright blue in the aura shows integrity, sincerity, and natural wisdom. Often, someone with predominant blue is involved in science or the arts. Royal blue also means a very loyal, devoted person. Consider the expression "true blue." It shows honesty, as well as good judgment in material affairs, and it can signal a very religious soul. Madonna blue, a light but not quite powder blue, shows obedience and fulfillment of duties. This person obeys God's will. Sapphire blue is one of the strongest healing colors and is seen around doctors and healers. Aqua is also a very healing color, high in vibration, and can indicate prosperity. Along with violet, it can bring in peace and help quiet the nervous system. Peacock blue shows talents and abilities. Blue-purple indicates accomplishment with God's power, as well as a person who is making an effective connection with his or her divine self.

Powder Blue

This is a light blue energy that brings in high, creative inspiration. It is one of the pearl luster colors, which means this is a very ethereal power. In the aura, it shows an artistic person who loves beauty. Light blue shows devotion to noble ideals. Great artists in the throes of inspiration will have powder blue strongly marked in their auras.

Turquoise

Turquoise is the energy of prosperity, and this is in all departments of your life—an abundance of ideas, friends, and material goods. It's a "good luck" energy. Turquoise holds you in the consciousness of wealth and freedom from limitation and restriction. A person with this energy in his or her aura thinks in unlimited terms and knows that the money or the resources will be there for them when they need it, even when the outside world appears to show the opposite.

Green

Green is the color of growth and renewal. Emerald green expresses balance in an individual and is a very important color to have. This individual has his or her life in order. Emerald green is also the color of harmony of mind, body, and soul. It's seen in a person who, growing in knowledge, experiences harmony in many facets of life. It reveals one's love of nature and the outdoors. Pale, delicate green is sympathy. Apple green shows new spiritual growth and hope, loving service, and cooperation. Green is restful to nerves and good for overcoming fear. Green-blue indicates a trustworthy, helpful nature.

Lemon Yellow

This energy brings in powers of concentration. It deals with the intellect. People who have this color strongly in their auras may devote their entire life to the study of higher truths. They will be able to embrace a subject and stick with it until it is learned and mastered. Lemon yellow in the aura shows mental vigor in artistic, creative, and scientific endeavors. Yellow, for example, will be seen in a schoolroom around children who are learning. Teachers, of course, have a great deal of yellow. Yellow represents a healthy body, mind, and intellect. It is beneficial in dispelling fear, worry, and nervousness. Bright, optimistic people have this lemon yellow in their auras. Yellow and orange together can be very inspiring.

Orange

This is a bright orange, like the fruit. The color orange means that the person has strong motivation, enthusiasm, and good organizational abilities. This energy can also show a burning desire or ambition. A very determined individual, one who almost always overcomes obstacles and meets his or her goals, will earn this color energy. Straight orange expresses thoughtfulness, consideration, and soul energy. The person is a dynamic leader, a live wire. Golden orange is wisdom and energy, heightened mental and spiritual abilities, and self-control—a high spiritual vibration not often seen.

Red

This is life energy, especially ruby red. It radiates a lot of vitality. Red is a color that can also mean righteousness. It indicates an enthusiastic individual with high aspirations. It's the passion part of us. People with red in their auras have insights into other people, and they work well with others. They are not defeated easily. Ruby red is usually physical vitality and endurance. Red invigorates the body. Rose red represents an active love; rose red and orange together help to create a glow of well-being, promoting a healthy outlook. These are predominantly strong and uplifting colors, bringing brightness and a feeling of warmth, a desire for living. Clear red is faithful; orange-red is a healing and cleansing color. Coral represents authority.

Scarlet red can indicate a soul with spiritual power. If the scarlet red is tinged with vitiated red, that can indicate egotism. Red-purple represents power over the body.

Violet

The person who has violet possesses an aura that is serene and calm. He or she expresses an inner and outer poise. This person is always willing to be of service to humanity. Violet brings in high spiritual power, true greatness, and unselfish efforts. Violet offers mental protection. If the violet moves into lavender, a worshipful character is revealed. Orchid, which is the slightly deeper shade, denotes humility and, as the first cousin to lavender, is holy and spiritual.

Purple

This color in a person's aura means deep peace. Also, a person with purple in his or her aura is deeply religious in a mystical way. Yet, purple also expresses an ability to deal with practical and worldly matters. Purple–indigo indicates that one is seeking spiritual power. Waves of purple bands under the feet show a person who has overcome adversity.

Indigo

This color gives inspiration and deep inner strength of a purely spiritual nature. It is an extremely high color and seldom seen to any marked degree. One who has this color has come a long way, as it means that he or she has awakened in the spirit self. It doesn't take much of this energy to have a powerful effect on the aura. Indigo-violet shows someone who is searching for a spiritual experience.

UNENLIGHTENED COLORS

Unenlightened energies show some type of defilement or corruption of the Divine Light. They are divine energies that have somehow been misused and are now void of the divine essence they were originally imbued with. For instance, a bright, clear mind would have the lemon yellow energy in it, but if the person became lethargic and lazy, then the bright yellow would degrade to a dirty, creamy, mustard energy.

The brightness would vanish because the person was not utilizing spiritual energy as it was intended to be used and there is no longer the divine essence in that light as there was before. This person would now have a difficult time making decisions. Mustard yellow could also signal sickness. If it gets very dull, it can even show a savage person. Bright orange is the color of drive, enthusiasm, and ambition, but if it turns into a burnt orange, the person has become filled with self-pride. Dark brownish orange shows a lack of ambition stemming from repression. In addition to the dark color, these energies have a repulsive, cold vibration. In other words, they're no fun!

If you recognize some of these energies operating in you, it's simply a sign of where you need to work to improve: you needn't worry or hit yourself over the head about it. Remember that your aura is constantly changing, and there's not one aspect you can't elevate and transmute. If your thinking is lethargic, it can become astute. If you're mean, you can become kind, and so on.

Every one of us, at one point or another, has created dark light. It's part of the human experience to rise above these conditions. The thing to remember about unenlightened energies is that they are not part of God's divine emanations. They're artificial and not part of your true, divine nature. You do not need to claim these negative energies as your own. You just need to clear them out of your aura and avoid creating any new destructive vibrations. The best part of all is that these negative energies are powerless before the Divine Light. They have no real influence unless you invite them to operate in you. The more good you do, the more of the high colors you attract and accumulate, and the more you displace these lower vibrations.

Gray

Gray energy is connected with fear, gloom, and depression. Gray is the color of illness. When someone expresses gray energy, that person can be a worrier. Gray appears in the auras of people who can't see their way out of whatever dark cloud they've fallen into. However, if there is silver moving in with the gray, it shows someone who has known despair and suffering but is fighting his or her way out. Charcoal gray indicates despair, and gray-black is heaviness, dullness, grief, and loss.

Vitiated Red

This energy comes through in a dark, dirty, maroon red. It shows lustfulness. This person is mainly operating from the lower animal, with instinctual levels of consciousness. The person may be intoxicated by sex and have an insatiable appetite for more. It can suggest perversion and a definite misuse of the sexual energy. Vitiated red also shows deterioration of the person. Deep, muddy red shows strong anger, nervousness, a domineering temperament, and strife.

Avocado Green

This is a very dark green, like the outside of an avocado. It reveals deceit in an individual. This is someone who is out to cheat and take advantage of people. A traitor would have avocado green in his or her aura. It can show a person who is greedy. Avocado green is also present in the aura of a person with a consuming jealousy. It is a very insidious energy I have seen too often in people. Olive green, which is lighter in shading, shows envy.

Dark Brown

Brown, especially cocoa brown, shows someone who is cruel and petty. This energy stimulates selfishness and selfish desires for power. It can show someone who wishes to achieve and grow with intense feelings, but in the wrong directions. Dull brown denotes avarice. Greenish brown shows petty jealousy. A brownish mass of color can mean miserliness. Brown can also express guilt and repression. The lighter clear brown, however, is not an unenlightened energy like the others; it indicates an earthly, sometimes material-minded person.

Black

Black is the lowest vibration of all the colors. It is totally absent from the higher vibrations. It indicates someone who is open to dark influences, even vicious evil. Inky black clouds around a person are indicative of malice and hatred. A soul with this energy may be prone to murder or may have already committed a heinous crime. This person is capable of committing even more terrible crimes without hesitation or conscience. Lighter, smoky black indicates a "dark night of the soul," someone in the depths of despair. It can mean sorrow and suicidal impulses.

A GALLERY OF AURIC PORTRAITS

Let's apply our knowledge of spiritual colors and the aura as we look at some illustrations of what the aura is like in activity. Some people have the mistaken impression that their aura is something impersonal or removed from everyday life. Nothing could be further from the truth. The aura is an intimate, dynamic, and active part of everyone's life.

Like snowflakes, no two auras are exactly alike because no two people are going to use the life force of God in exactly the same way. If you spend your life planting seeds of hate, you will not display the auric splendor of those who plant seeds of love. If you are a violinist and I am a stockbroker, our auras will not be alike because our jobs require different focuses and skills. Whether filled with strife or filled with love, our lives are entirely dependent on the kind of energy we have created for ourselves.

This gallery of auric portraits depicts auras of actual people I have known. I have chosen auras that show a dramatic use of spiritual energy, either for positive or for negative purposes. Again, these auric conditions are not static or permanent. The aura is active and changing constantly, its shades of expression as varied as the people who express them.

Romantic Love

Here we see the aura of a twenty-year-old college student who fell in love with a young musician. (See color Illustration 3.2.) The musician returned her affections and an intense romance began. In this aura, a cloud of pink above the girl's head shows that she is strongly thinking of love, and of her beloved in particular. Around the whole aura is a bubbly pink champagne energy moving in a circular motion, joyously expressing the perpetual state of euphoria her love creates. It also reveals that the love is being reciprocated and that she is experiencing a vibrantly loving relationship. For the energy to be as intense as this, love has to be reciprocated.

Notice the active emanations of emerald green, royal blue, and gold radiating from her Hermetic center, showing steadfastness, determination, and strength of soul. This girl could not be shaken from her feelings. Hers was an all-consuming love. Active emanations of pink radiating in star-points of light from her emotional center show the actual expression, the feelings of love. The two were constantly expressing their love for each other. Energy such as this will stay in the aura for as long as the bond of love is sustained.

In such a relationship, the lovers will do anything for each other. Feelings go beyond sexual attraction. They're best friends, and neither would dream of hurting the other in any way. They're always looking to please one another and enjoy what the other does for them. This aura is fun-loving, optimistic, and supportive. Sometimes there will be possessiveness, which can bring in some lower energies, but in this case, it wasn't there. Her feelings revolved around an intense desire to be with her love. This soul is monogamous and immune to outside temptation. I know this sounds like a fairy-tale romance, but it does happen. I have seen many auras expressing love, although I've seen it to this degree less often.

Intelligence

This is the aura of an atomic scientist I observed in one of my lectures. (See color Illustration 3.3.) Naturally, the energies in his mental division were particularly strong. He had a band of yellow light just below the gold band connected with his mental division. This band had been built up through constant use of his powers of concentration. Another salient feature often accompanying such a brilliant mind is the solid silver triangle within the mental center—a mark of exceptional intelligence, even genius. That he was in the midst of intense mental work is evident in the upper part of his aura, where equation-like thought forms, some of which were quite long and complicated, were being projected from his subconscious, because he was so focused on his work. Brilliant souls such as this also have a highly developed magnetic division.

The weak links I have found in studying the auras of scientists and intellectuals are in the emotions. One would think that highly intelligent people would also possess well-balanced emotions, but this is often not the case. Emotionally, this man still had things to clear. The imbalance in this case showed up as avocado green rays shooting out from his emotional center. Strong irritability, manifesting in jagged dark red lines, also projected from his emotional center. An absence of pink in his aura suggested that he probably was a little cold in his relations with people.

Hatred

This is the aura of a woman who'd been molested as a girl by her father. (See color Illustration 3.4.) Although many years had passed, the result was a basic distrust and hatred of men—not pleasant for the men in her life. This aura shows the misplaced hatred she was directing toward her boyfriend at the time.

When I first met this woman, her aura wasn't so bad. She was actually very artistic—shown here by the active magnetic division—but as problems in her relationship developed, they triggered this kind of auric reaction. It took several months for the energy to build to this degree. A black cloud began to form above her head, showing persistent thoughts of long-standing, festering hatred. The fact that it was above her head means that although the thoughts were focused in hate, her mind could nevertheless be clear in its dark thoughts. Occasionally, I will see a cloud of hatred in and around the head area, which is indicative of confusion and poor functioning, but this was not the case here. The woman owned her own business and was doing quite well. Lightning bolts of maroon and black were also in her aura, showing rage born of hatred. Black radiations from the Hermetic and emotional centers testified to the consuming and destructive effects of hatred: she was making life very difficult for herself and the people around her. Such an aura must be closely monitored because a person in this condition is prone to rash acts. This woman talked about how her boyfriend was no good, and how she thought about killing him.

And yet, this is by no means an evil aura. The woman actually had spiritual inclinations and, interestingly, clairvoyant abilities as well, but she was disturbing those energies by creating such dark light.

Anger

Anger is perhaps the most dramatic of the negative emotional states seen in the aura. This illustration represents the energies of a man who constantly lashed out at his wife. (See color Illustration 3.5.) She didn't have to give him much of a reason to launch into one of his tirades. The situation ended tragically. The wife eventually became ill because of all that happened and died.

This anger extended beyond the perimeters of the auric shell. Squiggles and thunderbolts of vitiated red shot through the aura, along with streaks of red and blotches of olive green—unmistakable signs of extreme disharmony. The Hermetic center held clouds of dark brown and other muddled colors, showing the heaviness he was carrying on a constant basis. Broken lines of brown energy moved from his throat center when he was on one of his tirades, yelling cruel words at his wife. His emotional center was one big jumble of jagged vitiated rays of anger and irritation. Black dots showed the hatred this man felt, even though the wife did nothing to warrant it. Of course, it wasn't only his wife he was angry with. He was like a walking time bomb that was ready to explode at the slightest provocation.

Wealth Consciousness

One of the most prosperous energy fields I've ever encountered was that of a prince of royal German lineage. (See color Illustration 3.6.) He was a man of immense wealth when he was forced to flee Germany after Hitler came to power. He managed to take a large chunk of that wealth with him to the United States. Highly educated and with many skills, he was a diplomat and geologist, as well as an astute businessman. He owned his own oil company. Above all, as evinced in his aura, even though he was displaced from his homeland, he maintained his high level of wealth consciousness. He was in his seventies by the time I met him but still very alert and active.

Looking at this illustration, you can see pronounced turquoise energy moving around him, which means that this prosperity consciousness was long-standing. There is also a foundation of turquoise at his feet, establishing it as a steady consciousness that did not waver; he would most likely carry his prosperity consciousness into every situation. The preponderance of turquoise in this aura showcases a man who has continuously attracted and manifested abundance. The turquoise around his Hermetic center shows the day-to-day activity of the prosperity flow. The orange active radiations express his enthusiasm and motivations—this man really enjoyed what he did and was not operating out of greed or pride. As a rule, this kind of aura is very upbeat and fun to be around.

Poverty Consciousness

This aura represents a negative reaction to a tragic event. (See color Illustration 3.7.) The illustration is based on a woman who was widowed and left with three children to care for. She found work as a maid and was good at it, but it was a rough go with three kids to raise. Fortunately, the people in the small town she lived in helped as much as they could, but it was still hard for her. To compound the problem, she developed a pessimistic, gloom-and-doom attitude. The reason her aura was adversely affected was not so much her trying situation as it was her negative handling of that situation. Depending on him totally, she had put all her trust in her husband, and when he was gone, her world fell apart. Had this woman been able to put her faith in God, or even in herself, at this challenging time, she would have fared far better and bounced back more quickly.

Notice the dark energy around her head area. She feels sad, downtrodden, fearful, and without hope. Most of us have experienced this feeling to some degree. There's a feeling of failure. One has to work hard to get out of this consciousness. Most people make the mistake of seeing financial woes as permanent, and here's where they make their big mistake: feeling stuck and with no way out, they marshal little motivation to make the necessary effort to make changes. Yet if the condition is seen as temporary, there is much more motivation, faith, and hope that better days are in the making.

By this woman's head is a heavy thought-form concentration of avocado green, gloomy blue, and cocoa brown, reflecting the constant darkness of her thoughts. I remember seeing it undulate in this darkened state, giving those unhealthy thoughts a life all their own. The woman was always sad and often belittled herself. The fact that this thought form obscured part of her head shows that the condition was definitely clouding her thinking. Above this blotchy energy, note the gray cloud of fear. When I knew her, she was constantly fearful of what might happen next.

Around the Hermetic center was a maroon energy that signified negative conditions in her personal affairs. There were also brighter colors of royal blue—loyalty to her children, despite a bleak outlook on life. Emerald green showed an attempt to keep balance in her life. She was not a bad person by any means, but had succumbed to the hardships that befell her. In her emotional center, pink radiations of love showed her to be a warm person who loved her children very much. Mingling with that love pink were gray radiations, signaling fear of the future.

Fear

This auric illustration is of a man who was afraid of losing his job. (See color Illustration 3.8.) Fear and worry energies are very similar in the aura. They can be about a particular thing or situation, a chronic condition, a phobia, or an anticipated event. The fear may be justified or not, but when present to this degree, it's all-consuming. This man's worries had been building for months, which was reflected in a charcoal gray cloud above his head. If his fear were to diminish, then the gray would also lighten. Drooping gray lines emanating from the emotional center suggest that this man was withdrawing from the challenge rather than facing up to it. The fact that the radiations were moving downward means that the experience itself was pulling him down, creating a devolving situation. Royal blue still emanated from around the throat, but the energy was broken, showing the lack of confidence and weak will that accompanied his fear. In this case, the man's fears were based on a real threat, but things ended up okay. He kept his job. Yet the energy he expended in his worry sapped him of valuable energy, which took time to rebuild.

The Spiritual Aspirant

The aura of the spiritual aspirant is one of growth, as the soul begins to develop its spiritual powers and potential. This aura belonged to a minister at a metaphysical church, an energetic, enthusiastic, and knowledgeable person. (See color Illustration 3.9.) This soul had begun its conscious pilgrimage to its Eternal Home and the woman was working on bettering herself. The aura had beautiful bands of apple green and powder blue radiations of light above the woman's head (but below the spiritual division). They were very bright, clearly showing she was advancing on the spiritual path and had already been adapting her life to be in alignment with her spiritual aspirations.

She had pronounced silver sparkles of light just above the head, showing she was being quickened in divine intelligence to expand her spiritual awareness and perceive the new ideas and inspirations that were coming to her. There was a strong lemon yellow energy in the mental center, showing her developed intellectual powers and the ability to learn new things and retain that knowledge. The purple light below her feet was very bright, showing she had overcome many obstacles to get to where she was; it didn't come easy to her. There were sacrifices.

The emerald green ray was strong in her Hermetic center, showing that not only had she worked through many of these challenges but she had effectively integrated her spiritual aspirations into the rhythm of her life. There was a brilliant orange ray emanating from the Hermetic center as well, indicating the excitement she was experiencing with her new spiritual discoveries. Above her head, her beautiful crown chakra had begun to open its petals of light. It wasn't fully open but this meant that she had started the process of awakening her conscious awareness of the divine. She was pulling all facets of her aura together, organizing the energy in beautiful ways through her dedicated efforts. Such an aura as this is heading toward the great goal of the enlightened aura.

While this minister was on the road to the higher life, there were still areas she needed to improve. Most notably was her emotional center. While she was a loving person, there still were areas of gray, denoting fear, and vitiated red, denoting anger, indicating that she was struggling emotionally with some personal issues and was trying to come up out of it. There was a battle going on between her higher nature, urging her upward, and her lower nature, which was still fighting the transformation. This internal drama is completely natural and inevitable. It will fight you until you have it under your control. The good news is that as long as this person stays on the path she will eventually work through these lower vibrations and resurrect the higher, divine nature. This type of aura is not uncommon, especially today, with more and more people waking up to the spiritual realities of life.

Part II

MEDITATING WITH
DIVINE LIGHT

CHAPTER IV

Three Keys to Working with Spiritual Energy

. . . .

A unique feature about tapping into your spiritual bank account is that you're drawing energy from a spiritual source outside yourself, and from a greater place and dimension. This is the reason the light can be so effective. Because the Divine Light comes from such an exalted realm, it has potency far beyond anything connected with physical life. As you explore the myriad ways to work with spiritual energy, keep in mind three simple keys. They represent the process you will use to employ light in any situation.

> KEY 1—Decide what you want the light to do for you.
> KEY 2—Draw the light into your aura.
> KEY 3—Apply the light to effect the change you desire.

KEY 1——DECIDE WHAT YOU WANT THE LIGHT TO DO FOR YOU

Before meditating, it helps to have a clear idea of how you want the light to help. When you meditate with light, meditate with a purpose. This is not to say that you won't sometimes simply get into the divine oneness and ask the Divine Light to bless you. Rather, it means that preparing your meditations ahead of time will help you be more effective in your light work. The clearer you are about what you want the light to do for you, the more definite your results will be.

There are countless situations in which you may call on the light for spiritual assistance, from meeting daily challenges to working out deeply embedded character flaws and traumas. If you already know where you want to focus the light, then you are ready to begin the meditation. However, since you're taking the time to develop yourself, I recommend that you first step back and take personal inventory of your strengths and weaknesses. This way, you can better see where you are in your consciousness and spiritual progress. As Socrates said, "The unexamined life is not worth living." As part of your normal routine, take time out from life's pursuits to reflect on what you're doing in order to gain a fresh perspective. The list you compile from this self-inquiry can become a reference point, not only for what you need to work on but also as a signpost of your progress.

Recognition Is Half the Battle

The first step in any type of self-inquiry is recognition. You have to recognize that there are parts of you that need improvement. Despite the desire many of us have to improve our lives, we often encounter resistance to the whole process. It's not easy to recognize a fault or weakness. Many people go through the greater part of their lives unaware that they may be doing things that are hurting themselves and others. Recognition of a personal strength or weakness is a giant step in the right direction. There is tremendous liberation in the simple realization of why things are the way they are.

In some fortunate instances, recognition alone is enough to break through whatever blocks you may have. More often, recognition is the critical first step toward transformation. Recognition doesn't have to be limited to faults. It can be the recognition of a virtue or strength that you want to make stronger.

Take Responsibility

The next step in conducting an effective self-inquiry is to take responsibility for your actions. You will not get far in your spiritual growth if you constantly assign blame for your troubles to other people or outside circumstances. In my counseling work, people come to me with endless complaints, sometimes accompanied by self-pity. I say to them, "Do you want to be the master or the victim of your life?" Stop projecting your own faults onto others and blaming the other guy for what's going on in your life. You may not always be able to control conditions around you, but you are in absolute control of how you handle the situations in your life. Take charge of your life and watch how things will change.

Listing Strengths and Weaknesses

To begin your self-inquiry, get a notebook and assign space for six categories. Label them:

> *Thoughts*
> *Emotions*
> *Personal Affairs (situations and conditions in your life)*
> *Relationships*
> *Career*
> *Finances*

Then list what you feel are your strengths and weaknesses in each category. After you write down your observations, check to see how honest you are with yourself. Are you being too easy, too hard, or right on target? Which trait seems to stand out the most? That's probably the one you should focus on first.

To look at yourself objectively, I recommend conducting a weeklong self-survey. Keep a log of these six qualities in action. Don't steer your observations in any particular direction or judge anything. Don't change any of your daily habits. Take the week just as it comes: boring, average, exciting. Any activity is going to bring out qualities in you. Just observe and keep track in your journal of what you're doing. At the end of the week review your survey. The beauty of this kind of survey is that there's no arguing with yourself. If you got angry a lot that week, you got angry. If you were impatient, you were impatient. Things are clearly seen for what they are. Of course, not everything will come out in these preliminary exercises, but what you need to know to begin your light work will be apparent.

Once you recognize an area to work on, you can plan the spiritual energies to work with. This book offers many examples to point you in the right direction. For example, say you decide you need to work on forgiveness. Maybe someone in your life has hurt you and you have a difficult time letting that go. Anger and resentment live inside you and you find it challenging even to be in that person's presence.

Each person's situation is unique, but a place to start is to work with the orange-red flame of purification (see chapter 6) to clear out the anger and negative energy that has been brewing in your aura. You would then follow up with the blue-white fire to build up new life force, because the resentment has depleted precious energy from your aura. Then you may work with the deep rose pink of spiritual love to build up a more loving energy in your consciousness and to see this situation from the eyes of spirit. Working with this energy is essential in any relationship entanglement. It can help you see things from a different perspective.

Then you would follow up with the forgiveness prayer. There is a very powerful one offered in this book (see page 214) that I have worked with for years. So the list of meditative work you would do in this meditation would look something like this:

> *Orange-red flame for purification*
> *Blue-white fire for new life force*
> *Deep rose pink for love*
> *Forgiveness prayer*

With this preparation you would be ready for key 2—bringing the light into your aura.

Another example might be that perhaps you recognize a lack of self-confidence. You don't believe in yourself as you should and you allow other people to take advantage of you. In this scenario, you will need to work a great deal with the energy of confidence, the golden ray of wisdom light. Perhaps something dampened your enthusiasm and you feel discouraged. In that case, the bright orange of motivation is needed. In addition, you notice emotional patterns of fear that need cleansing. So your list of meditative work might look something like this:

> *Orange-red flame for purification*
> *Blue-white fire for new life force*

Golden ray of wisdom light for new confidence
Bright orange ray for motivation and enthusiasm

There are countless combinations of energies to work with depending on the situation you are dealing with. Working with the Divine Light is an art as well as a spiritual science. Throughout this book are many meditative prayers to help you get started in your light work.

KEY 2—DRAW THE LIGHT INTO YOUR AURA

Once you know where you want to focus the light, you're ready to meditate. The beautiful thing about taking inventory is that not only does it give you direction as to which way to go with the light, it also helps to get you in the frame of mind to work with spiritual energy to begin with.

You may have several areas that you want to work on. I recommend focusing on one area at a time until you have made progress in that direction before beginning another. This way, you'll see results faster and build more confidence in the effectiveness of the light.

In drawing in Divine Light to your aura, follow the six-step process outlined in chapter 5. People ask me how long to meditate and how many rays can be brought in during a meditation. In starting out, I recommend meditating for twenty minutes. You can certainly do more, but the key is consistency. You want to meditate daily. It needs to be routine, like brushing your teeth. This way, you are giving time for the light to build momentum in your aura. It's far better to meditate even ten minutes every day than, say, to do one long meditation on the weekend.

The other key is the depth of your meditation. Your meditation is an experience with the Divine Light. When you finish a meditation, you should feel different from when you started. As you become good at meditation, this will become easier to do. The whole idea of working with the Divine Light is to uplift your consciousness, which will give you a new perspective on things.

As far as how many rays to work with, the guideline is to work with as many rays as you feel you can actually implement at any given time. If you're working with the love ray in your meditation, then it's your job to be loving! If you've brought in the emerald green ray for balance, then it's your job to express balance in your life, and so on. You want to bring enough spiritual energy to effect a change but not too many rays that you are overwhelmed with the process. Your meditation should feel balanced and in rhythm with the whole of your life.

KEY 3—APPLY THE LIGHT TO EFFECT THE CHANGE YOU DESIRE

Once you have completed your meditation, then there is one more key to complete your light work—apply the light in your life. Occasionally a meditation alone can make the change you desire, but for the most part, you're going to have to actively apply the light after receiving it. You can't expect the change to come just by doing the light work alone and not applying the spiritual energy where it's needed. You must become the example of what you want. The whole key with light meditation is to integrate the light received into your active life.

You will be spending the most amount of time applying spiritual energy in your life, so this is a skill you want to get very good at. Some people love to meditate, but too often don't follow through after the meditation because they mistakenly think the meditation is enough. Think of your meditation like you're a spiritual warrior getting ready for battle. In your meditation, you are gathering up all the spiritual arsenal you need. Then you are ready to go into the battlefield of life prepared.

Strive to be the living example of the divine consciousness you are requesting. If you called on the energy of faith and trust where once there was worry and doubt, then it becomes your job to express that faith. Maybe something comes up that would normally get you worried and upset, but this time with the support of the Divine Light, you catch yourself and refuse to fall back into that old pattern. You realize you have the power to do this and the divine powers will become a deeper part of your life and you will have conquered a part of your personality.

But if you go back into those muddy waters of worry, you will neutralize the light work you have just done and the light will have little positive effect. Unfortunately, those worry energies can reignite in the aura. It's like taking two steps forward, but then falling two steps back, leaving you where you started. So this means you need to be steadfast in your light work. You have to see it all the way through.

In practice, it takes persistent effort to transform and enlighten the various facets of your aura. This is why you need to make meditation a daily practice. If a meditation doesn't bring about the change you desire the first time, try again. Through repeated meditation, you build the power in your aura until it becomes a steadfast part of you. There is no place the Divine Light can't go and turn things around. Every facet of your consciousness can be blessed.

Remember, the spiritual path is not an escape from life's duties, but the fulfillment of them. It's an enhancement of all life's processes. The light gives you a much-needed spiritual booster shot, but it is not a shortcut to spiritual unfoldment. Regardless of your knowledge or talent, you still have to go through all the steps of growth. Tapping into your spiritual bank account simply helps you get there faster.

Be receptive after doing a meditation. Sometimes the light works for you in ways you're not expecting. There is great joy and freedom in the process. Once the light starts working in your life, you may see that some people you thought were friends are not really friends at all. You'll need the courage to forgive and let them go and to allow new, like-minded friends to come into your life. Or you may discover that you're in the wrong job and will need to start looking for a new and better one. Be adaptable, and trust the light. It will always steer you in the right direction. New desires may unfold; you may have revelations about yourself; talents that were latent may start expressing themselves. You may also start to witness spiritual gifts awakening. That is not a prerequisite to the light work, but many I have worked with have had direct experiences with the light. Once the Divine Light builds in your aura, a new life will gracefully unfold.

CHAPTER V

Six Steps to Change Your Aura

. . . .

*T*he six-step technique presented in this chapter is a simple yet powerful meditation to draw the light from your spiritual reservoir into your aura. It's a technique that's been a part of the metaphysical tradition for centuries. I have been practicing this meditation for most of my life and taught this technique to thousands of people with astonishing results. It has no formal name, but I call it the Higher Self meditation.

UNDERSTANDING THE HIGHER SELF

Before beginning the Higher Self meditation, there is one more part of your spiritual anatomy to look at—a very sacred part. As we have explored, you can change your aura by first tapping your spiritual bank account. Yet, how do you actually tap into this creative flow? You have this magnificent source of power, and you have the expression of this light in your aura, but what is the mechanism by which this light actually reaches you? There needs to be a link between you and your spiritual reservoir that can guide the whole light process. Fortunately, this link is already a part of you. It's a magnificent aspect of your spiritual design that already has the divine intelligence and awareness to relate to the light directly, as well as relate to the soul part of you. This link—or emissary of light—is your Higher Self.

The Higher Self has been mentioned so many times in spiritual literature that it has become part of the nomenclature of metaphysical study. Many teachers recognize it as a guiding force in humanity's evolution. Helena Blavatsky, the great metaphysician, cofounder of the Theosophical Society, and author of masterpieces such as *Isis Unveiled* and *The Secret Doctrine*, called the Higher Self "the divine prototype" and "the reflection of the universal spirit." The famous European mystic Rudolf Steiner called the conscious awakening of the Higher Self a "spiritual rebirth." Other teachings call it a "lifeline," or a beacon by which a ship lost at sea can find its way home; the awakened soul is answerable to and looks for guidance from the Higher Self alone.

All the spiritual light you receive from the celestial realms has to first pass through the Higher Self to reach you. The Higher Self does this automatically, but when the process is attended to in a conscious and direct way, it can greatly increase the light your Higher Self can transmit to you. If it were not for the Higher Self, you would have no direct way of connecting with the Divine Light.

The beauty of your Higher Self is that it's already in its divine awareness and therefore in a state of perfection. It's a greater part of you that is completely aware of the spiritual realms above it and yet keenly aware of what is happening to you, here and now. You can completely rely on the Higher Self. It has no blemishes, no human traits to disappoint you. It's totally reliable and is a guiding force in steering your soul in its evolution. The Higher Self is always with you and always working for you, whether you are aware of it or not. As you align yourself with its power, its effectiveness greatly multiplies.

The Higher Self is often contrasted with what is commonly termed the "lower self." The lower self refers to the unenlightened human parts of your consciousness. These are the parts of you that have not yet spiritually developed. For many people, the lower self is all they're aware of at this point in their spiritual evolution.

In addition to channeling light, the Higher Self is one of the tools you will use to help transcend your human awareness and reach into your spiritual knowing. This consciousness will help you awaken to the spiritual path and your divine potential. It also helps you to consciously become aware of the light process.

Fortunately, the Higher Self is not simply a metaphysical concept. It is an intimate and sacred part of you. In the aura, the Higher Self appears as a point of light twenty-four inches above the physical head. If you wish, you may call this the eighth spiritual center or chakra. Its full name is the Higher Self Point of Spiritual Knowing. (See color Illustration 5.1.) It's about three inches in diameter (similar to the other centers) but it does not rotate. It's gold, with a point of lighter gold in the center. From this center, thousands of gold and white threadlike rays shoot out about fourteen inches in all directions. Many depictions of spiritual blessings, such as *The Coronation of the Virgin* by Velázquez, interestingly place the source of the blessing at the Higher Self Point. The more developed and connected to the Higher Self the individual is, the more radiant and extended these rays will be. As a particular energy is drawn into it, many of the rays will take on the color and quality of the light being called upon.

Since it is above your head and above the mixed elements of your human aura, the Higher Self Point can receive the light clearly and directly. Think of the Higher Self Point as like a satellite in space. An orbiting satellite can receive a signal from deep space much more clearly than a receiving station on Earth can because the satellite has no interference from the atmosphere. In the same way, without the atmosphere of human interference, the Higher Self Point becomes a gateway to the greater realms of light and life. It's an indescribable sight.

THE HIGHER SELF MEDITATION

To begin the Higher Self meditation, first find a quiet, relaxing place. It should be a place where you feel good and can concentrate without interruption. You don't want to be around a lot of people when you are doing this meditation. If you don't already have one, find a spot in your home that is conducive to meditation. Ideally, it should be an area that others don't spend much time in. It may be a corner of your bedroom where you have your own special chair—anyplace where you can work consistently. This way, the energy will have a chance to build, which will make your light work all the more effective. If you live with other people, let them know what you are doing and that your meditation time is to be uninterrupted time. You may also work outdoors, which is excellent. Being in nature is certainly an effective way to work with the light. Again, find a place where there aren't many people nearby, such as your backyard or a park. I've even pulled my car off a main road, found a quiet neighborhood, and done a meditation right in the car.

The point of meditation is to become still and shut the world out, so you can tune into your own divine nature. Meditation is a way to get closer to God. In the activities of daily life, it's hard to feel your divine oneness unless you're able to tune out that activity periodically. I had a student once who said she was meditating every day, but that things weren't happening fast enough for her. So I went to her house, and she showed me how she meditates. To begin with, she had the radio blasting. She also had the phone right next to her and picked it up twice during her "meditation." She had food on the stove and would get up periodically to check it. In other words, she was doing everything but getting into her divine oneness. How could the light work be effective this way?

I've had people ask if they can meditate while they drive or exercise. Certainly you can ask that the light bless you during these activities, but this is not meditation. In meditation, you are physically still. The whole idea is to step outside the activity of the world to be in the God presence. Remember why you are meditating. This is your one-on-one time with God. If you find yourself saying you are too busy to meditate, that's like saying you are too busy to spend time in the God presence. Put your meditation time at the center of your life and watch how everything else falls into place.

The Higher Self meditation is actually a form of meditation and prayer. Prayer is a sending out, a petition to God. The goal of prayer is to connect with your divine source. Through the act of prayer you are reaching out to the divine. Then, in this divine oneness, you will be requesting the Divine Light and inspiration to flow to you through what are called meditative prayers. Meditation is getting into the stillness to receive. In your light work, you will be getting into the stillness to receive the light that you have petitioned to the Divine for. So meditation and prayer work hand in hand.

In first working with the light, twenty minutes is ideal. Light a white candle and place a bowl of water next to the candle. This will help to set the right vibration in the room for your work. You can place flowers near you if you like. It doesn't matter what time of day you meditate. I like to meditate in the morning because it helps to start my day. I suggest selecting some clothes that you will wear for your meditation time, such as a robe, because with each meditation you're putting light into those clothes. Over time, so much light will be held in your meditation clothes that you'll find yourself in the mood to meditate just by putting them on.

THE SIX STEPS TO THE HIGHER SELF MEDITATION

1. *Relax.*
2. *Establish protection.*
3. *Check your spiritual centers.*
4. *Connect with your higher self.*
5. *Down-ray the light.*
6. *Ground yourself.*

STEP 1——RELAX

Take a few moments to simply relax. Let go of the world's clamor and your own preoccupations. It doesn't matter what's going on around you. You're in a sacred place now, where you're making your connection with the Divine, and you want to be as clear and lucid as possible. This relaxed state is not a sleepy state, but an awakened calm.

If you're upset or disturbed by something, be sure to calm down first before starting the light work. You don't want to start angry or disturbed. Take a break and go for a walk or a drive, and don't think at all about what is bothering you. If you're having trouble relaxing, begin by playing some music to calm you. You can also start with some slow, deep breathing.

STEP 2——ESTABLISH PROTECTION

When you do any type of meditation, you're putting yourself in an open, receptive state of consciousness. Spiritual protection is important at every level of life and doubly important while in the meditative state. There's a lot of activity in the world, a lot of negative energies coming at you from people and places that can affect you if you permit them to. So, before you start your meditation, make sure to call for protective light around you.

To establish your protection, once you have found your place to meditate and are relaxed, place yourself in a bubble of golden light. To do this, stand up, hold your arms out, and envision yourself surrounded by a golden bubble of light just beyond arm's length from your body. This bubble of light is all around you—in front of you, behind you, above you, below you, and on either side of you. Envision seven flows of living light surrounding you and keeping you in perfect safety while you say the following prayer.

Golden Bubble of Protection

"Encircle me now in a golden bubble of protective light. I
ask for seven flows of this light to surround me, keeping me
in Thy perfect protection."

Once you feel you have established your protection, you can start. Over time, if you are consistent with your meditations, you will build your protection very strongly, and you won't need to stand. You will be able to reinforce your protection sitting down. In addition to the golden bubble, it is recommended to add to your protection by closing what is called the psychic door (see page 245).

STEP 3—CHECK YOUR SPIRITUAL CENTERS

In working with the Divine Light, you're most frequently going to be sending the light from your Higher Self Point to four spiritual centers. These are:

The mental center
The throat center
The Hermetic center (heart center)
The emotional center

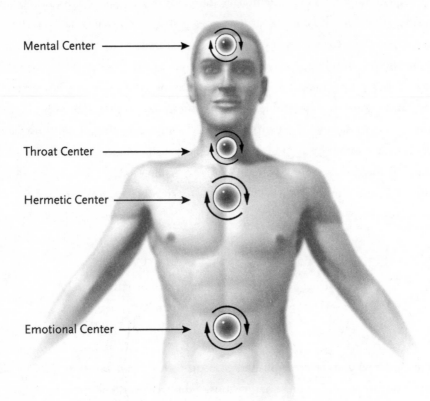

Mental Center

Throat Center

Hermetic Center

Emotional Center

ILLUSTRATION 5.2-*Moving the Centers Clockwise*

These four centers are going to be focal points for receiving and distributing the light throughout your consciousness. It's not that the other centers don't come into play; they're just not designed to be the kind of receiving and transmitting stations that these centers are.

When the centers are moving in their proper flow and rhythm, they should be spinning in a *clockwise direction*. (See Illustration 5.2.) Imagine a clock, attached to your chest with its face out, its hands rotating in their normal direction. Twelve o'clock would be straight up, three o'clock to your left, six o'clock below you, and nine o'clock to your right. This is clockwise. If your centers are moving *counter*clockwise, you are opened up to all sorts of disharmony and the centers make poor points of contact for the Divine Light. Even if only one center is moving counterclockwise, it can throw the others off.

To check your centers, begin by placing your hands, right hand over left, over the center you want to check. Start with the emotional center and work your way up. Become very still and try to get a feeling of how your center is moving. If you feel fine or sense that the center is moving clockwise, everything is good and you can move on to the next center. If you feel uneasy or sense that the center is off, envision the pure white light going into that center and changing its spin, moving it clockwise. Continue in the same way until you have checked all four centers.

If you do sense a center is off, by doing this you will know even better where to ask this light to go. In addition, checking the spiritual centers beautifully prepares the consciousness for the Divine Light you are about to call on.

STEP 4—CONNECT WITH YOUR HIGHER SELF

Now you're ready to make your connection with the light. To begin the Higher Self meditation, sit upright in a chair, with your legs uncrossed and feet flat on the floor. (See Illustration 5.3.) Take your shoes off so the energy can flow freely. In this type of meditation, it's important that your feet are flat on the floor. This will act as a strong grounding for the powers that will be flowing down from above you. During the meditation, keep your hands on your emotional center, right hand over left, to help polarize the energy as it flows through you. Begin your meditation by placing your attention at your Higher Self Point, twenty-four inches above your head. By effectively placing your conscious attention at this point, you are making a strong connection with your Higher Self. It's very possible you will feel elation, or a heightened awareness of the Higher Self, but such an experience is not prerequisite to conducting an effective meditation.

When you're ready, start by saying the following invocation out loud. This invocation is a signal that you are calling for help. It affirms your connection with your Higher Self Point and helps you to get in the divine state you need to work with the light.

ILLUSTRATION 5.3-*The Meditative Pose*

INVOCATION

"Heavenly Father, Holy Mother God, I raise my consciousness
into Thy consciousness where I become One with
Thee. I ask to receive that which I need and that which I
need to know now."

As you say these words, place your attention into your Higher Self Point, becoming one with its divine essence. Let go the world and any worries or concerns. You are on holy ground now. Feel and sense that you are in the clarity of spiritual knowing, a place of peace, serenity, and harmony. The centers within your body can be tainted and corrupted, but not this Higher Self. You have placed your consciousness above the human levels of your being and moved into a pure divine part of you.

STEP 5——DOWN-RAY THE LIGHT

Once you have established a connection with your Higher Self, you can petition the light verbally. Verbalization is important because it helps you to focus, while also making you a much more active participant in the light work. You're going to be calling on a particular light ray to do a specific task. If you say it silently, there's a tendency to let your mind wander a little.

Verbalizing your prayers is a strong affirmation of the light, and it also brings into play spiritual tone through your throat center.

In calling on the light, the key verb you will use is "down-ray." The Divine Light is going to be down-rayed from the higher realms to your aura. Remember, this is not a spiritual supply that comes from within you. Rather, it is energy that you are drawing from a source that is above and beyond you. As you ask for the energy you need, first see that energy down-rayed to the Higher Self Point. See the color of the energy you are working with touching into and activating this point. From the Higher Self Point, envision a beam of light moving down into the four spiritual centers you are working with (see Illustration 5.2), or wherever you're asking the light to go. As the light touches into each center, hold it there for a moment to feel the connection being made, knowing that these centers are being ignited with spiritual power. See the center completely filling with the colored light you're asking for, and out-raying about a foot in all directions. Then ask for the particular divine quality you want the light to bring you.

As mentioned, you will be calling on the light by saying a meditative prayer. These prayers give the directions you want the light to take. This book contains many examples of meditative prayers, suited to a variety of situations and conditions. I recommend using them verbatim in the beginning. Eventually you will get into the rhythm of the light work and come up with your own prayer for the exact need you have. Don't worry about goofing up the exact wording. Yes, there is a nomenclature to the light work, but as you work with it, it will come to you.

Working with the light will become an art as well as a spiritual exercise. If you can memorize the light prayers, that's great. If not, then simply read the prayers.

In working with the Divine Light, you can ask for the energy to bless a particular chakra or center or any facet of the aura and consciousness. Or, as you will often do, ask the light to bless all the centers, especially the four centers emphasized in this book. This way you bless all facets of your nature. Sometimes the attention goes to a particular facet of the consciousness you know needs help, but as parts of the aura are interconnected, you may find other facets that need help as well. By including the four main centers you are covering a wide area of your awareness.

As the light is being down-rayed to you, you may feel it as a rush of energy or a tingling sensation. You may feel heat, depending on what it's doing and the degree of your sensitivity. I repeat, even if you feel nothing, the light is still working for you. Eventually you will get into the feeling of the light. If you sense resistance, don't push against it. Be gentle, and go at a pace you feel comfortable with. If you're working with more than one energy, give yourself a few minutes between energies to allow each one to settle before calling on the next.

If you're not sure about something, ask divine intelligence to guide you. Don't worry about hurting yourself if you choose the "wrong" energy. Sometimes I have asked for one ray and seen a completely different ray come in. Your Higher Self knows exactly what your needs are. Always ask that you receive the light "to the degree of my need." You can't really overdose on the light because the Higher Self watches that you get only what you can handle, but you do want to be in the rhythm of the light work, and saying this is helpful. In addition, you want to ask the light to touch into "all levels of my consciousness." This way, the light can be directed to other areas of the aura that need work, in addition to the centers.

STEP 6—GROUND YOURSELF

After you have received the light, be still for a moment to let it stabilize through-out your consciousness. This way, you are grounded in the light. You don't want to suddenly jump up and get on with your day. When you feel that the light is estab-lished in you, ask that it be anchored into each point, sealing in the light. It's a good idea to ask that the golden ray of protection surround the light you have just received. Through your meditation, you have been blessed by the most precious energy of light. You don't want to lose that light or have it usurped. In closing, remember to use the following prayer to thank the Higher Power for all the work done for you, and to acknowledge all that you have received.

Closing Prayer

"I ask that the light I have just received be protected, sealed, and anchored into my centers and all aspects of my aura. I thank Thee that this is so, and so shall it ever be. So be it."

Once you feel yourself grounded, get up and go on with your day.

CHAPTER VI

Tapping the Power Rays

N ature is full of God's bounty. Everywhere you look you can thrill to God's richness and splendor. Nature produces an almost endless variety of physical creations—trees, flowers, insects, animals. Even physical light is not just one color but *many* bands of colors. The same variety holds true for spiritual light. There are myriad spiritual energies, each serving its own purpose. You need this diversity because each power ray draws in a different spiritual attribute, and there are many attributes of the spiritual life you need to draw on. The ten power rays described in this chapter represent ten different spiritual attributes to more deeply incorporate in your aura and consciousness. These spiritual energies have been specially designed to help you in your spiritual pursuits and all facets of life.

As you work with these rays, do your best to visualize their colors, as this assists you in tuning into their holy attributes. If you are naturally clairvoyant you may actually see the power; that's great but not necessary for an effective meditation. Your ability to receive the spiritual light will not be diminished if you don't spiritually see the energy. I have had students questioning whether they really got the energy and wondering why they couldn't see the light while others could. Doubting is counterproductive, as it can get in the way of receiving. Simply *know* that you are receiving. These power rays are no fantasy. This is not an intellectual exercise or a play of imagination. They are real. You really are drawing these energies to you, and as you work with them, you will get into a place of knowing.

The duties of these color rays can overlap. Sometimes, the rose pink love ray will purify negative energies more effectively than the orange-red flame. Other times, the gold will come in for illumination, rather than the pure white light. You'll get into the feeling and sensing of exactly how to use these rays. Best of all, your Higher Self knows just what you need. If you call in one ray but another is more appropriate for you at that moment, you will get what you need.

In describing these energies, a meditative prayer accompanies each ray. These are general prayers that you can use anytime you need these power rays. For example, if you're feeling jittery, you can use the meditative prayer for divine peace to calm yourself down. In the following chapters, we'll go into the various ways to work with the light in particular situations, and the individualized meditative prayers that go with them.

THE LIGHT AS CONSCIOUSNESS

As you work with Divine Light, remember what it is that the light is actually doing for you. As we have explored, the Divine Light is the conduit of *consciousness*. A conduit is a type of transmission or transportation system. It brings something from one place to another. A pipe, for example, is a conduit for water. It brings water to your home. Wire is a conduit for electricity. It brings the electrical current from the power plant to your house. In the same way, Divine Light is a transportation system to bring consciousness from the divine source to all facets of creation. So it's not the light itself that is so transformative, it's the divine consciousness that is *in* the light that is so powerful.

When you are working with spiritual energy you are working with consciousness. That consciousness is being transmitted from the divine source to you to elevate and enlighten your awareness.

PURIFICATION

The power ray to use for spiritual purification is called the orange-red flame. This ray is specifically designed to help release negative, unenlightened energy in the aura. The dominant energy is orange, which is the purifier, but the red is strong, too, which brings in purification quickly and with great vitality. The orange-red flame purifies by "burning up" negative energy in the aura. This ray breaks up the destructive energy into a fine powdery substance called black and gray atoms. Once cut loose, the unredeemed atoms are taken into the mineral kingdom, where they are reconstituted in the Divine Light. Nothing is lost. Even defiled energy is recycled.

Spiritual purification is essential in developing your aura. In physical life, the body can build up many toxins from a variety of sources. It must release these toxins or it will become increasingly polluted, stressed, and diseased. In spiritual purification, you need to release spiritual toxins for the aura to operate properly. These spiritual toxins are the negative energies you have either created or picked up from others. Such energies linger in the aura, disturbing and draining the entire energy field. Fortunately, the aura has a built-in self-replenishing system that operates on an eight-hour cycle to cleanse the energy field. Yet, sometimes this is not enough.

For example, say your aura is in great shape with no dark radiations to speak of. But you get into an argument and unleash a huge outburst of anger. The anger will change your aura, and some of those once-beautiful energies will now become vitiated red. You have dirtied your aura as a result of your emotional outburst. Eventually the negative radiations will subside, but this will take time. Even with the spiritual self-cleansing system working round the clock, an intense outburst of anger can take *two weeks* to completely leave the aura! During those two weeks, you can be susceptible to additional outbursts and other negative energies if you're not careful. If you succumb to more emotional outbursts, you build up more negative energy, thus restricting the natural flow of the aura. If you're not vigilant, you can attract other kinds of destructive energies, compounding the problem. The result can wreak havoc in your life, resulting in tension, accidents, illnesses, and other problems.

The orange-red flame is usually the first step in effecting change. So you're going to be calling on this ray often. Purification is an almost daily requirement; probably right up to the day you leave this world you're going to be purifying yourself. It's almost impossible not to create or pick up some negative energy along the way. There's always something that wants to come at you, and you can absorb these negative energies unintentionally. With the orange-red flame, you don't have to worry. This energy can get you out of any spiritual entanglement. The orange-red flame is also an essential tool for releasing the buildup of destructive energies accumulated from the past. You'll be using this spiritual scrub brush often in releasing bad habits and faults. It's a tremendous power ray. Without this energy, humanity could never rise out of the negative energy it has created or acquired.

MEDITATIVE PRAYER FOR THE ORANGE-RED FLAME

"Down-ray the orange-red flame of purification to all levels
of my consciousness, releasing me from all black and gray
atoms and taking them into the mineral kingdom to be
dissolved in the light."

NEW LIFE FORCE

The ray to call on for new life force is the blue-white fire of eternal life. This ray is very powerful and connected to what is called the "breath of God." It's one of the highest energies you can use. If you have time to use only one energy, use the blue-white fire. It's a powerful, replenishing energy that brings in new life force to your consciousness. It's a spectacular energy to see. The predominant color is a rich sapphire blue, almost like the blue flame of a gas stove, with sparkles of white and silver light shooting out, creating an electrifying effect. Again, it appears more like a ray than an actual fire, but it works in you very much as a spiritual life-giving fire. There are actually seven attributes to this power ray, and many times you can see a kaleidoscope of colors moving with the blue and white, which is why this ray is so beneficial.

The blue-white fire will be used very strongly in conjunction with the orange-red flame. After you complete your spiritual purification, follow up with the blue-white fire. Having finished using one ray, you are now replenishing with another. The blue-white fire has an amazing capacity to rejuvenate and charge up your aura, making other energies assimilate better. Like pulling up weeds from your garden before planting new flowers, you want to prepare the soil so the new seeds will grow well. Using the blue-white fire is like tilling in new soil.

The blue-white fire is the single greatest healing energy there is. So if you are using spiritual energy to help heal an illness or injury, you will use this power ray a great deal. It helps alleviate pain and distress. It contributes greatly in sustaining the physical body. Its power courses through the physical organs and bloodstream. Without the blue-white fire, the physical body would lose its vitality and not be able to function well. In essence, it's part of the cosmic life force, capable of healing and restoring life energy to all areas of your being. In truth, the blue-white fire has many applications. If you're depressed, the blue-white fire can help lift you out of that depressed state.

MEDITATIVE PRAYER FOR THE BLUE-WHITE FIRE

"Down-ray the blue-white fire of eternal life, charging and recharging all levels of my consciousness in a clockwise motion with new, electrifying life force."

WISDOM

The ray to call on for wisdom and illumination is the golden ray of wisdom light. It appears as a brilliant golden ray and is the spiritual essence of the dynamic power of God. Like the blue-white fire, there are many applications for this holy power. You will use this energy a great deal in conjunction with divine guidance. If you're trying to make an important decision, bring in the golden ray of wisdom light, especially to your mental body, and ask for illumination to help you make the right choice. If you find you're wishy-washy in general, the golden ray is the energy that will help you become more decisive.

Wisdom is one of the key attributes of a mature soul. True wisdom is born of experience. It speaks of spiritual insight and knowledge, strength of character, and strong moral fiber. A wise person makes decisions from a place of inner knowing. Spiritual wisdom is a result of applied knowledge and not repeated, drilled-in information. A student can memorize many spiritual principles, but this doesn't make him or her wise. Until that student has assimilated the knowledge into his or her knowing, it's not really wisdom. There's an old spiritual saying, "You know that you know that you know." It takes time to truly build wisdom. This is why an aura with the predominant gold in it is one of the highest auras of all. It shows that the soul has gone through countless experiences, tests, and trials and won the victory of true spiritual knowledge and mastery.

The gold light is the most dynamic of all the rays, and you need to be expressing your dynamic nature. It would be very hard to get anything accomplished in this world, especially anything spiritual, without dynamic energy.

Many people involved in spiritual work misunderstand the dynamic nature of life. They often confuse being spiritually dynamic with being humanly aggressive, and so they shy away from expressing their dynamic nature. The dynamic nature of life is the "giving out" aspect—the builder and the initiator of life. Being spiritually dynamic is a *divine* trait that operates under the direction of divine will so that your actions are in harmony with life. In this way, your actions are in no way detrimental to others. It becomes a win-win situation. People who are dynamically active will radiate a beautiful golden light.

Because golden light is such a dynamic power, it has many applications. The golden ray may be called upon to build a dynamic will, confidence, courage, divine power, faith, and inner strength. It's the best energy for protection, even better than white light.

Meditative Prayer for Wisdom Light

"Down-ray the golden ray of wisdom light to all levels of my
being, bringing forth Thy wisdom and illumination and all
the divine, dynamic attributes of this power that I need now."

SPIRITUAL LOVE

The deep rose pink is the energy to call on for spiritual love. As the golden ray brings in dynamic wisdom, will, and action, the deep rose pink draws in love, compassion, and kindness. Its essence is the magnetic nature of God. In the high spiritual realms there are basically two forces operating—Divine Mind and Heart of Spiritual Love. Love is the bond that holds the universe together. More than anything else, Divine Love brings you into oneness with God. Once you are in that unity, you will have love for yourself and compassion for others, because you will be connected to the source of love.

The love ray is one of the easiest energies to sense. When working with it, you can feel its softness and gentleness. There's often a feeling of bliss when using this ray, and people see its energy more often than any other. The deep rose pink ray may be used to create a more loving environment for yourself and others around you. It can also work as a great healing energy if you have been hurt or are feeling lonely or unloved. It's an essential energy to use in mending relationships, working on forgiveness, increasing your trust and understanding, and becoming less selfish. It's the great healer of the soul and can mend the deepest of wounds to the heart.

All human fears, frustrations, loneliness, and worries can be dissolved by the deep rose pink love ray. This Divine Love helps to inspire a selfless attitude toward life. It is the pure unconditional love that gives without thought of return. It's the sacrificial love, the love of service to humanity. This high love leads to the ultimate universal love of God, that loves all of creation equally and unconditionally.

MEDITATIVE PRAYER FOR DIVINE LOVE

"Down-ray the deep rose pink ray, quickening my spiritual
centers and filling my entire consciousness with this Thy
love, bringing me into perfect beauty, rhythm, and tone, as
one body in Thy body of Divine Love."

DIVINE PEACE

The deep purple is the ray to call on for divine peace. There is also a gentler version, which is violet in hue. The deep purple ray is essential for quieting the mind and emotions. It seems the word most often used in the world today is "peace." People are crying out for peace. In this stressful and fast-paced world, in the midst of the whirlwind, you need to quiet the consciousness and commune with your own divine nature and God. The only way to do this is to turn to God for your peace. This ray offers one of the best ways to help you release the stress and strain of the world and to get into that calm state. It releases any sense of burden or heavy-heartedness.

This is the energy to call upon to bring you into the divine stillness, the spiritual silence. When you're at peace with yourself, there is no conflict. There's a relaxation in divine knowing. You can only be truly at spiritual peace when you are in that divine knowing. A person with a lot of purple in his or her aura is very advanced indeed because that person has truly let go and let God take over.

Many people hold on to their worries and troubles to such a degree that they leave no room for God to enter their lives. They let stresses burden them to the point that they can barely function. When there's a lot of anxiety, the aura is affected. The energy doesn't flow as it should and becomes jagged and irregular. This ray can help smooth out these bumps in the aura. It's great for soothing the nerves. If you are grieving, or have experienced something shocking, the purple ray is the energy to use to help you come out of that grief.

MEDITATIVE PRAYER FOR DIVINE PEACE
. . . .

"Down-ray the purple ray of divine peace, touching into all

levels of my consciousness and bringing me into the silence

of peace and the peace of silence."

BALANCE AND HARMONY

The power ray to call on for balance and harmony is the emerald green ray. Without harmony and a centering of the consciousness, nothing will work right in your life. The more spiritually centered you stay, the easier things will go for you. The emerald green ray helps balance and harmonize all the different aspects of your life, so they move smoothly. In music, harmony is defined as the blending of two or more musical sounds in a pleasing manner. In the same way, you want the different departments of your life to be moving well together. You can use this energy to help maintain balance between mind, body, and soul.

The emerald green ray is very important in your day-to-day life. This energy helps to keep your spiritual equilibrium, no matter what obstacles you face. If you feel disoriented in your earthly affairs, call on this energy to balance things out. You undoubtedly have many things going on at the same time and need to keep them all moving smoothly. Maybe your home life is fine, but your professional life is chaotic. Your relationship with your friends may be strong, but not with your own family. You may have suffered a trauma that threw your life out of balance. These are all situations that need the emerald green ray. A person whose life is balanced will be able to handle many things with efficiency and ease. There will be fewer extremes in his or her life, and when extreme situations do come up, they will have far fewer devastating effects.

Your Hermetic center is in particular need of this ray, as there is so much activity in this center connected with the outside world. This energy also helps to reverse counterclockwise movement in the aura.

Meditative Prayer for Balanced Power

"Down-ray the emerald green ray of balanced power to
flow directly into my centers and entire being, bringing me
into perfect harmony of mind, body, and soul."

DIVINE INTELLIGENCE

The silver ray brings divine intelligence. Intelligence is different from wisdom in that it is based strongly on perception. There are people who are intelligent but not wise. Yet, you need intelligence to perceive wisdom. The silver ray works strongly on the mental levels of the aura to quicken your powers of perception. The silver ray facilitates clarity and is great for quickening perception when you're having trouble comprehending a lot of information.

This ray accelerates progress. Say you have a business transaction that seems to be dragging. It's clear what has to be done, but there is endless red tape. Papers are not getting signed, people are not returning phone calls. You can call on the silver ray to quicken the whole process and break through the stagnation. It's a powerful ray when you need guidance in your life. The silver ray works very well with gold, lemon yellow, and white light. It helps to enhance the effectiveness of other rays, so that you receive them more easily in the aura. You can call in this ray to help guide you when you're not sure which ray to use in your meditations.

A person who is utilizing his or her divine powers of intelligence will have uncanny understanding and insights when facing the challenges and problems that arise in life. Have you noticed how certain people seem to handle pressure very well, making clear decisions that seem to turn out right? This kind of person is very close to the divine consciousness of this power, whether on a conscious or unconscious level.

MEDITATIVE PRAYER FOR DIVINE INTELLIGENCE

"Down-ray the silver ray of divine intelligence to my mental
body, quickening my brain and flesh cells and all levels of
my conscious brain/mind thinking, sharpening my
powers of perception."

CONCENTRATION

The lemon yellow ray brings in powers of concentration. If you're studying for a test or trying to master a subject, this is an essential ray to call upon. It gives you the ability to focus on a subject without distraction. As you build this power, you will stimulate your ability to study and increase your enjoyment of learning. If you need to dispel mental lethargy, this is the ray to use. Although it's primarily a mental energy, it may be used throughout the aura to help steady the vibration and bring the energies into greater order if they are scattered.

The lemon yellow ray is important in becoming a trained clairvoyant. When I was developing my own clairvoyance, I spent nine months just working on concentration to get me to the level that I needed to develop my sustaining power. It's difficult to hold certain clairvoyant perceptions for any length of time. Without this level of concentration, I would not be able to sustain my spiritual vision throughout a whole lecture—which may include reading many auras.

MEDITATIVE PRAYER FOR CONCENTRATION

"Down-ray the lemon yellow ray into my mental body,
quickening my conscious brain/mind thinking and
bringing me powers of concentration."

PROSPERITY

The turquoise ray is the spiritual energy of prosperity, abundance, and supply. Its color is a bluish green, very much like the bluish shade of the turquoise stone. If you believe you are lacking the spiritual awareness of prosperity, this is the energy to work with. This power ray is especially designed to help you build the consciousness and flow of unlimited wealth. In physical life, there is often a tendency to limit oneself. This ray can help you get out of the narrow-minded thinking of lack and limitation and expand your horizons. With this power ray, you will step into an expanded flow of light. This energy works well in all the centers, especially in the Hermetic center, to multiply and amplify the positive conditions in your life. It can help you to create more material abundance, as well as attract friends, ideas, and assistance in building fresh new opportunities.

As explored in chapter 10, prosperity consciousness is one of the natural, inborn attributes of your consciousness. As a child of God, you have the power to create prosperity. To express these gifts of abundance is a matter of nurturing and developing those inborn qualities. If you're lacking in physical resources, it can mean you've disconnected from your spiritual heritage. Somehow, the turquoise energy is not balanced in your aura. To build your prosperity, you have to draw on this energy often. You must also think, speak, and feel prosperous. It's especially important to get into the feeling of this energy; you need to *feel wealthy* to establish it in your consciousness. Your emotional body needs to feel this spiritual richness, whether your pocketbook agrees with you or not.

If you're in a financial crunch, you can use this ray to build up a positive spiritual flow that will help generate income. If you're anxious about money, you can work with this ray to build a more spiritual consciousness of money. This way, your faith and knowing will carry you through any financial rough times. If you are in the true consciousness of prosperity, it won't matter how much you have, because you are directly connected to supply and know that you will always have what you need.

MEDITATIVE PRAYER FOR PROSPERITY

"Down-ray the turquoise ray of abundance and supply,
touching into my Hermetic center and quickening persons,
places, things, conditions, and situations, bringing me into
perfect prosperity."

THE PURE WHITE LIGHT

The pure white light is a wonderful elevating and redeeming energy. It brings in the very essence of God. It has a tremendous ability to transmute negative energies. If you have done something you know is wrong, you'll want to call on this energy to help lift you out of the dark energy you've created and repair any harm you may have done to others. It doesn't matter how deep the pit you may have fallen into. The white light can help uplift you out of any quagmire. This ray is strongly connected with your evolutionary climb.

The pure white light will bring you into the purity and holiness of the God experience. It works wonderfully with confrontation in relationships, helping to lift you out of that abrasive energy. It's essential to use during sex to keep the energy moving on a high level. It's one of the primary energies to use in developing clairvoyance. The pure white light is an illuminating and revelatory ray, especially when you're asking for illumination of a purely spiritual kind. It has protective properties, too, and works well with the gold for that purpose.

Like the orange-red flame, the pure white light can release negative energy, but it does this in a more gentle way than the orange-red flame. So it is a good purifying energy if you're feeling overly sensitive or resistant to the orange-red flame. As mentioned, it particularly focuses on *redeeming* energies. With negative energy you have a choice: you can either cut it loose or transmute it. In redeeming negative energy, you're restoring defiled energy to its divine essence. It's like the cells of the body. Some cells are discarded when they are old and beyond use; others are replenished because they're still useful and can be restored, even if some impurities have contaminated them.

MEDITATIVE PRAYER FOR THE PURE WHITE LIGHT

"Down-ray the pure white light to equalize, align, center,
and attune all levels of my consciousness, uplifting and
bringing me into the purity of Thy oneness."

CHAPTER VII

Guidelines for Effective Meditations

. . . .

*I*n the beginning, working with these rays may take a little getting used to. You have to become familiar with the whole process, as well as comfortable with the greater flows of energy you will be receiving. Yet, once you get into the rhythm of the light, it will quickly become second nature. What you are actually doing in the Higher Self meditation is following the natural course the light takes in reaching you. By working in conscious cooperation with this natural process, you're simply enhancing the spiritual power you can receive.

A wonderful artistry unfolds as you get into the rhythm of working with the light. In the beginning, speaking the words might feel like a recitation, but eventually those words will feel like your very soul expressing itself. The nomenclature of the light work will become your sacred language, and you'll find your own form and beauty of expression. Also, give yourself time to get used to the greater vibrations of light you'll be receiving. It will come in small doses in the beginning until you're acclimated to this new level of spiritual activity.

In your transformative process, the light essentially does three-fourths of the work while your own hard work takes care of the other fourth. The three-fourths entails a whole intricate process of sending the light to you. Your part consists in doing the spiritual meditations and, above all, keeping yourself as strong and as balanced a channel of light as possible. You can't work with the light by day and debauch yourself by night. I've had students say they decided not to work with the light because it was too much effort! As if all one had to do was wish for something to happen, and it would. As they say, "If wishes were horses, then beggars could ride!" You have to do your best to become the example of what you wish to be.

Some common questions I've been asked include how long one should meditate with light and how many rays can be brought in during a meditation. When starting out, meditating for approximately twenty minutes is excellent. You can build this to thirty minutes or more, once or twice a day, if you are motivated. Another thing to consider is not only the length of the meditation but the depth. When you finish a meditation, you should feel different from when you started. Meditating with Divine Light is an experience. If you step deeply into the meditative state and really tune into the spiritual energies, time will stand still.

As far as how many rays to meditate with at one time, usually three to four energies is excellent when starting out. Leave yourself a little breathing room between energy rays. Yet, again, the real question to consider is: how many of these living powers can you embody and express at one time? Remember, you need to apply the light for it to take hold. If you call in the deep rose pink ray of spiritual love, really embody that love consciousness, and be loving in your expression of this power, then you will have a much more successful meditation than if you were to bring in many rays but not really apply their powers. So pace yourself. Start simple to get into the rhythm of working with spiritual energy and build from there.

People have asked me how many meditations it takes to clear something from the aura. The answer depends on several factors. First, how deep is the situation? A recent irritation will clear more quickly than a long-term resentment. Another factor is the determination of the individual. A lackluster approach to light work will be far less effective than a single-minded approach. Another challenge is the element of backsliding. In a perfect world, even the most tangled of energies could be cleared in a relatively short time. Yet, in practice, there is almost always a seesaw effect. The light process begins, but then something reenergizes the negative condition, and the light process must begin again. This can go on for some time before the momentum swings in favor of the light.

Think of the light work as pouring clean water into a cup that's filled with dirty water. If you keep pouring clean water, eventually all the dirty water will be displaced, and there will be only clean water. Generally, a single isolated negative energy in the aura that has not gained momentum can be cleared in five to ten effect-ive meditations.

UNDERSTANDING THE DEFINITION OF SPIRITUAL ENERGY

Too many people misunderstand how the light works. They think the light is like taking a pill: once done, it works automatically. Your support of the spiritual power you bring in will be the key to your success. To do this, take time to understand the definition of spiritual energy as the conduit of consciousness.

Let me give an example of this with the turquoise ray. This is a favorite energy to work with. When people who are not familiar with the aura learn there is an actual power ray of prosperity, they are excited. They call on this ray a great deal and mistakenly think miracles will automatically happen. And while wonderful things can happen, they need to better understand how this works.

Let's say you are at your dining room table doing your monthly bills. You have your accumulated income for the month on one side and you have the bills on the other. It turns out you have more bills than income for that month. If you're not careful, anxiety and fear can creep in. You can fall into a poverty consciousness and start to panic. You can't pay all your bills—you don't have enough money— what will you do? These thoughts flood your head and stress quickly starts to build. This is a common scenario most of us have been in at one time or another.

But let's look at this scene from the point of view of consciousness and Divine Light. Regardless of what the physical situation is, in your distress where is your consciousness directed? It's focused on your fear and worry over money. Let's say that before doing your finances, you didn't realize how overextended you were. You were feeling fine until this realization hit you. And now your attention has been redirected to a distressed state. This state of worry will be reflected in your aura because the aura is reflecting your consciousness.

Now let's say you realize you let yourself fall into a state of financial anxiety and know you have to get out of it. You realize it's time to work with the Divine Light. You go into meditation and bring in the turquoise ray of abundance and supply. This is the God consciousness, the divine attribute of the infinite supply of wealth. Say you have the best meditation of your life. As this power ray comes down and infuses your aura, your fears and worries about money disappear. Through your light work, you have redirected your consciousness away from your financial concerns and you have embraced the wealth consciousness of God. When you finish your meditation, you feel great. You feel like a king and money is no longer a concern.

In this wonderful state of being, you finish your meditation, give your thanks to the Divine for this blessing, and get up and walk out of the room you were meditating in. You walk back into the dining room where you were working. And there are the bills still on the table untouched! At this moment, you have a choice. You can walk into that room full of the divine power of God, see the unpaid bills, and say, "Crap, what am I going to do? I still can't pay my bills. The meditation did nothing." In other words, you can fall back into the state of worry and stress that you were in before you brought in the Divine Light. Seeing that the physical situation hasn't changed, you can get all worked up again.

By reacting in this way, you'd be counteracting all the good light work you just did. You'd be letting the Divine bless you with this consciousness of wealth, but then right away dispelling that divine blessing by reigniting your worry and distress. Plus, because the light didn't immediately change your situation, you may even start to feel that your meditation was ineffectual. In the end, you'd be right back where you started from.

Yet, there is another choice in this scenario, another way to react. When you come out of your effective meditation, full of the God power of wealth, feeling connected to your divine source, you can walk into the dining room, see the bills on the table, but now affirm the divine blessing—regardless of how things appear—by acknowledging it with something like, "I refuse to allow the appearance of this situation to unbalance the divine consciousness of prosperity within me. I am prosperity. I hold to the consciousness of God's infinite wealth. I refuse all thoughts of lack and limitation." In other words, you recognize that, in consciousness, you are not the same person you were before the meditation. The situation may not have immediate changed, but *you* have changed. You are now in a higher state of consciousness. You are dynamic because you have the dynamic power in you, and you refuse to surrender that power.

By doing this you sustain the spiritual power just given to you. Then you will start thinking of ways to take care of your financial obligations, ways to turn things around. You do not see yourself as a victim. You take charge of your life. Then, by the spiritual laws of life, if you sustain that inner divine power, eventually the outer world will reflect that inner truth. It has to; that's the divine law. If you hold to the consciousness of prosperity and act on that awareness, your financial situation will heal and turn around. For some this can happen quickly. For others it can take time, depending on the dynamics of the situation, but it will turn around if you stay the course.

In practice it's not so easy to do this. This is why daily meditation is so helpful. It helps build and sustain the spiritual momentum.

EFFECTS OF THE LIGHT PROCESS—THE LIGHT IN ACTION

Most times, the meditation process is a catalyst for change. It generates the initial movement of spiritual energy that begins the transformational process. It's a little like a tiny snowball rolling down a snow-packed hill—it generates momentum and grows bigger and bigger. The light work gets the ball rolling. The initial destination for the light is the energy centers. The light comes down from the Higher Self to the extent that we need it and does the job it was designed to do. When it is finished, it withdraws and returns to its source of emanation. During this process, light is retained in the energy centers, where it shows up as active emanations; it is these emanations that can really help to get the ball rolling. (See color Illustration 7.1.)

But this energy is a blessing; it's not actually part of your aura yet. To make this energy part of your aura, you need to apply the power you have called on. This is why it's critical to use the energy you receive right away, or it begins to fade. As you integrate this power in your aura through use, it becomes part of your aura and you will truly transform that part of your life.

Over time and with constant effort, the aura takes on a whole new glow and vibration with the Higher Self meditation. One very dramatic example of this process could be seen in a woman I counseled before I began teaching full-time. I was working at an insurance company at the time, and she worked in my department. I didn't tell people I could see the aura at that point. Yet, since I could see problems, I would try to help people in an indirect way, or I would occasionally teach some of the principles to friends who were really in need and open to such ideas. I had to be careful, as I was doing this at a time before metaphysical ideas were as accepted as they are today.

I could see in this woman's aura that she had problems. One day, I asked in a casual way if something was bothering her, and she told me her troubles. It turned out her husband of thirteen years had just up and left her with six children to care for. They'd married when she was only seventeen, and now she was barely thirty and on her own with six children. Deeply shaken, she had fallen into a serious depression.

Her depression showed clearly in her aura. (See color Illustration 7.2.) Her mental center was spinning counterclockwise, and there was a creamy energy around it, showing mental confusion. In addition, there was a gray cloud above her head, denoting intense worry. The fanning rays in all of her centers were gray, the very color of her depressed thoughts and feelings. She also had dark blue active radiations emanating from her Hermetic center, expressing her gloom-and-doom attitude. Proceeding from her emotional center were avocado green active emanations, showing she was developing some darker emotions of deceit. This expressed in her trying to see what she could get away with on the job and in her personal life.

The orange-red flame and blue-white fire rays were used to cut loose depression and the pessimistic assumption that she would never find another love. Emerald green light gave her balance because desertion had left her shaky and very disoriented. The deep rose pink was needed to boost her self-esteem. This was probably the hardest part for her. More painful than the anger toward her husband was the feeling that no one would ever want her again. The fact was, she was still a young and attractive woman, and there was no reason she would not fall in love and marry again. I told her there was an excellent chance that she would remarry. She'd always answer, "Who would want me, with six children?"

After about eight months from the start of this whole process, her aura looked great. The dark clouds and muddied areas were completely gone. Her mental body was sharp and clear. Instead of gray clouds, there were now silver diamond points of light, attesting to the development of much keener powers of perception. Lemon yellow fanning energy coming from her mental center showed alert and focused thinking. Her Hermetic center had emerald green fanning rays, illustrating the balance and harmony she had achieved in her life. There were beautiful bright blue active emanations coming from this center as well, signifying dedication and loyalty to her children. Her emotional division was also in great shape. There was a beautiful rosy pink fanning energy coming from her emotional center, expressing her new love of life. There were also bright blue active emanations in this center, showing the now-steadfast and stable quality of her emotions. Of course, her whole outlook on life was much rosier.

One day as we were having lunch, I saw the image of a man in her auric field. I couldn't see any specific features, but I intuitively felt that this was a man she would meet. I told her, "You're going to get married!"

She looked at me incredulously and said with an amused laugh, "Who's going to marry me with six children!"

"I don't know," I said. "But you're going to meet someone soon."

Before a month had passed, she received an invitation to her high school reunion. She went, and there she met an old high school sweetheart. It turned out he had married, fathered two children, and was also divorced. The attraction was still there. A month later, she married him, with her six children and his two children participating in the wedding ceremony, the littlest girl being the flower girl! This experience had a profound effect on me as well. Helping her marked the beginning of my teaching career because, from then on, this woman kept telling people, "I don't know what that Barbara knows but she knows something!" As a result of her prompting, I began conducting some of my first public metaphysical lectures.

DEVELOPING A SPIRITUAL POINT OF VIEW

One other point I wish to reemphasize is the importance of working with the light from the spiritual point of view. Remember that life works from the inside out. Everything we experience in physical life was first created on the spiritual plane. This is why the aura comes first in any transformation. What often hinders our spiritual unfoldment and lessens the effectiveness of our connection with the light is that we look at life from a physical point of view. Even when it comes to spiritual matters, most of our knowledge and understanding is perceived and interpreted through the five senses. I have seen the aura described as an electromagnetic field, as if it were only a radiation of the physical body. People have tried to equate spiritual light with physical light. It's natural to do this because we're comfortable and most familiar with our physical surroundings and experiences.

The spiritual light and aura will make little sense if viewed strictly from the physical standpoint, because the Divine Light is not of the physical world. It can greatly affect the physical world but the light is part of the inner, spiritual world. Although the spiritual and physical worlds are part of the whole of life, in practice they operate very differently.

The spiritual world is the creative world, the originating world. It's the world of God. Everything we see physically was conceived and originated in the spiritual world. So the spiritual dimension existed before the physical one. It's from this divine source that we draw the light, and it's in this spiritual life that the aura exists and is perceived. Because the spiritual world is the original world, it is not dependent on the physical life for its survival: its life is independent of physical existence.

In addition to being creative, the spiritual world sustains life as well. It sustains all life on Earth, including each one of us. Without this divine power holding the universe together, all of creation would cease to exist in an instant. The spiritual world is, therefore, in a constant state of giving. The Divine voluntarily pours out its life that others may partake, which places us in intimate and constant contact with the source of our being. There is great joy in this process because it is in giving that there is creating. This creative nature of giving is the essence of our spiritual character as well. When we are spiritually minded, we are always creative, original, and in a selfless state of giving.

The physical world, on the other hand, is a created world. It's the result of creative acts that originated in the spiritual realms. It has no power of its own. Without the spiritual world to nourish and sustain it, the physical world could not maintain its form and would return to its source of emanation. Because of this, the physical world is in a constant state of receiving. In receiving life from the spiritual world, the matter of the physical world is organized and sustained. So, the nature of physical life is to take. As spirit wants to give, matter wants to take. The physical world will seek to draw into itself all it can to maintain itself and will resist any idea that compromises that goal. Form is always seeking to hold its own. In this way, it's inherently selfish. It depends on this holding power to survive. The same is true of us. If we are thinking only physically, we will always be narrow-minded, selfish, and with no true understanding of what we're doing to our fellow man.

The secret of understanding your aura lies in the recognition that if life is first spiritual, then it follows that you are, above all, a spiritual being. This means that the same attributes that apply to the spiritual world apply to you. Your spiritual character, then, is the essence of who you are. It's the core of your being, the real you. And all the spiritual qualities you admire are already your true nature.

The only reason you're not automatically aware of your divine nature is that you're in a process of spiritual unfoldment. This unfoldment is part of your design. The divine attributes in you are *potential* powers, waiting to be developed. And as you develop these powers, they become more and more a part of your active life. If your life does not presently reflect the spiritual essence within you, it's only because you have yet to develop those qualities.

The part of your spiritual essence that's unfolding is what we call the soul. The soul is like a seed planted in the ground. A seed starts out as a tiny thing. Yet, all the potential for developing into a beautiful rose or a mighty oak tree is already there. All that is needed are the right elements in which to grow: air, water, sun, and earth. The seed, if nourished and undisturbed, cannot help but become that great flower or tree. In the same way, your soul is like a seed that God plants in the garden of creation. All the potential for realizing its divine nature is already in the core of the soul. To realize that potential, the soul must embark on a pilgrimage through creation, where it grows and eventually makes its way back, fully realized, to God. And like the plant that needs water, the soul needs the spiritual nourishment of Divine Light to grow.

To effectively change something, you must start from the spiritual foundation, even though it may seem unrelated to your immediate physical problems. By working from a spiritual perspective, you can improve anything. Problems, character flaws, and dilemmas are the result of a disconnection from the divine root of life. Fix the connection, and you correct the problem.

Part III

UNFOLDING YOUR

SPIRITUAL POWER

CHAPTER VIII

How to Change Mental and Emotional States

. . . .

Thoughts and emotions are the most important areas in which to begin your auric transformation. You will find that the majority of problems in your life stem from some unhealthy thought or emotion lurking somewhere in your consciousness. For that matter, most of the problems in the world today can be traced to wrong thinking and feeling. By working on these areas, you will be adding immeasurably to uplifting your aura and relieving yourself of much stress.

A negative mental or emotional condition is never permanent—you can change any condition you find yourself in. It doesn't matter if a thought or emotion appears overwhelming or has been with you for a long time. Because these negative states are not the spiritual reality of who you are, they can be transformed. In the same way, you are in control of your reaction to outside influences. No one can tell you how to think or feel unless you permit that to happen. Yet, this is exactly what many people do. They let others run their lives, and then wonder why they have problems.

Fortunately, the Divine Light is extremely effective in transforming mental and emotional states and cutting loose those negative energies at their core. If you're careful not to re-create negative conditions, you will be clear of destructive momentum altogether. The light can also help to build new spiritual power that sustains high levels of positive thinking and feeling.

The first step in your process of transformation is to recognize that the spiritual part of you is the true guiding force behind your entire thinking and feeling. If you try to divorce thoughts and emotions from their spiritual foundation, you will be creating wrong thinking and feeling that will take on a life of their own. This can only produce problems, and you will never receive the answers that you seek. You may see the problem, but its resolution will always elude you because you are not connecting with the source that can really help you.

Thoughts and emotions have enormous power in the auric field. Together, they play a vital role in keeping consciousness moving harmoniously. The mental and emotional divisions are also where you see the greatest fluctuations in the aura. This is especially true of the mental division because you're always thinking about something. As you change the tendency of your thoughts, your auric colors change, and as you emotionally react to your thoughts, your emotional colors change as well. The thoughts of an unenlightened mind are like monkeys in a cage going all over the place. This is exactly the way it looks in the aura—chaotic and disoriented. Of course, the emotions will react accordingly.

In working with thoughts and emotions, keep in mind the following principle; it describes the fundamental operating relationship between your mental nature and your emotional nature. This principle is always in action and by understanding it, you will possess the key to creating the mental/emotional harmony you seek. This principle can be stated simply as:

$$Think \rightarrow Feel \rightarrow Do$$

First you conceive something mentally, then you have an emotional response to that thought. Based on that reaction, you act. This sequence of activity is so simple, yet so many times the relationship is confused—with disastrous results.

In the spiritual context, the mental part of you is the director of your consciousness. It is the part that's meant to guide your emotions. The emotional, feeling part of you is the doer. An emotion doesn't just happen; there has to be a thought behind it. I first have to think, "I love this," or "I hate this," for me to react to that thought emotionally. From this emotional response will come action.

THOUGHTS—THE KINGDOM WITHIN

In the New Testament, when confronted by the Pharisees as to when the kingdom of God would arrive, Jesus gave them an answer they were not expecting: "The kingdom of God cometh not with observation . . . for, behold, the kingdom of God is within you" (Luke 17:20–21). This statement has come to be interpreted in different ways. For some, it means acknowledging the God presence or divine spark within. For others, it means to look within rather than to the outside for change. These are all wonderful interpretations, but in understanding thoughts, this statement is a particularly important revelation.

In metaphysics, your mental body *is* the kingdom within. It's the king-*dome*, the dome being the head, which houses your thoughts. Your mental division is the highest part of your conscious nature. It bridges your higher Divine Self and your lower human self. The mental body is the deciding factor in your evolution as to whether you will rise up into higher, Divine Self or stay in the lower self.

How you think controls the rest of you. So, the first place to make changes in your life is in your thinking. If you know *how* to think, you know how to live. Mind is the builder. You imagine, design, and create everything in your life from mind first. Thoughts create the world you live in and every aspect of your nature. The entire universe was a divine idea before it was a physical reality. So by redesigning your thoughts, you can redesign any part of your life. Without mind, you're like an amoeba. This is why you must keep your thinking sharp and refuse to become slack in this area. Thoughts are far more than just little currents of electrical activity in the brain. They are living entities with energy behind them.

Thoughts are as real as your physical body. They are *more* real, in fact, because there is less constriction with thoughts. They create as you permit them to enter your consciousness and become part of you. Enlightened thoughts can take the form of radiant crown jewels of light. They shimmer with pearl luster colors and beautify the aura. Devolved thoughts can take hideous forms, choking and constricting the auric field. The sad fact is that most of us are confused in our thinking. Even when we think we're clear, there can be confusion or delusion. The key to dealing with negative thoughts is to remember that they are artificial in origin. They were created at some moment in time, somewhere in your experience, but they are not part of your true nature. At some point, you entertained and accepted a false perception, creating a dark thought and allowing that thought to take root.

Thought is the first step in the think-feel-do process. Mind always comes first.

Some people try to reverse this process by putting their emotions first. Yet, even when you "act without thinking" you still have to give yourself mental permission to do so. So thought still comes first, even when you permit your emotions to run rampant. It's ignorance of this principle that can mess things up and permit your emotions to rule your thoughts, instead of the way it was meant to be.

In metaphysics, there are three levels to our thinking self. These are the higher (divine) mind, the conscious mind, and the subconscious mind. When we're dealing with change, we're using our conscious mind. The conscious mind is our intellectual mind. Its focus of power is, as we have explored, in the mental center. The conscious mind is the part of us that reasons things through. It has the power to accept or reject thoughts. The conscious mind is the part of us that exercises our free will by making conscious choices. You can be reading this book and rejecting or accepting the ideas presented. No one can take that right away from you without your consent. By your acceptance or rejection, you're either altering or reinforcing your perceptions, and hence your experiences of life.

The word "conscious" is very important. It indicates the ability to be self-aware. We have to be self-aware to make a conscious choice. Animals make choices, but they do it instinctually. They have yet to develop the capacity for self-awareness. We also have the subconscious, but of course, we're not self-aware of our subconscious mind unless we bring something from our subconscious to our conscious mind. We have our instinctual levels as well, but these are also subordinate to our conscious thinking.

God gave us this ability to choose in order to learn the difference between right and wrong, to distinguish the enlightened from the unenlightened. We are learning how to embrace the enlightened thoughts that strengthen the mental body, and we are also learning how to reject the negative thoughts and energies of others, as well as our own. Until we really learn this lesson, the lines may be blurred. Very often we unintentionally accept negative ideas and reject good ideas, then pay the price down the line when the effects of our thoughts are not to our liking. Eventually, by trial and error, we learn the difference and enlighten the mind.

As the mental body becomes more enlightened, spiritual power can establish itself more easily. The light expands, creating radiant colors and bands of light. The beauty of enlightened thinking is its effortlessness. There's clarity, decisiveness, and true inspiration when the conscious mind is enlightened. This is the goal of our thinking. Look back on times when you were in a very clear mental state, and remember how well things went. It all seemed effortless, didn't it? That's the state of mind you're meant to be in on a regular basis.

Most of us bog down our conscious mind with a lot of stuff we really don't need, or we ask it to do things it's incapable of doing. The conscious mind also becomes colored and conditioned to think along certain lines and in habitual closed loops. Upbringing, environment, and our own mental tendencies create this conditioning. As the mental body gets weighed down with negative thoughts, it becomes harder for the Divine Light to get through. The mind become confused and clouded and moves further away from the clarity of enlightened thinking.

SPIRITUAL ENERGY AND THOUGHTS

Abraham Lincoln is purported to have said, "Most folks are as happy as they want themselves to be." In other words, *you create the parameters* of what you will and will not allow yourself to do, and you do this through your thinking. You must recognize that, in whatever state you find your thinking, you can always change that thinking if you so desire. You are in control of your thinking! If you have relinquished that control, you must reclaim it. Then get the attention off your particular negative preoccupation and concentrate on a positive quality or trait that you want to have. If you have a persistent bitter thought about someone, you obviously don't want to start your meditation thinking of all the ways in which you dislike that person. You need to see yourself free of that bitterness and hatred. Better yet, simply see yourself in a place of spiritual love where that bitterness doesn't exist.

You will be working a lot with the orange-red flame to cleanse the mental center. Not only can this power ray cut loose specific negative thoughts, it can also cut through clouds of negative energies that may encircle you. You can work with the orange-red flame to release specific destructive thoughts or to conduct a general mental cleansing. The following meditative prayer is excellent for general cleansing. Use it anytime you feel mentally clouded or confused. If you've had a tough day at work or at home and you don't know which end is up, this is a great meditative prayer to use. Also use this meditation if you're trying to clear your mind before making an important decision. I suggest that you memorize it; let it become your anthem for cleansing the mental body.

MEDITATIVE PRAYER FOR MENTAL PURIFICATION

"Down-ray the orange-red flame of purification into my mental body, releasing me from all mental confusions, illusions, delusions, all superimposed, distorted, and upside-down images. Let it out-ray in all directions, freeing me of all mental bombardments and impingements. I ask that all these black and gray atoms be dissolved in the mineral kingdom, in the light."

Feel and sense that flame going into the nucleus of your mental center and out-raying throughout your whole mental division, bathing it in this flaming light and breaking up all negative energies. If you can visualize or actually see the process happening, all the better. Feel and sense those black and gray atoms being released from you and see those atoms going directly into the mineral kingdom, dissolved in the light and forever out of your consciousness.

From the mental center, let the light shower your throat, Hermetic, and emotional centers to clear out any interconnecting debris. Let the light fill and activate these other centers, while also dissolving any negative energy in the mineral kingdom.

You may be surprised at how much negativity you've been holding in and how good it feels to let it all go. You don't have to qualify or justify anything. If it's a negative energy, you want it out of your life. As the orange-red flame is releasing negative thoughts, images or emotions may pop up unexpectedly. This is all part of the releasing process and simply means the light is doing its job. Look at these images as if they were a movie that you're just watching. Acknowledge them for what they are, but give them no power. If you feel inspired, you can name any specific thought you want released as it comes up. Simply add at the end of the meditative prayer: "Free me of . . ." and name the thought you want to be released from.

This purifying work can take on the quality of a confessional, discharging whatever torrent of negative thoughts you have been holding in. This is the time to surrender it all to the Divine Light, to the very altar of God. You may receive revelations you didn't expect. And yes, the old part of you may fight to hold on to those dark thoughts, but just keep letting go. Before going on to the recharging process, let's look at some of these negative thoughts more closely.

CONFUSIONS

This word comes from the Latin, meaning "to mix together." Confused thinking comes about when two or more thoughts vie for attention and supremacy. You may be telling yourself you want something and at the same time telling yourself the thing you want isn't good for you. These conflicting thoughts create confusion in your thinking, and the result is inaction. Confusion shows up in the aura mainly as a creamy energy similar to the tan colors of lethargic thinking.

ILLUSIONS

Illusions are ideas and perceptions that you have accepted as real, but which are not real. At some point or another, we all have illusions about something. Most of the time, we're unaware we're in an illusionary state. When you wear rose-colored glasses about someone, you're in an illusionary state. You can have illusions about your parents, friends, love interests, and yourself. There can be a feeling of disappointment and disillusionment when your bubble bursts. Nevertheless, part of the beauty of spiritual work is stepping out of these illusions and into greater realities.

DELUSIONS

Delusion is similar to illusion, but there is more intent in delusions, more purposeful action. You delude yourself because you don't want to face something and you choose to escape from it. You might be under the delusion that things are fine at your job, when they are not. Or you might delude yourself into thinking you have great talents or abilities, when in fact you don't.

SUPERIMPOSED IMAGES

If you take two images, place one on top of the other, and look at them, you'll see a jumbled mess. This is an example of superimposed images. I may hold a wonderful image of something. Then you come along and tell me that what I love is terrible. If I accept your image, I now have a conflict with the image I've held. Superimposed images tend to come from the outside rather than being self-imposed.

DISTORTED PICTURES

Here you're twisting things out of their natural shape, creating scenarios that may have little or no bearing on reality. Paranoid people most often have distorted pictures of things, painting normal situations as doomsday scenarios.

UPSIDE-DOWN PICTURES

This is seeing something as the total opposite of what it really is, as in "Greed is good" or "Wrong is right." Upside-down thinkers have taken their distorted pictures to the extreme. This kind of thinking can be very dangerous. You see a friend where there is an enemy. Note how satanic imagery often involves inverting images to mean their opposite, as in upside-down pentagrams and crosses. This is no accident but rather a deliberate intent to invert natural laws for unnatural purposes.

MENTAL BOMBARDMENTS

These are thoughts coming at you from the outside world. It could be people thinking negatively of you, knowingly or unknowingly. The problem with bombardments is you don't usually know they're coming. You may believe you're "under the weather" when actually you're under attack. This is why spiritual protection is so important.

IMPINGEMENTS

Whereas bombardments can come at you from anywhere and everywhere, impingements are much more targeted. They come at you like stilettos, sharp and pointed, penetrating your aura. Certain people are very sharp in their thinking, and you can feel it. Impingements are not as common as bombardments but are still something to watch out for.

Once you've finished your purification, bring in the blue-white fire. This energy will recharge the areas depleted by the negative thoughts. It will also serve as new spiritual soil, making room for a fresh crop of new thoughts and ideas.

MEDITATIVE PRAYER FOR RECHARGING THE MENTAL BODY

"Down-ray the blue-white fire of eternal life to charge and
recharge all depleted areas in my conscious brain/mind thinking
with new life force, breathing in new spiritual thinking."

Give yourself time with the blue-white fire. You may feel a shifting and upliftment as it's doing its work. Again, feel and sense this energy radiating out from the mental center in all directions, charging and recharging all levels of the mental division and out-raying through the brain cells, drawing in new life force.

See that electrifying life force sparking new currents of divine life into all aspects of your mental being. Again, let it touch into the other centers as well. Once you've replenished yourself with the blue-white fire, you can begin your building-up process. The key rays to work with are silver, lemon yellow, gold, and white light. Silver brings in greater powers of perception and a faster-thinking mind. The lemon yellow brings in powers of concentration, especially if there's been disorientation or laxness. Gold carries new wisdom, inner strength, and whatever dynamic qualities are needed. White light is especially good for lifting all the vibratory frequencies to bring in greater powers of illumination and vision.

After your meditation, watch your tendency of thought. Are your thoughts more positive, or are you still in the same negative state? Follow up your light work with positive action to establish new, constructive thinking, giving the light you have attracted the chance to express in every area of your life.

EMOTIONS—THE SPIRITUAL MOTOR

Emotions give life to thoughts. They are the engines that propel thoughts into action. Once an emotion is wed to a thought, that thought has tremendous power and will move into motion. To put anything into action, you need the combined effort of mind and emotions. You may have a dream to be an artist or a doctor, but unless you attach a strong emotion to that dream, it has no chance of becoming real. Emotions may be likened to gunpowder, and thoughts to bullets. Without the fire-power of gunpowder, the bullet will just sit in the chamber, no matter how intently we point and pull the trigger. Mind designs the plan of what is to be created, but once that design is in place, it is the emotions that get the energies going to realize that design.

It's not always easy to balance emotions with thoughts. We tend to lean one way or the other. Those who stay too much in the mental are more intellectual and will conceive more than they create. "Doers," who stay too much in the emotional, can often paint themselves into corners because they don't think before they leap. Balance the two in a positive way, and you're steady, focused, and dynamic.

Emotions do not think. This is perhaps the single most important thing to remember about emotions. Emotions *feel.* That's their job. Emotions need thoughts to guide them. Have you ever tried to reason with a person who's in a rage? You can't, because that person is not operating from a thinking level at that moment. It's emotions talking. You have to approach the person gently, from a loving place. Let him or her calm down so the thinking levels are back in action; then you can communicate.

Your emotions are meant to flow in clear streams of love, compassion, inner strength, and all the higher attributes of life. In this mode, the emotional division of the aura radiates tremendous light. When you're in your higher emotions, you're expressive, and others are attracted to your positive emotional force field. Yet, many times emotions are filled with hates, jealousies, fears, and angers. When you are in these dark states, your aura is darkened and weighed down, and the energies move out in a swirling, chaotic manner.

You have to really work at rooting out negative emotions. You can't just say, "I'm not angry," for example, when trying to deal with anger. You have to free yourself of that anger, because that anger will be smoldering inside, waiting for a chance to express itself. As with thoughts, the Divine Light can reach into the root of negative emotions and release them. Often when you think you're operating from your mind levels, you're actually moving from your emotions. In this condition, you're bound to make wrong decisions. Most people live nearer their emotional self than their mental self and allow their emotions to rule their thoughts. When you make decisions solely by your emotions, it's like throwing yourself to the wind. It may blow you where you need to go or it may not.

For example, say you are the manager of a company and decide to fire one of your employees. You give several good reasons why you must do so, and you claim to regret the decision. However, on closer examination, it becomes clear that job performance is not the real issue. The truth is, you're jealous. Although new to the job, the person you wish to fire shows great potential, and you're afraid that once your superiors catch wind of how good this employee really is, he may be promoted above you. So by getting rid of him, you're no longer threatened. Since you refuse to see yourself as a jealous person, you have to come up with a plausible reason for firing him, one that you can believe. So you scrutinize his performance, looking for—and magnifying—little faults. Though the driving force behind your actions is jealousy, you're convinced it's a logical choice. In the think-feel-do principle, the sequence of this situation would look like this:

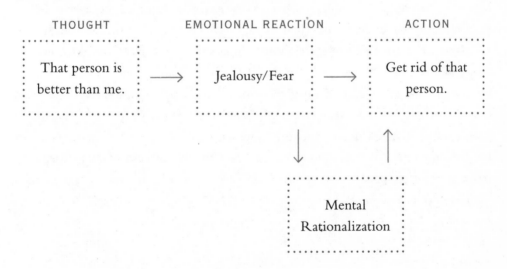

ILLUSTRATION 8.1-*Mental/Emotional Pattern*

In this situation, there is the added step of mental rationalization before action, but the results are the same. Your rationalization has led you to believe that you are coming from thought, when your actions really stem from emotional reactions to the original negative thought—which you have put out of your conscious awareness altogether.

Once we have an emotional response to a negative thought, we can do one of three things. First, we can act on that negative emotion, which will only compound the condition and create more destructive energy. Second, we can restrain ourselves, which shows control and discipline. This is better, but the negative energy will still be inside us, waiting to come out in other ways. Or third, we transmute our thoughts and feelings. No matter what the emotional reaction, we can always intervene with our thoughts and turn that reaction around. We can always "count to ten" and "turn the other cheek" to avoid acting rashly. Unfortunately, the majority of people automatically go with the first option and act on their negative emotions with little or no thought.

Negative emotions are deceptive. It's easy to feel justified in our negative feelings. If someone does us wrong, we feel justified in becoming angry or hateful. And herein lies the trap: as spiritual students on the path, we must train ourselves not to react with our lower emotions when wrongs have been done to us. Do your best to redirect that instinctual urge, matching wrong for wrong, blow for blow, eye for eye. "Two wrongs do not make a right." Whether we are "right" or not, what are we doing when we react to that negative energy? We're tying in to the very situation that created that energy—which can only generate more negative energy. The result is that we're dragged down into the mud with the person who "started it." As humans, of course, we're going to have a reaction. It's unavoidable. The idea is to learn to react constructively. Then we will have become the masters rather than victims of our own emotions.

SPIRITUAL ENERGY AND EMOTIONS

When you're unbalanced in your emotional center, you'll feel it most in your abdominal area. It could feel like a stomachache or nausea. Expressions like "sick to my stomach," "tearing my guts out," and "ripping me up" refer to feeling the emotional centers moving counterclockwise.

As with thoughts, the first energy to call on is the orange-red flame. This spiritual energy can reach deep into the emotions and cut through all emotional entanglements. If you find you're an overly emotional person to begin with, this energy can help to release the negative emotions that may have accumulated. The following meditation is for general purification of your entire emotional nature.

MEDITATIVE PRAYER FOR EMOTIONAL CLEANSING

"Down-ray the orange-red flame to my emotional body, cutting
me loose from all destructive emotions, disturbances,
confusions, false sympathies, and bombardments. I ask that
all these black and gray atoms be taken into the mineral
kingdom and dissolved in the light."

Feel that spiritual energy reaching into the core of your emotional nature and out-raying through your entire emotional division, cutting loose all negative emotions. Working in this center can feel like taming wild horses. If you are asking for a specific emotion to be released, name that emotion and see it being dissolved in the light. If any other emotion pops up that you want to release, name that emotion and ask the light to release it from you. As with work on the emotional center, let this light touch into your other centers as well, purifying all interconnecting destructive links.

Before going on to the blue-white fire, let's look more closely at some destructive emotional energies.

DISTURBANCES

A disturbance is a counterclockwise movement within the emotional center that is usually caused by an upsetting situation. There's a problem at home that doesn't go away and you carry the disturbance wherever you go. Someone may have made a cruel comment that disturbed you. It's sometimes hard to trace where the disturbance came from, or what kind of emotion it is exactly. Yet you know it's there and that it's interfering with your normal activity.

EMOTIONAL CONFUSION

Emotional confusion comes about when two or more emotions are vying for attention. Love-hate relationships are an example of emotional confusion. Like mental confusion, emotional confusion tends to cause indecision and paralysis because you don't know where to go with your feelings.

FALSE SYMPATHIES

It's so easy to tie into the emotional energies of people around you. This can wreak havoc on your emotional body as well as your entire being. You can work hard to keep your aura clean and high, then mess it up by opening to outside influences. Although the entire auric field may be vulnerable to outside influence, the emotional division can be especially so through false sympathies. For example, you can be feeling peaceful, but if an agitated person comes near you, you pick up that agitation if you are open to it. This can happen especially when close to someone, like a spouse, parents, or children. If you have a sympathetic tie with someone, you will relate to that person emotionally. If that person feels sad, you will feel sad. If that person feels happy, so will you. This transference can happen quickly because, in this case, there's little thinking involved.

EMOTIONAL BOMBARDMENTS

Like false sympathy, bombardments involve taking in outside emotional energy that has nothing to do with you. Whereas false sympathy deals more with people you care about, bombardments may come from any source. There are so many emotional currents in the world you can unintentionally connect with. Bombardments can also be intentional—negative emotional energies directed specifically at you. If someone dislikes or hates you for any reason, that person will be transmitting an emotional current to you. You can easily pick up this energy if you're not paying attention, and absorb and aggravate the whole condition. By cutting loose these emotional bombardments, you steer clear of muddy waters.

Once you have finished your emotional cleansing, you are ready for the blue-white fire. Chances are, your emotional body will drink in this energy with gusto. Really feel it recharging all your emotions and replenishing all depleted areas, bringing them into a more vibrant place—especially if you are feeling emotionally exhausted.

MEDITATIVE PRAYER FOR EMOTIONAL REPLENISHMENT

"Down-ray the blue-white fire of eternal life to charge and
recharge my emotional body, filling it with new life force so
that my feelings and actions are in a positive, creative place."

Give yourself all the time you need to replenish yourself with the blue-white fire. Feel it out-raying throughout your entire solar plexus area and drawing in new spiritual power. Also let it flow into the other spiritual centers. In addition to the blue-white fire, you will want to draw in pure white light as well. The pure white light can help to bring the emotions into the poise necessary to sustain positive, creative emotions. Use the following meditative prayer to help transmute any hidden traces of dark light not cleansed with the orange-red flame.

MEDITATIVE PRAYER FOR EMOTIONAL UPLIFTMENT WITH THE PURE WHITE LIGHT

"Down-ray the pure white light into my emotional body to
steady all the feeling levels of my consciousness, bringing
them into perfect poise and alignment."

Sometimes an emotional reaction can catch you off guard. You get sudden bad news and you're thrown completely for a loop, which throws off your emotional body as well. If you can bring in the spiritual light right then and there, you can save yourself a lot of grief later on. You'll handle the situation much better, especially if you have to make an important decision and need a cool head. In this situation, you want the purple ray to still your emotions. The following meditations are for emergency situations. If you can get to a quiet place for your meditation, great. But if you can't, simply close your eyes and just visualize that soothing purple ray right where you are.

MEDITATIVE PRAYER TO STILL THE EMOTIONS

"Down-ray the deep purple ray to bring forth peace and
serenity, quieting my emotional body."

If the negative emotion has had enough time to gather momentum, ask to receive the emerald green ray as well, to balance things out.

MEDITATIVE PRAYER TO BALANCE THE EMOTIONS

"Down-ray the emerald green ray to bring forth Thy balance
into my entire emotional body, and move this emotional
center clockwise."

CHAPTER IX

Transformational Meditations

. . . .

*T*here will be many times when a general mental/emotional cleansing will not be enough to turn a negative condition around. You may find yourself in a specific destructive state of mind that resists your conscious efforts. In these cases, you'll need to *target* your meditations to focus the light on the particular aspect of your mental or emotional nature that needs transmuting. The beauty of targeted meditations is that they show how well the light can be applied to the most intricate and demanding of situations.

In these challenging conditions, try to identify the thought that originally started the negative momentum. Most of these conditions are a result of seeing things with physical eyes rather than spiritual eyes. By identifying the original misconception, you're that much ahead of the game. Both mental and emotional states are included in these meditations because they're so interconnected. However, if you notice the condition is more emotional, then focus more light there, and vice versa. In all cases, ask the light to touch into the four main centers and throughout your entire consciousness, permeating your entire auric field.

For most mental and emotional conditions, you'll start with the orange-red flame and follow up with the blue-white fire. I've included slight variations on these meditations to show how petitions to the light will vary according to the specific need.

Please keep in mind that if any mental or emotional condition is severe or chronic, you should seek professional help. Don't try to remedy the situation all on your own. Personal light work will help a great deal, but when problems are intense, you will need the expertise of a doctor, counselor, or skilled healer. Seeking help is an essential part of the spiritual growth process when the situation calls for it.

RESENTMENT

Resentment is strongly rooted in anger that is held in. Usually resentment is directed at someone who is close to you, whether it's a parent, spouse, child, or friend. The feeling of being wronged often takes the form of hurt that turns into anger, and then resentment.

Resentment is one of those tricky, stubborn, and self-justifying emotions. You can say, "This person did this to me, and therefore I'm right in feeling this way." Now you've fallen into the emotional trap. All you accomplish when you give way to resentment is to spawn a host of negative reactions such as hurt, bitterness, anger, and revenge, which will only tear at you and debilitate your aura. It takes energy to resent someone, energy that could be used for constructive, life-enhancing purposes.

In the aura, resentment usually shows up as vitiated red and gray energies in and around the emotional and Hermetic centers. These energies have a distorted, menacing quality. They're held in the Hermetic center, because you've let them into your heart. The dirty red shows anger; it will sometimes darken to a black if the resentment is very intense and veering toward hatred. The gray appears because the energy is turned inward. Resentful people don't always express their feelings. In some cases, depression can accompany that anger or hatred. Some of the spiritual centers could be spinning counterclockwise, and if the resentment were to persist, it would show up in other parts of the energy field as well.

To break the spell that resentment puts on you, first evaluate the situation. What really happened? Did that person really do this to you? Many times, resentment can build around imagined slights or misunderstandings. You may resent someone who got a promotion that you feel you deserved, when, in actuality, he or she may be better qualified. You must also make sure you have the full picture—that someone hasn't told you lies, or that you haven't misinterpreted events. You can work with spiritual illumination to reveal the truth, so that you're coming from a place of clarity.

However, let's say someone has definitely offended you, and you resent that person. The first energy you would bring down is the orange-red flame to purify all the negative energy that came at you or was generated by you.

MEDITATIVE PRAYER FOR PURIFYING RESENTFUL ENERGIES

"Down-ray the orange-red flame of purification to cut me
loose from resentment toward (*name the person*) and any
negative energies coming at me from (*name the person*). I
hold to the knowing that this energy is being released from
me and is being dissolved in the light. I am now free of all
resentment and animosity."

After you've called on the light, become very still and receptive to the purification. See all the hurts, angers, hatreds—all the things that led up to this moment—being cut loose from you. If you want to verbalize, let your heart spill out your feelings, allowing this negative energy to be purified by the orange-red flame and dissolved in the mineral kingdom. Whatever images, words, impressions, or memories come up, let them all go into this cathartic light. Try to make the release as vivid as you can. Feel divine energy flowing freely, touching all the dark places created by this resentment. Hold to the knowing that this energy is going through all the centers and all aspects of your being, releasing every stickpin of resentment.

Give yourself a few minutes after you've finished to let any residual energy be cleared out, and then follow up with the blue-white fire and the following meditation.

MEDITATIVE PRAYER FOR SPIRITUAL REPLENISHMENT

"Down-ray the blue-white fire of eternal life to reestablish
new life force at every level of my being."

Again, become still and feel the rush of this electrifying, life-giving energy. Now you are coming into a complete restoration of your aura from the ravages of energy-sapping resentment. Feel that new freshness entering your consciousness, bringing zest and enthusiasm, motivation and desire. Feel the restoring power of the blue-white fire going to every place touched by the orange-red flame and bringing those areas up to the energy level where they should be. You are beyond that dark thinking and feeling now. That energy is no longer a part of you. Let the healing quality of this divine life force restore your spiritual equilibrium and permeate every aspect of your being. Feel it recharging you, giving you a new positive outlook on life.

Once this work is done, you can follow up with any additional energy you feel you need. Spiritually strengthened, you are now ready to begin your forgiveness work (see chapter 11). Depending on how open you are and how deep the resentment, it may take several meditations for the light to take hold. If the resentment is long-standing, you also have to work strongly on the mind levels, because thought forms and patterns have had a chance to set in. It will take more work on your part to cut them loose, but the light work remains the same.

Once the situation has been placed in the light, you must decide what to do. You may decide to confront that person from a place of love, and you may be surprised by that person's reaction. If you're somehow unable to meet, and/or that person is not responding to the light, then you have to let the situation go, and ask that it be gently laid in God's hands. If the person who offended you isn't around, or alive, then send the light to that soul wherever it may be, and continue to practice forgiveness.

HATE

Hate is the lowest and most destructive of all emotions. No negative emotion is good, but hate operates on the very lowest vibratory frequency. It brings so much misery to all involved. In the aura, it presents itself in inky blacks. A person in a hate energy field is capable of just about anything, including murder. Like resentment, you hate something or someone who has done something to you, imagined or actual. However, unlike resentment, which can be understated and secretive, hate tends to express itself. People in such a state are more willing to tell you they hate you—unless they have a specific reason to hold back. If they don't tell you, they'll tell other people. The one advantage to such outspoken behavior is that you know where you stand with such a person. The bad thing is hatred tends to want company. If you tell someone that you hate this or that, you're encouraging the other person to respond the same way. And since hate is such a strong energy, the passion of your hatred can influence others, even if they don't feel that way.

Hatred is especially strong on a mass scale. Most of the world's atrocities can be traced back to hatred. Look at aggressive rulers and evil dictators, and you'll find hate as their motivating force for conquest. The terrorist who is willing to kill others as well as himself mistakenly thinks he is sacrificing to please God. Yet what actually makes him pull the trigger is not love of God, but hatred for the misperceived person or idea that stands in his way. The hateful person can also be methodical. An angry person might do something impulsively and then it's over, but the hateful person can stew for a long time, giving ample opportunity for premeditated acts.

Hate operates void of divine essence. That's why it's so menacing. It's an active absorbing energy that, like a black hole, wants to draw things into it. You can't mess around with hatred. The same is true if hatred is directed at you. It's an aggressive energy that you must counteract with the highest attributes of the Divine Light. In the aura, hate can take on different forms, but the predominating energy is always black. Look at color Illustration 3.4 to see what hatred can look like. It is totally out of harmony with the divine nature of life. And as we know, hatred can harbor cruel and sadistic thoughts.

If hate is in your aura, you must make it a top priority to work on it. With such an energy in your aura, it will be very hard for you to progress spiritually. Hatred can be very difficult to let go of. As with resentment, chances are, you are justifying your hatred. The wrongs committed are usually extreme. I'm certainly not excusing the behavior of those who have intentionally hurt you, but it's *your* choice how to react. Hatred is something you can control. You are choosing to hate.

Several steps are involved in clearing yourself of hatred. Once again, start by calling upon the orange-red flame. You need this energy to come down dynamically to cut loose the black energy in the aura.

MEDITATIVE PRAYER FOR PURIFYING HATRED

"Down-ray the orange-red flame to strongly cut me loose
from all hatred directed at me from (*name person*), and
release me from all hatred and animosity anywhere in my
consciousness that I have created and directed at (*name
person*). I ask that Thou takest these black and gray energies
into the mineral kingdom to be dissolved in the light."

You must be definite in calling in the orange-red flame, and then ready to surrender these negative energies so they can be cut loose from your life. Then become still and feel this power working in you. With intense emotions such as hate, you will most likely have to repeat the exercise several times to get the job done. With each meditation those dark energies will gradually lighten until they finally disappear. You must be very careful to not reenergize the hate by dwelling on it. Otherwise you will have to repeat the work until you stabilize your consciousness.

After the orange-red flame, follow up with the blue-white fire, and feel the blue-white fire lifting your consciousness.

MEDITATIVE PRAYER FOR SPIRITUAL REPLENISHMENT

"Down-ray the blue-white fire of eternal life to charge and
recharge all areas within me, bringing forth new life energy
and lifting me into the consciousness of Thy light."

After the blue-white fire, do the forgiveness work presented in chapter 11. You may also work with the deep rose pink ray of spiritual life to bring in compassion and understanding.

If you have acted on your hate, it's especially important to finish your work using the pure white light. It will help to release any stickpins where hatred may still be lodged and to defuse any negative momentum you may have generated. It's also an uplifting energy to help take you out of the hate consciousness you've been living in.

MEDITATIVE PRAYER FOR UPLIFTMENT WITH THE PURE WHITE LIGHT

"Down-ray the pure white light to go into all levels of my
being, lifting me into the vibration of Thy holiness."

Depending on your sensitivity to the light, you may feel relief during this process as you shift out of the dark state you were in. You will also begin to realize just how destructive that hatred was.

ANGER

Anger is a common emotion that everyone has felt at one time or another. Some people get angry quickly and forget their anger just as quickly. If unchecked, anger can build and turn into rage. People with this type of anger are like a bomb waiting to go off. They can blow up at the least provocation. There's an uncontrolled quality to anger. People don't plan to get angry, it just seems to happen sometimes against their will, and after the outburst they feel bad. This shows poor control of the emotional nature.

Anger is an explosive energy in the aura. Color Illustration 3.5 shows the firecracker-like energies of the vitiated reds and dark greens generated by sustained outbursts of anger. As mentioned before, one strong outburst of anger can linger two weeks in the aura. An angry person is hard to be around. He or she is usually insensitive, irritable, and likely to say terrible things, lashing out at people for no good reason. Many unpleasant personality traits can come through with anger.

To clear yourself of anger, begin with the orange-red flame to start clearing those streaks of vitiated red. See this energy bathing your entire aura as well as your energy centers.

MEDITATIVE PRAYER FOR PURIFYING ANGER

"Down-ray the orange-red flame of purification into my
entire being, releasing me of all anger connected with
(*name person or situation*) and dissolving all negative
energy in the light."

Follow up with the blue-white fire.

MEDITATIVE PRAYER FOR SPIRITUAL REPLENISHMENT

"Down-ray the blue-white fire of eternal life to charge and
recharge my entire being, bringing me new life force and
creative energy."

In addition, you will need to work with the love ray to help bring you into the consciousness of divine oneness and to release the irritations associated with anger.

MEDITATIVE PRAYER FOR DIVINE LOVE AND COMPASSION

"Down-ray the deep rose pink of spiritual love, touching my
entire being and transforming anger into love so that I may
have compassion. Let it flow into all levels of my being,
bringing me into Thy body of Divine Love."

I also recommend bringing down the violet ray, which is a subtler version of the purple ray. This ray is excellent for bringing in a gentle peace. In anger, there is a harshness and agitation that the violet ray can help smooth out.

MEDITATIVE PRAYER FOR GENTLE PEACE

"Down-ray the violet ray of Thy peace into my entire being,
releasing all irritations and bringing me into a serenity and
divine poise."

There is something called righteous anger. You may express righteous anger over an injustice done to someone who cannot speak for himself or herself, or for unkindness being directed at you. Say someone is gossiping about you, lying and hurting your reputation. You have a right to tell that person, in no uncertain terms, to cease and desist. In this case, the emotion is not an uncontrolled outburst but a definite controlled expression. No one has the right to push into your aura, and you have every right to defend your good name. Righteous anger is not the same kind of anger that we have been speaking about. Righteous anger appears in the aura as bright red, not dirty red. It is a positive energy. You'll know the difference between the two, because with righteous anger you won't feel upset or displaced afterward.

JEALOUSY

To be jealous is a sign of low self-worth. If you're jealous, you believe that someone has something you don't—but should—have. This can create all sorts of deceit and underhandedness as you go about trying to get the things you want.

The spiritual understanding missing is that what you desire on the outside is something you already possess *within*. If you find yourself feeling jealous of someone's talents or abilities, you must recognize that the very same talent can unfold in you—if you desire it enough. Just because a talent is active in someone else doesn't mean it can't be active in you. It's simply that the other has already worked at it, while you have yet to do so. In life, there will always be those who are farther along the path than you are, just as there are others who are not quite as far along. This is all part of the natural evolutionary link that ties us all together, and it's why you can never compare yourself to others. If you do, "you may become vain or bitter," as the poem "Desiderata" warns. You will always be looking over your shoulder at what the other guy is doing.

In the aura, jealousy presents itself as a dirty, avocado green energy. It's a very ugly color to see. It throws the aura off-kilter. There are often splotches of brown and vitiated red, because with jealousy, meanness and anger can be involved. If the jealousy is more like envy, then the shade will be a lighter olive green.

Being jealous can destroy friendships. I remember two sisters who got along very well together until they became interested in the same man. Both were in their early twenties and only a year or two apart. The man was interested in the older sister, who was prettier, and the younger one became very jealous. She did everything she could to win the man's affection, but it just didn't work. When she talked about her sister, I could see the avocado green energy coming out of her emotional center. It was an ugly sight. Of course, she had no idea what she was creating. Eventually the man married the older sister. The younger sister, still seething with jealousy, couldn't take it and ended up moving away without resolving her feelings toward her sister. These sisters lost their friendship, and their once-beautiful sisterhood, to the "green-eyed monster," jealousy.

Jealousy can be insidious. Begin with the orange-red flame and ask it to cut you loose from all feelings of jealousy, wherever they may be lodged in your consciousness.

MEDITATIVE PRAYER FOR PURIFYING JEALOUSY

"Down-ray the orange-red flame to release me from all jealousy
and envy wherever they are lodged in my consciousness.
Take all these black and gray atoms to the mineral kingdom
to be dissolved in the light."

Feel it showering your entire being. If you feel it more in the emotions, let the light stay there a little longer. If you've been talking about it a lot, you might feel it strongly in the throat center. You might be surprised at how much negative energy your jealousy can build. But don't dwell on that. Just feel the releasing. Afterward, come in with the blue-white fire to recharge the areas depleted, asking to retain the power where you need it to fortify your energy field.

MEDITATIVE PRAYER FOR SPIRITUAL REPLENISHMENT

"Down-ray the blue-white fire of eternal life to bring in new
life force to all levels of my being, and sustain its power
wherever I need it."

Then use the love ray to bring in more compassion for you and the person you've been jealous of. Also ask for gentleness to come in with this love, because chances are you were harsh in your handling of the situation.

MEDITATIVE PRAYER FOR EMOTIONAL UPLIFTMENT WITH DIVINE LOVE

"Down-ray the deep rose pink of Divine Love to bring compassion
into my entire being and to bring me into a consciousness
of Divine Love."

To crown your efforts, finish up with the emerald green ray to bring you into a harmonious state and to balance your aura. Ask that this ray bring in serenity with the harmony. If you feel you also need to bring down the peace ray to really establish that tranquility, then do so.

MEDITATIVE PRAYER FOR BALANCE

"Down-ray the emerald green ray to harmonize and balance
all levels of my being."

After you have finished your light work, make an effort to remove your attention from the object of your jealousy until that negative energy is completely out of your consciousness. If there's been active friction, you may want to get the issue out into the open. If it was jealousy over someone else's abilities, for example, pay a genuine compliment about that person's talent. Confess to your feelings and ask forgiveness. The person may surprise you and turn out to be your friend. Remember, the divine spark shines in everyone. Admiring the God spark in others is a holy trait. Mother Teresa saw Christ in everyone she met. How can you be envious of Christ?

You can also work with divine guidance to help create the things you want. If that quality, object, or situation you coveted is still a strong desire, then you begin the building process for yourself. If it turns out you don't want it as much as you thought, then you will know it wasn't that important to begin with. And if it is something that is meant to be part of your life, then you will be able to pursue it more effectively.

DEPRESSION

Depression is a complex problem. It is usually due to taking in too much of the conditions around you. Even if you're watching yourself, it's hard not to absorb the outside world to some degree. Strong disappointments, sudden loss, and unresolved traumas can easily bring on depression. Physiological conditions can also bring on depression.

A spiritual principle often overlooked in depression is that events or conditions in your life are never permanent: "This too shall pass." When in a depressed state, you're not seeing the full spiritual picture. The negativity that seems to be engulfing you is a created condition that is temporary. In your true spiritual essence, these states do not exist, and therefore are not part of the originating reality. In God's kingdom, all is in its perfect flow, and since you are part of that perfection, part of you is in that perfect flow right now.

Unfortunately, depression is one of those conditions you can become strangely comfortable with, which can lead to many destructive habits. Alcoholics usually have depression as a motivating force that drives them to drink. Some people seem to love looking at the world fatalistically or cynically. Yet, having a fatalistic or pessimistic view will only serve to cloud the spiritual reality of life and make it easy to slip into depression. The negativities you harbor stay with you only as long as you choose to keep them.

Granted, sometimes you may feel that you don't have the spiritual power to rise out of your present condition. This is where the spiritual work really comes to your assistance. The Divine Light will give you that "booster shot" to help you reconnect with your source, so you can see things in their true perspective. In addition, you now know that by connecting with your Higher Self, you're tapping into the higher spiritual awareness that is above the discords of Earth life. By stepping into that greater consciousness, you're letting go of your problems and putting them into God's hands. He will steer you over all the bumps and roadblocks along your spiritual path, and release the heaviness from your heart.

In the aura, depression most often shows itself as a gray cloud above the head. If the depression is severe, it can appear as a gray energy circling the entire person. Depression shows a lot in the Hermetic and emotional centers because of its connection to disturbing events and the emotional response to those events.

You must first cut loose these clouds with the orange-red flame. Like most of the work you will be doing in this section, it may take several tries before the gray clouds begin to dissipate, especially if the depression is long-standing.

MEDITATIVE PRAYER FOR PURIFYING DEPRESSION

"Down-ray the orange-red flame to cut loose any gray clouds of depression and any negative energy, wherever it is lodged in my consciousness, dissolving it in the mineral kingdom in the light."

After the purification has done its job, follow up with the blue-white fire—one of the most effective energies to use for depression. If you have time to work with only one energy in connection with depression, use the blue-white fire. Its uplifting power is truly dramatic.

MEDITATIVE PRAYER FOR SPIRITUAL UPLIFTMENT

"Down-ray the blue-white fire of eternal life to charge and recharge my consciousness, lifting me out of any depressive energies and into Thy renewing, electrifying, and everlasting life force."

If there has been a lot of stress connected with your depression, you may want to work with the purple ray as well. It will help you break away from whatever it is that depresses you, almost as if you were going on an island cruise and dropping away all your cares.

MEDITATIVE PRAYER FOR PEACE

"Down-ray the purple ray of divine peace, releasing me
from the burdens and pressures within my being and bringing
forth Thy peace."

Once you feel the light breaking up the depressive energy, you will start to see things differently. If you can, take a little time off to give your psyche a rest. Your body and nerves will recharge, and that will help the whole process.

Depression can take time to be fully resolved; it's hard to say how long this process may take. The light will certainly begin the process of release and upliftment right away. If the depression is not severe, the light can clear it up within a relatively short time. But as with any condition that persists, if the depression is severe or chronic, seek professional help as well, whether it be from a doctor, psychiatrist, or healer.

At some point when you feel stronger, start to work on resolving any condition that may have contributed to the depression to begin with. It might involve letting go of something that's bothering you or gathering the courage to face something you've been avoiding. If there is more than one thing going on at the same time, take each challenge one at a time. Use your energy work with everything that comes up. Above all, cultivate a spiritual, optimistic outlook.

GUILT

Guilt is directing anger or hostility toward yourself. Regret and remorse are often cousins to guilt. The funny part about guilt is that it usually becomes a form of self-punishment. By feeling guilt, you feel you're atoning for some wrong you have done.

In the aura, the basic color of guilt is gray. It can appear as a small gray cloud above the head or around the heart center and emotional center as well. Usually remorse is there, too, which will show up in tinges of darker, charcoal gray. The gray will be mixed with the color of whatever wrong was done. If you deceived someone, dark green will be mixed in with the gray; if you were mean or cruel, cocoa brown will tell the story. So the energy of guilt is rarely seen alone. This is what often helps to distinguish it from the gray clouds of fear or depression.

Guilt can be expressed in strange ways. I once knew a woman who owned a restaurant where I worked when I was very young. She had the strange habit of leaving the cash register open, which of course enticed customers and employees to take money from her, which they did. She would also make large accounting errors in employees' favor. It was as if she were deliberately inviting people to steal from her. One time, she made a thousand-dollar accounting error in my favor. I brought the matter to her attention and instead of being surprised or grateful, she was indignant! I could have just kept the money, but that's a form of stealing and I wasn't going to get caught up in that. I thought, "This is it. I'm going to find out what's going on here." I could see certain energies moving in her aura and knew something was happening.

It took a little work, but finally she told me her story. When my employer was a child, her mother had become hooked on morphine during a hospital stay. After using up all their money to satisfy her addiction, she would have her daughter steal. If they were visiting at a friend's house, the mother would be downstairs chatting while the little girl would sneak upstairs, go into people's bedrooms, and take what she could. Other times her mother would have her crawl through windows at night or when no one was home and take money. The guilt of what she did weighed heavily on her, and she carried it into adulthood. When she found herself in a better financial situation, her way of reciprocating was to allow people to steal from her. It made her feel better and was her way of paying back the money she'd taken.

Of course, if you make a mistake or hurt someone, there's bound to be regret and guilt. What you want to do as soon as you can is replace guilt with compassion—both for the person wronged and for yourself. You can't control what you did in the past, but you have complete freedom to work on things now. Forgive yourself for what you've done and certainly make amends. Recognize that the soul part of you is still growing and not fully perfected yet, so you will inevitably make mistakes. Sometimes you will make *big* mistakes. That's part of your life experience. What you want to do is learn and grow from those mistakes, so you won't repeat them. Begin with the orange-red flame. Ask it to cut loose not only the gray energies of guilt but also the negative energies that created the condition bringing about the guilt. If the wrong you did was severe, divide this process. Work on guilt separately as one purification, and then work on the negative situation.

MEDITATIVE PRAYER FOR RELEASING GUILT

"Down-ray the orange-red flame of purification to cut loose
all thoughts and feelings of guilt, wherever they are lodged
in my consciousness, and the accompanying destructive
energies that created this guilt in the first place."

Follow up with the blue-white fire.

MEDITATIVE PRAYER FOR SPIRITUAL REPLENISHMENT

"Down-ray the blue-white fire to replenish all depleted
areas of my consciousness with new life force."

Once you've revitalized yourself, you'll want to bring in a strong flow of the deep rose pink as a healing and uplifting love, so that you feel the Divine Love. Remember: no matter what you've done, God forgives you, because He always sees you in the highest possible light—as the divine spark that you are. Regardless of any mistakes, God's love is unshakable. By working with this ray, you are opening up to that love flow. People often feel they don't deserve God's love because of some of the things they've done. Yet, Divine Love is always with us: it's already a part of us. Many people try to separate from that love and deny it to themselves. This only serves to draw them further away from their spiritual objectives.

MEDITATIVE PRAYER FOR DIVINE LOVE UPLIFTMENT

"Down-ray the deep rose pink ray as a healing love to bring
me into the oneness of Thy love, releasing any self-hate or
anger and uplifting me as one body in
Thy body of Divine Love."

Finish up your light work with the emerald green ray to help harmonize your consciousness, especially if the guilt has been long-standing.

Meditative Prayer for Balance

. . . .

"Down-ray the emerald green ray to balance and harmonize
all the levels of my consciousness—mind, body,
and soul—with spirit."

Once you've cleared your energy field, begin your forgiveness work (see chapter 11). Pray for yourself and the other person or persons involved.

After the light work, it's time to turn around whatever situation you created. Look at it as objectively as you can and see what you can do to make things right. If you cheated someone, pay him or her back. If you were cruel to someone, apologize and show kindness. If you deceived someone, come clean. Make every effort to take effective action. And if you can't help the person you harmed, find someone else or someone in a similar situation and help that person.

GRIEF

It's impossible to go through this life without suffering a loss that brings grief. Everyone will lose someone or something dear to them at some point and feel sorrow when that person or thing isn't there anymore. After all, this life is a visit. You and I are not meant to stay here forever. Yet, it's easy to forget this fundamental reality when we're caught up in the activities of the world. Although loss of loved ones can occasion the strongest form of grief, people grieve over many things, including lost youth or ability, a bygone time when life was especially idyllic, and so on.

Grief is one of the most heart-wrenching experiences you will ever have to face. Anyone who has lost a child or a spouse will attest to that. And because it is so difficult, so overwhelming, it also becomes one of the greatest spiritual tests. Grief is an inevitable emotion; but when prolonged, that's a different story. I've lost many dear ones in my life and understand grief very well. In love I tell you—excessive sorrow is selfish. When you grieve in such a way, you're grieving more for yourself than for the other person. Should you be sad that the person you love is free from pain or old age? Do you mourn when a caterpillar turns into a butterfly? Your loved one has graduated from this existence and is free to go on to a greater existence. This Earth life is not the only life there is. When you pass on from Earth life, life does not end. You go on to the spiritual life from which you came. This is why one of the greatest services you can do for a loved one who has died is to let him or her go. Death cannot part you from your loved one—you will meet up again in the spiritual realms.

Prolonged grief will hold you back because it keeps you in the past. And if you're in the past, you cannot be moving forward. Understandably, if you've lost someone very dear to you, someone who's been an important part of your life, you're going to feel great sadness. It's only natural, and it's a good idea to give yourself time to mourn. There is a spiritual tradition that allows forty-four days to mourn, and I highly recommend taking this time. But after the mourning period, it's wise to make every effort to move on.

Grief is another emotion that shows up as gray in the aura. I've seen it as a gray bubble in the heart center and sometimes above the head as well. If the person is angry with the person who died, there will be vitiated red in the aura. Self-pity or depression would bring in a darker cloud of charcoal gray and even black. The grieving soul might have unresolved issues concerning the deceased, bringing up a lifetime of feelings and thoughts, all of which will show up in the aura.

Begin with a thorough cleansing and replenishing, to lift you out of the heavy vibrations that deep grief brings.

MEDITATIVE PRAYER FOR RELEASING GRIEF

"Down-ray the orange-red flame of purification to cut loose
all feelings of grief and loss everywhere in my consciousness,
and dissolve all black and gray atoms in the mineral
kingdom in the light."

Grief is another mental/emotional state that may be countered by a strong re-charging flow of the blue-white fire.

Meditative Prayer for Spiritual Replenishment

"Down-ray the blue-white fire to replenish all depleted
areas of my consciousness with new life force."

You will also need a strong dose of the emerald green ray to bring you back into harmony. With loss, your psyche will be thrown out of balance. Your world may feel upside down. You'll need the emerald green to bring things back into perspective.

Meditative Prayer for Balance

"Down-ray the emerald green ray to balance and harmonize
all the levels of my consciousness as one body in Thy body
of Divine Light and Love."

Of course, you will want spiritual love. This will help to uplift your soul and get you out of the loneliness you may feel. It also will help to strengthen your compassion so you can see things more from the level of Divine Love. Divine Love also brings in spiritual joy.

Meditative Prayer for Divine Love Upliftment

"Down-ray the deep rose pink ray as a healing love to bring
me into the oneness of Thy love, embracing me as one body
in Thy body of Divine Love."

Perhaps the most helpful energy of all is the deep purple ray of spiritual peace. If you have time to work with only one ray when in grief, use the deep peace. When you lose someone, there is almost always shock involved, and this ray can reach deep within to soothe and calm your soul. There may also be impulses to act rashly; this ray can put you in a place of serenity where you will see things more clearly.

MEDITATIVE PRAYER FOR PEACE

"Down-ray the purple ray of divine peace to all centers,
especially my heart center, to give rest to my soul and to
touch into all aspects of my being, releasing all grief and raising
my consciousness into a state of harmony and peace."

After you have completed your light work, you're ready to start using the light in your life. After a grieving period, start filling your days with fresh new thoughts and experiences. Surround yourself with positive, supportive people. Reassert your connection with God. Feel joy for the person who has passed on. Take care that you're not isolating yourself too much. There are as many ways of grieving as there are people. Some bereaved people develop a desire to die themselves, in the erroneous belief that it may bring them closer to the loved one who has passed on. Being around people and having good friends always helps. If you have unresolved issues with the person who passed on, be patient about that, too. Just because he or she is no longer in the body doesn't mean you can't still work things out within yourself.

FEAR

Of all the negative emotions, fear is one of the strongest impediments to reaching your spiritual goals. Fear can cut to the very core of your being and paralyze you. Whereas hate can spur you on to negative action, fear encourages no action at all. How can you progress and go after the life you want if you're afraid to take the initiative?

Fear reaches deep into the instinctual levels of your consciousness. Yet, your fear doesn't necessarily have to be a big fear. You can have small fears that accumulate and even go unnoticed at first. But after a while, they add up. You can fear something very real or have neurotic fears wherein an innocuous situation sparks apprehension. If it persists, fear can breed related emotions such as worry and depression. Worst of all, fear can breed more fear.

To fear something, you have to see yourself as separate from your divine source.

Fear, by its very nature, creates a sense of separateness. In fearing something, you're accepting the belief that something or someone has power over you and that you're powerless to do anything about it. If you return to your spiritual point of view, you can better see the fallacy in this type of thinking. You are an essential part of the creative process of life. How can there be any power greater than that?

In the divine realm, you are part of the One. You are "under the shadow of the Almighty." There is no separateness in the divine world. There is only one unifying, all-powerful source. This doesn't mean that you don't take normal precautions; it does mean that you're not coming from a place of fear and trembling. To the degree that you're in your divine oneness do you feel confident and courageous. You'll face adversity with dynamic power and courage. Look at the life of Saint Francis, who tamed the wolf and became his friend. Francis was a gentle man, yet he was able to save an entire village from a vicious predator without any bloodshed. If he had been afraid of what the wolf might do to him, what would have happened then?

You have to face your fears in order to conquer them. Most people will do just about anything to avoid a condition or situation they fear. Never allow fear to lodge in your being. It impairs your judgment, clouds your reason, and constrains your very being.

You're going to need a lot of spiritual power to get out of the fear state. Begin by asking yourself: Is what I fear a real or imagined situation? Try to identify the original experience or thought that created the fear. Once it's clear, you'll know where to start.

Fear shows very clearly in the aura as a gray energy, mostly in the emotional center. It can move in an odd, swirling motion from all the emotional turbulence involved. When the fear is strong, I have seen a whole band of it swirling around the aura itself. A very fearful person will also be lacking in some of the uplifting and dynamic energies, such as gold, orange, and red.

In working with the energies, bring down the orange-red flame and blue-white fire to do a clearing and cleansing and to build up your aura. You want the orange-red flame to touch into every thought, experience, and sensation that's producing the fear. The process may unloose some very specific pictures that evoke the emotion. If so, ask that they be cleanly cut away from your consciousness.

MEDITATIVE PRAYER FOR RELEASING FEAR

"Down-ray the orange-red flame to cut loose all vibrations
of fear wherever those negative energies have taken control
of my life, and dissolve these black and gray atoms in the
mineral kingdom, in the light."

After you're finished, bring in the blue-white fire.

MEDITATIVE PRAYER FOR NEW LIFE FORCE

"Down-ray the blue-white fire to charge and recharge my
consciousness with this electrifying life force at all
levels of my consciousness."

Fearful experiences tend to pull you out of spiritual alignment quickly, after which it's hard to let any new energies take hold. Ask that the emerald green ray touch into your centers and entire being, especially your emotional body, bringing you into mind, body, and soul balance.

MEDITATIVE PRAYER FOR BALANCE

"Down-ray the emerald green ray of balanced power to any
areas of my consciousness that were thrown out of alignment
by fear, and bring me into a divine centering and harmony
at all levels of my consciousness."

Now you have to build up the aura with the gold light. Gold will help you to develop faith, courage, and strength. Bring in this ray very deliberately to establish the dynamic light. It was your lack of faith that put you in fear to begin with, but when you are in unity with God, you will feel nothing resembling fear. You will be handling situations with a swift keen hand and a sure step. The gold light will help you to reclaim that self-confidence.

MEDITATIVE PRAYER FOR INNER STRENGTH

"Down-ray the golden ray of wisdom light to touch into all
aspects of my being, bringing me the inner strength,
courage, confidence, divine faith, and inner knowing to pull
me through negative states of consciousness, so that I
am in dynamic oneness with Thee."

Once you are in your spiritual power, use that energy. Face your fears one by one—ideally as they come up. Acknowledge the God power and the supreme power. Spiritual affirmations are of great assistance in restoring confidence and courage (see chapter 17). Use the gold as often as necessary to reestablish that gold and the divine faith, and eventually you will conquer your fears.

WORRY

Worry and fear show up very similarly in the aura. The gray is the dominating energy, but with worry the gray is lighter and not so oppressive. If the worry is chronic, it might also show itself in the color division as gray specks.

Some people are worrywarts. They feel that somehow it accomplishes things, protects them, or prepares them for the unexpected. Of course it's important to be alert and prepared for the unexpected, but this can be accomplished without worry. When you worry, you can exhaust yourself so much that eventually you must relax, and in your relaxed state come your answers.

When you worry, you're expressing a lack of spiritual trust, a lack of faith. If you are one with God, then you know for certain that God is working things out for you. If you really have confidence in God, there can be no worry. If you're unsure about what to do in your life, you need to consult your Higher Self to receive divine guidance (see chapter 12). Be patient for that guidance to come. You can do only so much on your own. You are the channel through whom God works—which is all that's expected of you! We too often expect too much of ourselves and become stressed when answers aren't forthcoming. If you worry too much, you will block the flow of light. If you really want resolution, stay quiet, and receive. Then act.

Follow the same steps that dispel fear, outlined earlier, to clear your aura of worry. Unless the worry is habitual, you don't have to use the emerald green ray.

MEDITATIVE PRAYER FOR PURIFYING WORRY

"Down-ray the orange-red flame to cut loose all patterns of
worry and all anxieties and irritations connected with worry,
and dissolve these black and gray atoms in the
mineral kingdom, in the light."

After you're finished, bring in the blue-white fire.

MEDITATIVE PRAYER FOR NEW LIFE FORCE

"Down-ray the blue-white fire to charge and recharge my
consciousness with electrifying life force
at all levels of my being."

Then you'll want to work with the gold to increase your faith and spiritual trust in God.

MEDITATIVE PRAYER FOR INNER STRENGTH

"Down-ray the golden ray of wisdom light to touch into all
aspects of my being, bringing me the inner strength and
confidence, faith, and guidance to direct my life so that
I am in dynamic oneness with Thee."

Then retrain yourself so that whenever conditions arise that call for you to act and make decisions, those old patterns of worry don't creep in. Once you start to really establish your dynamic nature, a lot of your fears will simply disappear.

PRIDE

It has been said that one of the first great sins committed by humankind was inspired by pride. Throughout history, pride has been the cause of so much strife, yet many people regard pride as a positive quality. They ask, "Why not feel proud of an accomplishment well done? If I work very hard for something, I should feel proud of what I did." From a physical, human point of view, this would seem to make sense, but a deeper look at the spiritual root reveals the fundamental error in this thinking. Pride is an overbearing feeling of self-accomplishment. The keyword here is "self" and it is in "self" that you can be deceived. Of course you want to acknowledge a job well done. It's important to know your skills and talents. This is not pride. Pride is when you acknowledge and congratulate yourself as the creator of your achievements, and you put the emphasis solely on *you*. This immediately moves you away from God consciousness and gives you a sense of being independent and disconnected from your divine source. You believe that the success is coming from your own efforts alone, forgetting the wellspring from where your inspiration came. If you continue along those lines, you will inevitably build the illusion of your superiority over others, which can quickly lead to arrogance.

The spiritual truth missing in pride is humility—the understanding of your relationship with God. Humility is your ability to see your rightful place in the great cosmic plan. This relationship is not always easy to act on. The grass always seems to be greener on the other side. Even Jesus' disciples felt a sense of personal accomplishment when they felt their spiritual powers over evil growing ever stronger. Jesus quickly rebuked them, saying, "Rejoice not, that the spirits are subject unto you; but rather rejoice, because your names are written in heaven" (Luke 10:20). In other words, marvel that God has allowed you to be an instrument of spiritual power, but do not claim this power as your own personal possession.

When you are in tune with the Divine, many things will happen for you, and if you're not careful, you may start to claim these accomplishments as your own, or even as your God-given rewards for being such a marvelous person. This is a big test to see if you clearly understand the relationship between you and your divine nature.

When you begin to recognize the spiritual root as the life-sustaining power behind all your accomplishments, and give all credit and glory to your divine source, then you have begun to overcome pride and master humility.

Some people have a hard time accepting humility because they think of being humble as a form of debasement or as an affront to their dignity. They confuse being spiritually humble with being humiliated. This confusion is understandable because of the way the word is most often used. Yet, humility is just the opposite of debasement. Spiritual humility is seeing yourself where you belong in the spiritual scheme of life—as an instrument and co-creative being of God. If anything, true humility creates a greater sense of worth, because you understand how precious you are in God's eyes.

The Greeks have a word for when pride gets the better of you. They call it *hybris*, from which the Anglicized "hubris"(overbearing pride) is taken. Everyone has felt hubris at some time or another.

Pride usually shows up in the aura as burnt orange and distorted avocado green energies radiating from the emotional body in a jerky motion. Begin your light work with the orange-red flame. You may feel a little resistance to this energy, especially if your human ego has built up a lot of pride in your talents and achievements, but stick with it.

MEDITATIVE PRAYER TO PURIFY PRIDE

"Down-ray the orange-red flame into all levels of my consciousness
to cut loose all insidious energies connected
with pride, all feelings of arrogance, or feelings that
I'm better than someone else."

As you follow up with the blue-white fire, feel how this divine power is the very source of your life force.

MEDITATIVE PRAYER FOR NEW LIFE FORCE

"Down-ray the blue-white fire of eternal life and recharge all
levels of my consciousness, breathing in the very life of God

and helping me to recognize Him as my true source
of being."

Once this is done, balance is important, because if you are acting under the delusions of pride, you are out of rhythm with the spiritual pulse. The emerald green can help you get back into harmony with the God flow.

MEDITATIVE PRAYER FOR SPIRITUAL BALANCE

"Down-ray the emerald green ray of spiritual balance to
touch into all levels of my being, balancing all conditions in
divine order and harmony."

Along with the harmonious green ray, you will need to work with the white light to bring you back into a spiritual understanding of your relationship with God. You can also work with the gold light if you feel resistance and need more dynamic power to establish this consciousness in you.

MEDITATIVE PRAYER FOR SPIRITUAL AWARENESS

"Down-ray the pure white light to touch into all levels of my
consciousness and to cut loose all unnaturalness and all
pretenses so that I may come into a spiritual inner knowing
of my true relationship with God."

I would finish this work with the deep rose pink ray to bring in more spiritual humility through its gentle and compassionate flow. When you are very proud, you cut yourself off from others, putting yourself in a special category, so you'll need to bring yourself back into unity and oneness with God and others.

MEDITATIVE PRAYER FOR SPIRITUAL HUMILITY

"Down-ray the deep rose pink ray of spiritual love, bringing
in more compassion and understanding for others, releasing

all feelings of arrogance or superiority, and establishing
spiritual humility at all levels of my being."

In applying the light work, start by giving God the glory and thanking the Divine for allowing you to be a channel of all good that is in your life. If you are having great successes, give credit to God. Look for all the ways in which you were inspired to follow the course you are on. If you are facing failure or difficulties, watch that hurt pride isn't getting the better of you. Affirmations are a great help. They can keep your mind focused on your spiritual priorities.

Pride is not easy to release. You may even have a hard time recognizing it as something that needs to be worked on. You have to stay on top of this very subtle enemy and strive to develop a more humble attitude. This is not easy. Ben Franklin put it best when he said, "Even if I could conceive that I had completely overcome it, I should probably be proud of my humility."

CHAPTER X

Improving Personal Affairs

· ·

*I*n the grand scheme of our evolution, Earth is a schoolhouse for spiritual learning. We are students here to learn the lessons this schoolhouse provides. Behind our day-to-day affairs and dealings with each other lies the true purpose of these interactions—our spiritual growth. Earth then is the testing ground of our spiritual mettle; it's the divine laboratory where we develop and unfold our soul's potential. With such a mission, every action takes on divine significance, however great or small it may be.

It's in our daily affairs that you put the tools of spiritual light to work. Divine Light is the key to success in all earthly endeavors. To create any condition in your life, you must have the energy for it already present in your aura. And if it isn't there, you must generate the spiritual power so that it becomes a part of you.

I have worked with some very famous and successful people in my life, and have always found it clear from looking at their auras that their success was no accident. Their talents were already a part of them—already in their aura. So, it was no freak of nature that Mozart was a master musician or that da Vinci was able to paint the *Mona Lisa*. In the same way, it wasn't the apple that fell on Newton's head that gave him the concept of gravity. The accomplishments of great men and women down through the ages were born of spiritual power, and the passion to use that power for the greater good.

In the aura, the nucleus of all your relationships and personal world affairs is the Hermetic center. This center is responsible for directing spiritual energies that power your outside activities. All of your worldly conditions are reflected in some way in this center. This means that the energies of your relationships, your job, your finances, and your personal and spiritual life all converge at this point. In this energetic flow, you're the center of your world—not *the* world, but your *own* world.

The Hermetic center is your manifestation center. It is through this chakra that you project the spiritual energy to objectify what you have in your heart and mind. To handle the activities of life, the Hermetic center has twelve built-in power rays, representing the twelve avenues of your world affairs. This tells us that the affairs of our life involve many facets. There is an art to living; and learning to balance all departments of life is the key to spiritual success. Too many times we focus on one part of our lives to the detriment of other parts of our lives. Balance is the key to living and to the Hermetic center. This is why the nucleus of the Hermetic center is emerald green. This is the hub that regulates and steadies all departments of your life.

Because the Hermetic center has so much to do, it can become burdened to the point that you can feel overwhelmed and helpless. In this state, the Hermetic center can become obscured by clouds of dark light, making it hard to create. As with the other centers, you must work extra hard to keep the Hermetic center moving in a positive flow even if there is turmoil around you. You will not always have control over what's happening in your life, but you have total control over how you react to those conditions. People often make the mistake of judging their lives in terms of what's happening to them, rather than by how they're handling what's happening to them. If you're facing a difficult situation with courage, fortitude, and humility, you're brightening your aura and will be strengthening the Hermetic center.

The Hermetic center is the seat of the soul. It's here that the soul registers and absorbs all of life's experiences and lessons to grow and mature. So the first step in strengthening this center is to stay in your own divine harmony and rhythm, and not take on the world's woes. Of course, don't ignore the outside world. You need to be an active participant in life if the soul is to grow, but don't claim world conditions as your own. If you're *of* the world, you're going to do what the world requires, and your primary allegiance will be to the world. Your first allegiance must be to

God. We live with one another, but it is God who sustains us, and God to whom we shall one day return.

It's very easy to put trust in each other first, because we're so close to one another. For example, it's very easy for you to look at your boss as the source of your income. If you offend that person, you could lose your job, and therefore your income. You might wonder, "Where does God fit into this picture?" From the spiritual point of view, your employer is the *instrument* through whom God's prosperity is made manifest to you. There's a big difference between being the instrument and the *source* of something. If you see God as your source and your boss as the instrument, your focus changes. You respect your boss, but know that if this channel were taken away for any reason, your spiritual supply would still be there. It would find another channel of expression. So your approach to life is strongly reflected in your heart chakra.

The key to a harmonious Hermetic center is to make sure it is spinning *clockwise*. You want all your centers to be moving clockwise, but this is especially true of the Hermetic center. If you're not sure what clockwise is in relation to your Hermetic center, review step 3 of the Higher Self meditation (see chapter 5). If this center is spinning counterclockwise, something is "off" in the way you are handling a situation or condition. Maybe there is an urgent problem that needs your attention, and instead of dealing with it you are running away. Maybe you are pursuing something for the wrong reasons and are stubborn to correct that mistake. And if one aspect of your life is off, that counterclockwise momentum can extend to other aspects as well. For example, your career may be going great, but if you're having troubles at home and those troubles are not resolved, eventually they can affect your work life.

When this center is moving clockwise, the rays of light move out in beautiful flows. Depending on the development of the individual, energetic radiations can extend well beyond the body. When the center is moving counterclockwise, the light doesn't radiate nearly so far. It's more restricted and generally looks jumbled. And there will be darker hues of color as well.

If you're facing life's challenges, even if they are not yet resolved, your Hermetic center will rotate clockwise, but you have to be *really working* on your problems! You can't just sit on the fence and hope that things will somehow work out. If you have a problem, resolve that problem or be earnestly working toward resolution to keep this center moving clockwise. This is God's way of keeping you involved and active. Otherwise, you might be tempted to sit and do nothing, mistakenly thinking your meditations and prayers alone can do it all. In my counseling work, when someone comes to me with a problem and I see the Hermetic center spinning clockwise, I know that this person is doing his or her best to handle the situation. Most likely things will work out, regardless of present appearances. However, if this center is spinning counterclockwise, it means not only is there a challenging situation going on, but the person is not handling the situation properly. There's something he or she is not doing or is doing incorrectly that is generating the counterclockwise motion. This means there is something urgent that the person must do to remedy the situation.

To start building up more power in this center, begin with a cleansing to cut loose the tangled energies that can disrupt your spiritual flow and throw apparent obstacles in your path. The light will help to harmonize and organize your many activities.

Meditative Prayer for Purifying the Hermetic Center

"Down-ray the orange-red flame of purification into my
Hermetic center to cleanse all my comings, goings, and doings;
touch into persons, places, things, conditions, situations, and the conditions
that constitute situations, releasing me from all destructive energies
and obstacles in my path. Dissolve all these black and gray atoms in
the mineral kingdom, in the light."

This is a very effective meditative prayer that covers a wide range of activities. It is recommended that you memorize this prayer, as the wording is common to many applications of the light in this center. You can add any specific situation to your prayer that you feel needs purification. Upon finishing, bring in the blue-white fire. Feel the life force touching into all areas of your world affairs, drawing in new, divine energy to give you a fresh outlook on life.

MEDITATIVE PRAYER TO REPLENISH THE HERMETIC CENTER

"Down-ray the blue-white fire of eternal life to charge and
recharge all twelve avenues of my human Earth affairs,
establishing new life force and creative energy in all
aspects of my activities."

The emerald green ray is one of the most essential rays you can use in this center. Even though emerald green is already part of this point, you will be using this energy a great deal to keep all your activities in balance. This power can help you stay steady, especially if something suddenly pops up that throws your life off-kilter.

MEDITATIVE PRAYER TO BALANCE THE HERMETIC CENTER

"Down-ray the emerald green ray to balance all twelve
avenues of my human Earth affairs, establishing divine harmony
and rhythm in all of my activities."

In addition to the emerald green ray, I recommend using the white light to uplift and bring in the holy vibration to this center, as you can feel disconnected as a result of so much earthly activity.

MEDITATIVE PRAYER TO UPLIFT THE HERMETIC CENTER

"Down-ray the pure white light to bring forth Thy divine
radiance in every avenue of my world affairs, spiritually
uplifting me into Thy divine consciousness and activity."

Because this center is so active, it is easy for stress to build, especially if sudden or unexpected things happen. In these situations, bring in the deep purple energy to still your consciousness. Even if you haven't the time to call down any other ray, bringing in the peace ray will help soften the shock element so that you can think more clearly.

"Down-ray the deep purple ray of spiritual peace to touch
deep into my heart levels, stilling any stress and shock and
bringing me into the silence of peace and the
peace of silence."

BUILDING PROSPERITY

We go through the greater part of our lives earning, saving, and spending money. Money facilitates so many of our daily activities that it seems like a basic operating principle of life. Although money does indeed occupy a central place, many of us understand little of its spiritual operation. It's no wonder that we often have problems with finances in one form or another.

To understand how to work with spiritual energy to build both supply and a consciousness of supply, we'll need to look at the basic spiritual principles of abundance. Prosperity, by the way, is not limited to finances. We can enjoy a wealth of ideas, rich friendships, and abundance in just about every avenue of expression, but here we'll focus on prosperity as it relates to finances and money supply.

Where You Stand Is Your Prosperity

This is the first principle of supply. It means that all the prosperity you'll ever need is already with you. And since it's with you, you don't need to look outside yourself to generate prosperity. Prosperity is with you even if it's not yet manifest in your outer world.

Following the spiritual point of view that all physical manifestations are the result of inner, spiritual causes, it follows that all physical expressions of wealth result from an inner spiritual root of prosperity. As with everything in life, wealth and supply originate in the spiritual realms. By touching into your spiritual source, you're touching into the divine source of all supply. This places you in the midst of an unending fountain of supply. This supply can materialize in a variety of ways, but regardless of the channel of expression, be it a person or a job, the true connection to your prosperity is always the Divine within you. If you look to the outside world for your fortune, your success will be hit or miss.

To activate this spiritual power of abundance, God gave you a special power ray. One of the twelve power rays of your Hermetic center and your human Earth affairs is the turquoise ray of supply. It's your own special connection to the divine reservoir of spiritual wealth. This power ray gives the jump-start you need to move the prosperity principles into action. Without this ray, it would be hard to draw on spiritual power to create what you need. This turquoise ray is with you always, whether you use it or not. You could be dying of starvation or be homeless, and this ray would still be with you. Again, it's a matter of using or not using the power that's already there. When I was a little girl living in Minot, North Dakota, there was a woman who walked around town like a beggar, scraping for money. It turned out she had a mattress full of cash at home. In our own way, this too often happens. Though blessed with the potential for unlimited power and wealth, we often choose to live as if we were paupers.

How you handle prosperity is one of life's greatest challenges and opportunities. Money is a form of energy. It represents your Earth power, and by mastering the art of Earth power, you are showing your capacity to handle one of life's most essential divine powers. The principles of prosperity exist at every realm of life. It expresses itself even more wondrously in the higher planes of existence. In these higher dimensions, prosperity can manifest through the power of mind and divine will. In order to develop this kind of consciousness, develop your power of prosperity here and now by mastering the conditions that now face you.

What does it mean to master the lessons of prosperity? Does it mean accumulating a great sum of money, becoming a king or one of the wealthiest persons on Earth?

Certainly these things can and do happen. Yet the real goal of mastering prosperity is to reach the point where you know your supply is there for you whenever you need it. This knowing is not an idle affirmation that can waver at the first sign of adversity, but a steadfast inner knowing. When you are steadfast in that divine knowing, you can manifest what you need, when you need it. However, the demonstration of that divine knowing won't always assume the form of great wealth. It will take the form of expression that best serves the divine purpose.

Becoming the richest man or woman on Earth doesn't mean you have mastered the art of prosperity. A surprising number of extremely wealthy people live in a constant state of fear that their money isn't enough or that it will be taken away from them somehow. This is not a demonstration of the divine consciousness of wealth. When you are in your true wealth, it won't matter how much you have, because you will be in direct connection with the very source of abundance.

Give to Receive

This second great principle is best expressed in the adage "The more you give, the more you receive." Notice the word *more*. The more you give, the *more* you receive. Not the *same* you receive, commensurate with your giving, but the *more* you receive! The spiritual principles of prosperity dictate that if you give a dollar, *two* dollars, in some form, will come back to you. When you send the energy out initially, not only do you create the conditions for its return, you create the conditions for its return *multiplied*. This is one of the great laws of the universe and may be seen operating at every level of life. By lending a hand, in some way you will be offered *two* hands to help you when you need them. This principle of spiritual multiplication is part of the ascension principle in your spiritual evolution and light work. As you climb the ladder of life, not only does your light expand, it expands exponentially.

Most people have trained themselves to think in reverse. They try to collect as much as they can. They hoard money and then give it out with great reluctance. There may be fear connected with money. When money gets short, what do you tend to do? You hold your money back, right? The tendency is to withdraw out of fear of losing what little you have. But this has the opposite effect of what you want. By holding so tightly, you're actually "strangling" your consciousness of supply and ensuring less for yourself. Now, I'm not saying to spend money recklessly. If funds appear low, sure, you might have to cut back on expenses, but you must still keep the principle of giving very much alive.

Start by being generous. Open your heart. If someone asks for help, give it. Don't judge that person's merit, or do it begrudgingly. Give with your heart. The gift without the giver is bare.

You Are the Steward of God's Supply

This principle is most often overlooked. It simply states that you are the channel—and not the owner—of God's abundance and supply. Most people like to think in terms of things being *theirs*. They live in their own houses, drive their own cars, and have their own bank accounts, their own families, and so on. In truth, they are the stewards of all these things. There's nothing in this world that belongs to you. All that you appear to possess is a result of a spiritual root that was alive long before it showed up in your life. It's by your alignment with the spiritual laws of life that you enjoy your things and circumstances.

This knowledge can relieve you of much stress in relation to money. First, it takes some of the responsibility off your shoulders. As long as you're following the laws of supply, you can leave the rest to God. Did not the Christ say, "Take therefore no thought for the morrow" (Matt. 6:34)? Or, as it has been metaphysically interpreted, "Take no *anxious* thought for the morrow." Being a steward of money rather than its owner releases you of possessiveness. It makes you aware that, as a steward, some of your money is obviously meant to go to others. It was brought into your life for just that purpose. Many times that's how God can reach those people—through you.

POVERTY CONSCIOUSNESS

Before getting into the meditative work, let's look at familiar behavior that stops us from being in this wonderful awareness of wealth. In two words—poverty consciousness.

Poverty consciousness is the mental conditioning wherein we accept a negative, physical perception of a seeming lack as real. Poverty consciousness is so pervasive and automatic that we don't realize how often we actually talk ourselves out of abundance. For example, if your bank account has a balance of two dollars, it would be natural for you to say you have no money. This negative affirmation would then begin a chain reaction, because you've accepted this condition as real, when in truth, you are seeing things as they physically appear and not as they are spiritually. Regardless of your physical situation, spiritually your wealth is unlimited and unchanged. The only reason you're experiencing a sense of lack is that somewhere there has been a disruption in your spiritual connection that you now must correct. Once that connection is reestablished, the condition will work itself out.

When you are in poverty consciousness, you'll feel like there's never enough money. You'll be thinking in terms of how limited your funds are, that you don't have enough to do the things you want. And you will think all these conditions are permanent, or next to impossible to change. Maybe the bills are stacking up with no apparent money to pay them. Maybe your clothes are getting old or your home needs repairs or your car is on its last legs. These are strong images, and if they're around you all the time, it's easy for you to let them make a deep impression on you.

Poverty consciousness, by the way, is not limited to "poor" people. Wealthy people can entertain feelings of lack and limitation just as easily. These people may be worth millions but still worry about money. There was a man who founded a multimillion-dollar company, yet still lived in the simple house he grew up in. He even kept the same rotary phones he had when he started the business! Why didn't he enjoy his wealth? Because he still saw himself as the struggling young man with little money, even though he had long passed that point. Proverbs 13:7 says it best: "There is that maketh himself rich, yet hath nothing: there is that maketh himself poor, yet hath great riches."

This mental conditioning of poverty can come from a variety of sources. It may be that you grew up in a family with little money and you came to accept that as a normal fact of life. You may have associated with other poverty thinkers who influenced and reinforced your thinking. Or it may simply be your own mental tendency to think in terms of "never enough." There are many outside influences that encourage the consciousness of lack and limitation.

When you accept poverty, you have poverty. It's as simple as that. Be alert and reject thoughts of poverty as soon as they come to your awareness. Poverty consciousness, if allowed to grow, will have a paralyzing effect on your life. It creates low self-esteem and a feeling of futility that will stop you from going for the things you want in life. In addition, it creates a host of other negative emotions, including anxiety, fear, worry, and desperation. The longer you stay in such a consciousness, the more you will think that the condition is permanent.

There is a famous story about two brothers, both born into poverty. They were separated while still young. One went on to become a successful businessman while the other continued to be plagued by financial troubles. Now why did one brother rise above his situation while the other didn't? The brother who succeeded believed he could rise above his conditions, while the brother who struggled accepted his poverty condition.

Poverty Being Holy

One of the false conceptions of how money works comes from a deeply entrenched notion of poverty being holy. Many spiritually minded people have adopted the idea that having money somehow inhibits their spiritual growth and have thus chosen to do without money or earthly luxuries in order to be spiritual. Many spiritual philosophies and anecdotes appear to support this idea. There's the familiar Bible misquote: "Money is the root of all evil." The actual words are, "*Love* of money is the root of all evil" (1 Tim. 6:10). It is not money itself. That is as much a part of the Divine as anything else. It is the *attachment* to money above all else that is the root of so much unnecessary pain and suffering. Jesus spoke of how it was "easier for a camel to go through the eye of a needle, than for a rich man to enter into the kingdom of God" (Matt. 19:24). There are even some religious sects in India that believe having furniture is a sign of decadence and moral corruption!

Metaphysically speaking, there is nothing inherently evil or wrong with having money. Quite the opposite is true. Money is a form of energy like everything else, and being in the flow of prosperity is sharing in God's light and power. If God is infinite wealth, why wouldn't the Divine want you, as the beloved child, to partake of that holy wealth? You're meant to partake of all God's blessings, and prosperity is one of those blessings.

Where the confusion sets in is when you worship money as an end in itself. *Worshipping* money is an evil that will eventually bring spiritual and/or financial bankruptcy. If you make a false god of money, you are sure to have trouble. It's not that a rich man cannot enter the kingdom of God, but rather that a man who is *attached* to his possessions will not be able to enter the divine kingdom until he learns to let go of material attachments. If you worship possessions of any kind, it's much harder for you to come into your spiritual consciousness because your mind is focused on material things. You need to reverse your priorities and direct your attention to the spiritual life. Then your prosperity will flow, and it will be in balance with other aspects of your life.

There's a wonderful story about a young Indian boy who left home to search for the guru who would teach him the mysteries of life. He looked in many places but couldn't find his spiritual teacher. One day, he had come to a palace to ask for some water. As he was leaving, he heard a voice inside the palace asking, "Where are you going, little boy?"

The boy looked inside and saw the owner of the palace coming out. He looked like a raja and was dressed in the finest clothes and jewelry. "I stopped for some water and must leave to find my guru," was the boy's response.

"What makes you think you haven't found him?"

The boy looked at the man in his fine raiment. "You? No, you can't be him. What do you know of spiritual things?"

"Why don't you come in and stay for a while. If you don't think I have something to teach you, you can go on your way."

The boy agreed, and the master of the house started teaching the boy many things. The boy was impressed, but still could see only the man's wealth and couldn't imagine how a man with so many material things could be so spiritual.

One day, as the master was teaching, a servant ran into the room crying, "The palace is on fire!"

The master didn't move an inch and simply replied, "Don't bother me; I'm busy."

A few moments later, the servant came up again yelling, "But, Master, the fire is growing and coming up the stairs now!"

Again the master said, "Can't you see that I'm busy? Please, leave me alone."

Finally, the servant came again, beseeching the master, "Master, the fire's coming down the hall! You must do something or the palace will be lost!"

The man still did not move, but the boy, hearing such news, picked up his books and started running for the door. Suddenly, the master said, "Aha! I was willing to lose my whole palace and perhaps my life, and you were worried about your three little books."

So you are the one who passes judgment about what is spiritual and what is not. Clearly, in this apocryphal story, the guru was not interested in threatening the boy's life or boasting of his own spiritual development. He was using this situation to provoke the pupil to help him break the illusionary picture the boy had regarding wealth and spirituality. This story also demonstrates that not only can a misapprehension of prosperity block the flow of prosperity, it can actually hinder spiritual development as well.

God is not interested in making you suffer. After all, the Creator knows very well that you need material things. Even the great Buddha, when he was searching for enlightenment, was said to have tried at one point to deny himself every physical dependency and live on one grain of rice a day, only to learn that this was not the way to enlightenment. This experience helped him to choose instead what he termed "the middle way" to spiritual maturity.

For every Mother Teresa who chooses to give up worldly possessions, there is also a King Solomon who is both spiritual *and* wealthy. It all depends on the soul's particular lesson or mission.

TAPPING THE TURQUOISE RAY

In working with spiritual energy to build prosperity, you first want to clear misconceptions from your mind because poverty consciousness starts on the mental level. The orange-red flame is wonderful at clearing away these invasive weeds. Again, include the four main centers in your spiritual cleansing.

MEDITATIVE PRAYER FOR RELEASING POVERTY CONSCIOUSNESS

"Down-ray the orange-red flame of purification to cut loose
all sense of lack and limitation, especially in my mental body,
cleansing me of poverty consciousness wherever it is
lodged in my being."

Feel those unenlightened thoughts dropping away from you. You will be surprised at how much you've been holding on to that needs releasing. You might find that you resist this process. Chances are, you've built a strong image of whatever your condition is, and it's not so easy to just let it go. In this case, pace yourself. Follow this meditative sequence to the degree to which you feel comfortable. Later on, you can repeat the entire process as often as you feel the need.

After you finish using the orange-red flame, bring in the blue-white fire to help establish new positive flows of Divine Light.

MEDITATIVE PRAYER FOR REPLENISHING THE CONSCIOUSNESS

"Down-ray the blue-white fire of eternal life to charge and
recharge all levels of my being, bringing me new life force."

Once you have replenished yourself, you're ready to build up your aura with the turquoise ray. This is a marvelous energy, one you can never use enough when building your prosperity. You may work with all the centers, but there is special emphasis on the Hermetic center when working with this energy. As you bring it down, you want to get into the feeling and knowing of this divine flow of supply. Envision yourself as a mighty monarch who can buy anything.

MEDITATIVE PRAYER FOR PROSPERITY

"Down-ray the turquoise ray of abundance and supply into
all levels of consciousness, especially my Hermetic center,
quickening all twelve avenues of my world affairs,
and establishing this Thy prosperity in my
human Earth affairs."

Sense and feel the activation of this center. If you like, you can add a short visualization to fully establish this energy in your aura. If you have seven cents in your bank account, see seven hundred dollars in your bank account. See this ray touching into your money supply and quickening in this light. See all your sources of income receiving a quickening with this spiritual flow. Ask that the light "multiply and increase *this Thy money*." And hold to the knowing that this is actually happening for you.

To finish your work, add the silver ray to quicken the turquoise and help manifest prosperity faster.

MEDITATIVE PRAYER FOR QUICKENING THE PROSPERITY FLOW

"Down-ray the silver ray of divine intelligence into my Hermetic center, quickening this Thy prosperity. Guide me in the intelligent use and application of Thy holy abundance."

Once this power is established in you, give thanks, and trust that the energy is in motion. Feel that power attracting the things you need. If you find yourself falling back into worry patterns, repeat the light work. You can do this three times in one day to get the energy moving and really make the connection. Of course, you can complement this work with any other light work you feel you need to strengthen this spiritual abundance.

Once you feel the energy is there for you, focus on the goals you want to achieve, the things you want to create, knowing that financial resources will be available as you need them. Visualizations are a great help at this point to create the conditions you want (see chapter 17).

CAREER

Most people probably spend more time at their jobs than any other single pursuit. In many professions, the forty-hour week has turned into the fifty-, sixty-, and even seventy-hour week. That's a lot of time to be focusing on any single activity. Because your career takes such a big chunk of your life, you want to be sure the time you're spending at it is time well spent. Directing the light into your career can help build your dream job, create harmony in the workplace, remove stumbling blocks, alleviate stress, and keep moving your profession in the right direction.

The dictionary defines "career" as "a chosen pursuit." It comes from an old French word for racecourse. In staking your claim in the work world, a career can certainly feel like running a race or, as some call it, a "rat race." The first thing to recognize when doing spiritual energy work is that your career is not an identity; it's an activity. It's not you. You are a divine spiritual being in the process of unfolding your spiritual powers. To do this, part of your purpose is to express yourself in focused activities that strengthen your abilities. That's the spiritual purpose of a career. Your job is an important part of your life, but you are not your job. If you identify with what you do rather than who you are, you will always be at the mercy of that activity. And there will inevitably come a day of reckoning, because no pursuit can satisfy all your needs.

A common misunderstanding about a career is that it must be money producing. A "chosen pursuit" can mean anything that you diligently focus your attention on. It's come to be associated with a chosen profession, but any serious pursuit is a career. Motherhood, while not a revenue-generating job, is one of the most sacred and important careers a person can undertake. It's unquestionably a career in the best sense of the word.

Your chosen pursuit is strongly connected with your purpose in life. If Earth is a spiritual schoolhouse for the soul, then a career is one of the most important "courses" you'll be taking while attending this earthly school. Like any other aspect of your human Earth affairs, your career is a spiritual activity designed to help your soul grow. You may be here to develop your creative side, in which case you'll be attracted to artistic careers. Or it may be that you need to develop your social skills, in which case you will choose a profession where you'll interact with a lot of people, such as in business or the social sciences.

A positive attitude is an important prerequisite to pursuing a career. There must be joy in work because work without joy is drudgery. Create joy even if it's not your ideal work. Of course you should strive with all your heart for what you want, but in the course of reaching that goal, you may have to do work that is less than ideal. So attitude is everything. When there is love in what you do, it's not work at all.

Many people do not have a good attitude toward their work. In focusing the spiritual light on your career, cultivate a positive attitude about the work you're doing. From the spiritual point of view, no honest work is low or base. All work is valid and worthy in God's eyes. There is a story about Saint Francis of Assisi being confronted about work ethics. Saint Francis was sweeping a walkway to a church. It was a simple task, but he did it as if it were of great importance. A person came up to him wondering why he didn't assign that menial job to one of the monks in his order. When the man didn't get the response he wanted from Saint Francis, he tried to provoke him by asking what he'd do if he found out he was going to die in an hour. Saint Francis calmly replied, "I'd finish sweeping."

The way to maintain joy in your work life is to enjoy the process without being attached to results. This is work for its own sake more than for the rewards you may reap. This doesn't mean you don't pay attention and strive to reach the career goals you've set. It simply means that you don't identify those goals as your primary motivation. You are not always in control of how things turn out. If a job doesn't work out the way you envisioned, you might feel like a failure and believe that your time was wasted. But if you put your heart into the process of work and recognized that your spiritual growth was in the journey itself as much as in the destination, then you'd know that no time was wasted at all. What appeared to be failure would contribute to success in the next try. The Bhagavad Gita puts it well: "To work alone thou hast the right, but never to the fruits thereof."

One of the twelve power rays in your Hermetic center is the ray of career or purpose. It appears as pure white light. This ray quickens you to help manifest your purpose in life. It helps in all facets of your work life, such as position, advancement, finding a new job, etc. Without this ray you might have the thought or desire to do something, but there would be very little power to actually manifest those dreams. This ray works automatically for you. Yet when you work with spiritual energy to strengthen the Hermetic center you can greatly strengthen this career Hermetic ray.

When someone is at full throttle in his or her career, happy and productive, the Hermetic center will be very bright. It will be moving in a strong clockwise motion and show active emanations of gold, red, and orange energies radiating from the center at least a foot in all directions. The white ray within the Hermetic center will be very strong and pronounced.

THREE ENERGETIC PHASES OF BUILDING A CAREER

In building your career, there are three distinct spiritual energy flows in the aura connected to this process. They are:

1. *Internal building*
2. *Projecting spiritual energy*
3. *Manifesting*

The first stage is building the skills to be good at your work. Whether you are going to school, interning, or learning on the job, you need to build the energy in your aura to be successful at what you wish to do. In my own case, I was clairvoyant almost from birth, but it was only after many years of gathering experience and study that I was a *trained* clairvoyant and ready to teach metaphysics to others.

Depending on the type of career you are building or strengthening, working with spiritual energy can greatly help, especially calling on spiritual powers related to your type of profession. Remember, when you are learning something new, there is a spiritual energy associated with that activity. This power builds as you keep your attention on that pursuit. If you are studying to be an artist, you are building the spiritual power rays connected to creative activity. If you are pursuing the healing arts, you will be developing different types of energies as you build your healing powers.

Once the spiritual power has built to a certain level and your skill set has reached a certain competence, then it's time to start moving that power into your outer life. A new set of energies starts showing up in the aura for this second stage. Maybe you have just finished school and now get your first job in the "real world." It may not be your ideal work, but it's working in the field you have studied in. In the aura, the energies that have been gaining momentum in your aura now start projecting into your outer world. Remember, your career is not an isolated pursuit. You pursue your career in cooperation with other people. We are all playing our part in the divine plan and our careers need to be in harmony with that plan. This is why when

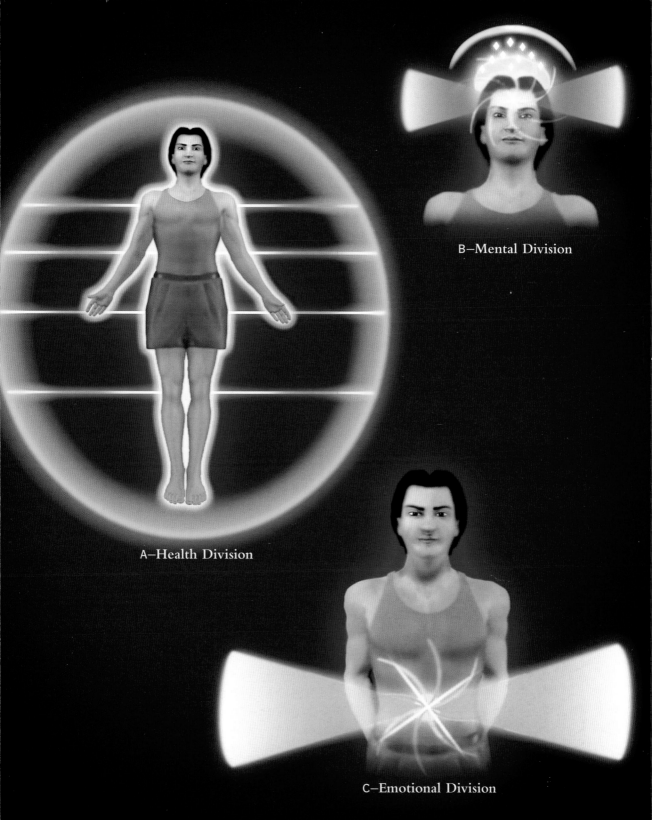

A–Health Division

B–Mental Division

C–Emotional Division

ILLUSTRATION 2.2: Divisions of the Aura, A-C

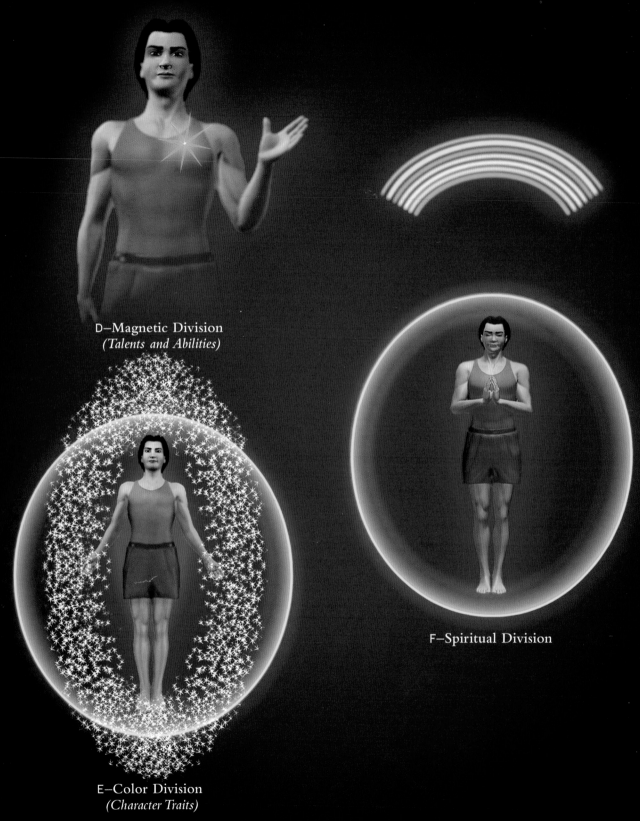

D—Magnetic Division
(Talents and Abilities)

F—Spiritual Division

E—Color Division
(Character Traits)

ILLUSTRATION 2.2: Divisions of the Aura, D-F

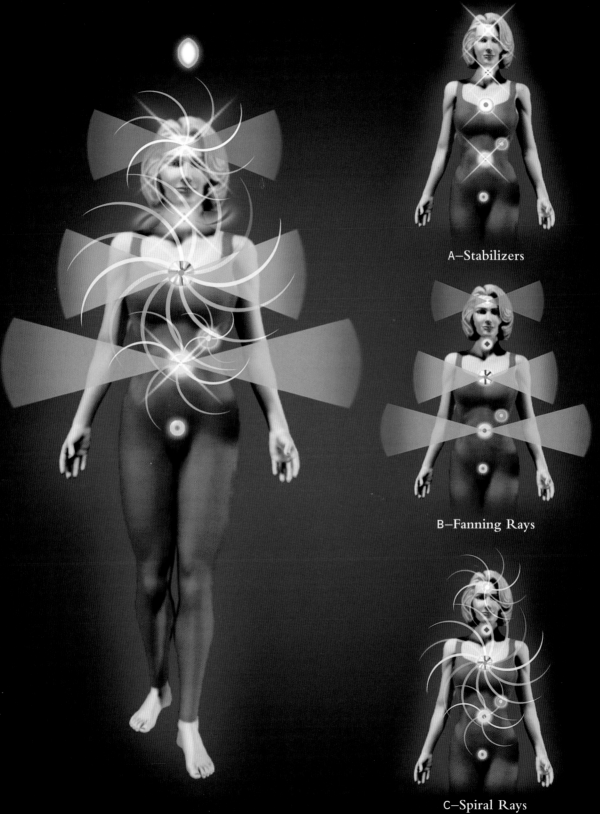

A—Stabilizers

B—Fanning Rays

C—Spiral Rays

ILLUSTRATION 2.4: Energy Center Radiations

ILLUSTRATION 2.5: The Mixed Aura

ILLUSTRATION 2.6: The Devolved Aura

ILLUSTRATION 2.7: The Enlightened Aura

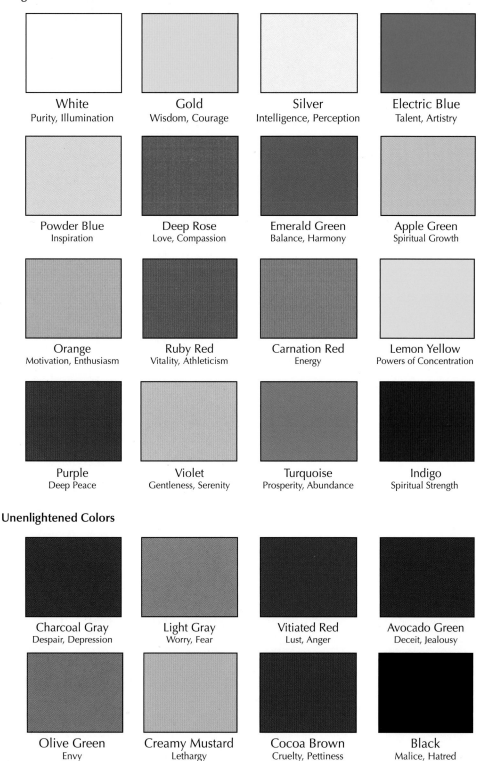

Enlightened Colors

White Purity, Illumination	**Gold** Wisdom, Courage	**Silver** Intelligence, Perception	**Electric Blue** Talent, Artistry
Powder Blue Inspiration	**Deep Rose** Love, Compassion	**Emerald Green** Balance, Harmony	**Apple Green** Spiritual Growth
Orange Motivation, Enthusiasm	**Ruby Red** Vitality, Athleticism	**Carnation Red** Energy	**Lemon Yellow** Powers of Concentration
Purple Deep Peace	**Violet** Gentleness, Serenity	**Turquoise** Prosperity, Abundance	**Indigo** Spiritual Strength

Unenlightened Colors

Charcoal Gray Despair, Depression	**Light Gray** Worry, Fear	**Vitiated Red** Lust, Anger	**Avocado Green** Deceit, Jealousy
Olive Green Envy	**Creamy Mustard** Lethargy	**Cocoa Brown** Cruelty, Pettiness	**Black** Malice, Hatred

ILLUSTRATION 3.1: **Auric Color Chart**

ILLUSTRATION 3.2: Romantic Love

ILLUSTRATION 3.3: Intelligence

ILLUSTRATION 3.4: Hatred

ILLUSTRATION 3.5: Anger

ILLUSTRATION 3.6: Wealth Consciousness

ILLUSTRATION 3.7: Poverty Consciousness

ILLUSTRATION 3.8: Fear

ILLUSTRATION 3.9: The Spiritual Aspirant

ILLUSTRATION 5.1: The Higher Self Point of Spiritual Knowing

Light Process During Meditation

Light Just After Meditation

ILLUSTRATION 7.1: The Divine Light Process

Original Condition

After 8 Months of Light Work

ILLUSTRATION 7.2: Releasing Depression with Spiritual Energy

putting anything to action you ask that it be done "according to divine law and love for the good of all concerned." It needs to be a win-win situation for all involved. This doesn't mean there isn't some healthy competition involved. But it does mean you are aiming to fulfill your part in the divine scheme of life through productive collaboration.

In the aura, this projecting energy appears as rays of white light moving out from the Hermetic center in every direction, 360 degrees. The rays can extend quite far when strong, almost half of arm's length. When a person is emanating this power it means he or she is dedicating a lot of personal power and motivation to succeed. You could see this type of energy in a woman, for example, who has spent years in college developing business skills and now is starting her work life and putting everything she has into being productive in her job. Her first or even second job may not be her dream job but she is applying herself diligently. She is putting herself into what she does. In doing this, this person is projecting her Hermetic energy into the vibrated ethers and this is working to attract her ideal work to her. Like attracts like. As long as this person stays on track and does not become discouraged to the point of changing direction or giving up, that energy will eventually lead into the third stage—manifestation.

In this third stage of career building, life is now giving back what has been given to it. The inner spiritual prompting is now projecting into outer manifestation. Perhaps that person does get the job offer she's been dreaming of or the business she started is now taking off. The momentum has built and although there may be more to do, the aspiring soul is now seeing the results of her steadfast and sincere efforts.

This third phase can present itself in fascinating ways in the aura. The gallery of auric portraits in chapter 3 shows wonderful examples of manifested success in the aura. Someone who builds great wealth can develop a prosperity aura similar to the one in color Illustration 3.6. This kind of prosperity energy can only be developed to this degree in the aura if the power is manifest in life. The scientific equations seen in color Illustration 3.3 would not be that extensive unless those equations were producing something in outer life. Even the love energy seen in color Illustration 3.2 would not be so strong unless the love were reciprocated. When our inner spiritual efforts find expression in the outer world, that energy reciprocates back to the aura blessing it.

Now, there are some people who do everything right when it comes to their careers, yet, because of circumstances beyond their control, they do not get to see the full fruit of their labors. What happens here? First, by divine law, sooner or later, in this or another lifetime, good deeds find their reciprocal flow. The "good karma" that has accrued must eventually find expression. While it may not fully be able to reflect itself back into the aura or your life initially, eventually it will. The soul is strengthened and its part in the divine plan is served. There have been many cases when pioneers in any field of life do not get to see the results of all their hard work. Later generations gain the benefits. Yet that energy still blesses those who pioneered such things. The spiritual lesson here is to pursue what you know you are meant to do, even if you are not immediately seeing the rewards of such efforts. Eventually you will see the effects of your efforts and your aura will reflect that manifestation. Life balances out.

Essential rays you'll need to work with in strengthening your job avenue are the gold light for strength and courage, the white light for upliftment and illumination, the bright orange for motivation and healthy ambition, and the silver light for guidance and direction and to stimulate activity. Let's look at some specific job situations and how to work with the light in relation to them.

CHOOSING A PROFESSION

It's interesting how some people know exactly what they want to do in life while others are not so sure. For the ones who know what they want, there are few questions concerning which direction to take. However, for a great many people, deciding what to do is not such a straightforward matter. Fortunately, all of us have a purpose in life and this purpose is reflected in your aura. Your aura can show you where your strengths and talents lie. A child who has pronounced musical ability would be a natural fit for a career in music. Someone who is very focused, with a sharp, analytical mind, would have what it takes to become a very good scientist. By following your natural gifts and desires, you avoid "barking up the wrong tree" when it comes to a career. By working with spiritual energy you can gain a clearer perspective on your career potential. Whether bricklayer or architect, all are part of the divine plan.

For tuning in to the kind of career you are meant to pursue, work with divine guidance and direction (see chapter 12). When it comes to a career, there is a spiritual plan for each of us. Recognizing your true calling is a matter of tuning into that purpose. The reason some people are so clear about what they want is that they are in touch with their spiritual purpose. So, if you are unclear about your goals, it's time to get to work and open up to inspiration and illumination. This can take time and repeated effort. Also, our purpose is not always one single thing. You may already have completed several things in your career life, but something is left unfinished. Regardless of where you are in the journey, by building up the spiritual power and staying with it, eventually you will connect with your full career destiny.

I recommend starting your light work with a thorough cleansing with the purifying rays to release any mental confusion and stress that may be blocking the clear picture of what you're meant to do. Once that clearing is done, the two key rays to work with are the gold and silver energies. The gold will help bring in the illumination to get a clear picture of the direction you should take and the silver will give you greater perceptive power to understand what your Higher Self is saying to you. Start with the golden ray to touch into your Higher Self Point. Then see that energy going into your mental body, quickening it with the light so that you connect with the guidance given.

MEDITATIVE PRAYER WITH THE GOLD LIGHT TO FIND A PROFESSION

"Down-ray the golden ray of wisdom light into my Higher Self
Point of Spiritual Knowing, to receive guidance and direction
in finding my chosen profession." (*Hold for a moment to feel
the connection being made.*) "I ask that this light down-ray to
my mental body to connect me with the guidance being
given so that I may envision what my true profession is."

After your meditation, hold to the knowing that your right work is forthcoming. As with all types of divine direction, the answers may or may not be given to you at that moment. Either way, you have begun generating the power to manifest the work you are meant to do. Continue with whatever job search you are on, but try to feel which way the light is directing you. Generally, you will sense the light moving more strongly in one career direction than another. This is God's way of inspiring you to your right occupation and livelihood.

Then add the silver ray to quicken your mental body so that you are receptive to spiritual inspiration and illumination. Silver is also a guidance ray and can bring in clarity of mind and heart.

MEDITATIVE PRAYER WITH THE SILVER RAY TO FIND A PROFESSION

"Down-ray the silver ray of divine intelligence to quicken
my mental body to perceive and better comprehend the
divine inspiration of my true profession being given to
me. I also ask that this silver ray touch into the
Hermetic center to open my heart and desire to
pursue my highest good."

GENERATING A NEW JOB

If you're already clear about what you want to do, and you are looking for a specific kind of job, you can work with the light to help you create the job you envision.

As we have seen, to generate a new job you first need to start generating that energy on the spiritual level. Everything that manifests physically was first created on the spiritual plane. By building the light for your new job in the spiritual dimension first, you are taking the first step in creating that job on the physical plane.

Both the gold and white rays are helpful in generating a profession. The golden ray of wisdom light has the ability to quicken your Hermetic center and open your path. Sometimes you can be right for a job but there is outside interference. The golden light gives you extra power to break through any dissenting energy and open up the right path for you. Gold can also give you stamina when you may feel like giving up the fight.

Raise your consciousness into your Higher Self Point and ask the golden ray to touch all levels of your consciousness, especially to touch into your Hermetic center.

MEDITATIVE PRAYER WITH THE GOLD LIGHT TO GENERATE NEW WORK

"Down-ray the golden ray of wisdom light to touch into my
Hermetic center and generate new avenues of work, cutting
through any negative blocks and giving me the inner
strength and divine power to pursue my path and open
up the job that's right for me."

Then work with the pure white light. This ray will help to open the actual flow of whatever job you're seeking, thereby helping you to connect with it. Sometimes you can be a little out of tune with the job you seek. It may be what you want and are good at, but you're just not clicking with the marketplace you're trying to enter. The pure white light can help you synchronize with the work you are seeking. It can also help to release internal blocks. However, if you notice a lot of internal strife, work on clearing that energy separately from this work. Primarily with the Hermetic center, but ask the light to touch into all the centers.

MEDITATIVE PRAYER WITH THE WHITE LIGHT TO FIND NEW WORK

"Down-ray the pure white light into my Hermetic center,
activating it in a clockwise motion to quicken all my human
Earth affairs, helping me to tune in and open up to the work
that's right for me, and giving me the vision to recognize
that work when I see it."

Adding the silver ray can help your new job open up quickly.

Meditative Prayer to Generate a New Job Quickly

"Down-ray the silver ray of divine intelligence directly into

my Hermetic center and out-ray into my human Earth affairs

to bring forth my new job quickly, according to divine law

and love for the good of all concerned."

It's also a good idea to work with the bright orange ray of motivation (not to be confused with the orange-red flame of purification). The bright orange ray will bring in ambition to success. It is especially helpful if something has dampened your spirits—this energy will bring in new enthusiasm.

Meditative Prayer to Generate a Motivation

"Down-ray the bright orange ray of motivation and enthusiasm

into my Hermetic center to stimulate this center with a

greater desire and ambition to succeed."

Once your light work is done, you need to trust that the light will do the job you've asked it to do. Conclude with the following prayer: "I hold to the knowing that the work I love is forthcoming. So be it."

DEAD-END JOBS

When I was still in college, I had many plans for my future. Financial troubles at home forced me to postpone my dreams and take up temp work to make ends meet. I was despondent, thinking I'd never do the things I really wanted to do in life. I went to ask the advice of well-known spiritual teacher and philosopher Manly P. Hall. One of his many inspiring aphorisms was "The universe always has work for those who are qualified to perform it." I respected his work and could see by his aura that he was a spiritually advanced soul. I met him in his office and started to pour my heart out, telling him all that was going on with me. I kept saying to him, "I have all these obstacles." He stopped me at one point and simply said, "What obstacles?" That stopped me dead in my tracks. I recognized then that he was right. I was allowing these immediate concerns to obscure my long-term goals. If I saw them as obstacles, I'd never get past them. Well, I did go through some tough times, but sure enough—things did eventually open up for me.

If you are in a dead-end job, the first thing to do is acknowledge that you need to make a change. You have to make an effort. This will take courage, but there is no other way. You need to get back to what it is you want in life and not let the momentary necessities cloud your vision. When you're doing work that you know is not your calling, it can feel frustrating. Yet, here is where you have to apply the principle of spiritual joy in the workplace. There are many times when you have to do things that are not to your liking, but there's always a lesson to be learned in these experiences. They only become stifling when you maintain that bad attitude and do nothing to change these conditions. No matter what the job, you still need a positive attitude and must respect the work at hand. Then these present job experiences will not seem so frustrating or permanent.

Work with the golden ray to help create the courage needed to break the cycle you're in and to begin generating the job you need. Again, if there are emotional or mental blocks, you'll need to work on those separately. Also, work with the love ray if you're being too hard on yourself.

Meditative Prayer for Courage in Finding Work

"Down-ray the golden ray of wisdom light into my Hermetic
center and out-ray into my human Earth affairs to dispel any
negative work patterns and to give me the courage and
dynamic power to pursue the work I love."

Once you get the light working for you, you can follow the Divine Light recommendations for generating a new job or for finding your chosen field.

UNHAPPY AT WORK

I have counseled many people who have good jobs but still are unhappy at what they do. They are unhappy because of friction with other people or because they simply are not enamored with their work. I have found that sometimes people who are unhappy with their work are not really suited for their jobs and chose that line of work for the wrong reasons.

Too many people choose a career solely for the money. For example, there are doctors who practice medicine not because they love the healing arts, but because the pay is good, the prestige high. A tremendous amount of dedicated work and responsibility go into being a doctor. Anyone whose motivation is money soon discovers that he or she has paid a steep price for doing something without love. People also pick jobs because they appear glamorous. Or they may choose to enter a profession because others have influenced their decision. A father may want his son or daughter to follow in his footsteps, despite the child's wishes to the contrary. Too often that son or daughter complies out of love or for fear of disappointing the parents. What inevitably follows is rebellion, a life of "quiet desperation," or, with grace, an awakening and shift to their true calling.

Review your inventory list and see if you picked up on anything about your work by direct observation. If not, you need to do some reflecting to gain some insight into what about your job is bothering you.

Until you've identified what's bothering you, it's hard to know exactly which power rays to work with. If the situation turns out to be more a people problem, turn to the chapter on relationships to see how to work with the light in professional environments. If the condition results from dislike of the actual work, then you need to call upon the gold and white, as you would to get out of a dead-end job. Even if you're in a high-paying job, if it's not for you, that job's not going to help you much in your spiritual growth. You'll need courage and vision to branch out in new directions.

Another reason people are unhappy at work is that jobs are becoming more all-consuming. It seems that any job worth its salt these days demands ten to twelve hours a day, or even more. Many people love what they do but still become frustrated at their work and eventually "burn out" because the stress is just too much. Such demands put enormous pressure on your personal life as well. By working so intensely, it's easy to fall out of the spiritual rhythm. And when you're out of rhythm, anything can happen.

Watch out for jobs that demand too much of you. If you're already in such a job, work with the emerald green ray of balance to keep harmony. To help relieve stress, do your best not to carry your job home with you. Give it your best effort at work, and then cut loose when you go home. Change the pace. Release your mind, especially in bed at night. Don't let your last thoughts before going to sleep be stressful ones about work.

GETTING FIRED

There's certainly a strong element of shock in getting fired. If you are fired—for whatever reason—you'll want to work with the peace ray to release that shock. You'll also need to do some mental/emotional work with the emerald green, because once the shock has worn off, there's bound to be some sort of reaction such as anger, resentment, or depression. It's also easy for you to start feeling sorry for yourself and fall into a state of self-pity. This is the time to work things out. Don't give yourself time to sulk. Why did you get fired? If it was politics, then you know it was not about you. If you were fired because of something you did or didn't do, then you must take responsibility. Don't beat yourself over the head or feel humiliated. Instead, find out where the problem is and fix it!

Here are two meditations to help you overcome the shock of losing your job and to help maintain your spiritual equilibrium.

Meditative Prayer to Overcome Shock

"Down-ray the purple ray of spiritual peace to touch into all
levels of my consciousness, releasing me from all shock and
establishing the silence of peace and the peace of silence
throughout my entire being."

Follow up with the emerald green ray to help keep things in perspective.

MEDITATIVE PRAYER FOR SPIRITUAL BALANCE

"Down-ray the emerald green ray to all levels of my being to
balance my entire consciousness so that my thinking is clear
and my actions are moving in divine rhythm and order."

CHAPTER XI

Strengthening Relationships

. . . .

Spiritual energy has a beneficial effect on all types of human relationships. The light helps build friendships, dispel discord, clarify misunderstanding, and keep relationships moving harmoniously. It can also help to draw the right people to one another. Working with Divine Light won't necessarily resolve every dilemma, but what it will do if you are diligent is help to resolve your part in that dilemma. Most of all, the light gives you the power to see other people beyond their personality self and in their true, divine self.

The primary element in any relationship is love. Without love, no relationship can work beneficently. Love connects us to each other, to creation, and to God. When dealing with others, you're going to work a great deal with the deep rose pink ray of spiritual love. I don't think there's such a thing as getting too much of this loving energy.

Love comes in many forms. Regardless of the expression, if love is real it emanates from the same spiritual source—God. Along with Divine Mind, God's Divine Love is the most powerful primary force in the universe. It emanates directly from the heart of God. Divine Love is the bond that holds all creation together. It's the heartbeat of life itself. Without this love, there'd be no purpose to life, no desire to create or act on anything. There'd still be Divine Mind, but no reason to express it. An act of Divine Love created each of us. God's love is what carries us through the trials and tribulations of our pilgrimage through creation and back to God.

The expression of Divine Love can be described as pure and unconditional when you love without thought of return. We see this love when people put others before themselves or risk their lives for others. This high love leads to the ultimate universal love. Divine Love embodies all the attributes of the spiritual life, such as gentleness, kindness, understanding, and compassion. There's a tremendous exhilaration and upliftment that accompanies such celestial love. Best of all, Divine Love is eternal. It's always there for you. It will never disappoint or let you down.

Human love is also spiritual, but it's graded down to the physical level. This love is more restrictive. Human love desires things of this world. People may love having a big house, a fast car, the money they make, the way their spouse looks, or the things that are done for them. There's nothing wrong with loving such things, but they are temporal and usually conditional. If the quality or thing that the person is getting is diminished or taken away, then the love can fade.

The goal of all your relationships is to transform them into acts of *Divine Love*. As part of your soul development, you're in the process of developing your love flow. When you give love before getting love, when you express love without thought of return, you're building that Divine Love state. Sometimes, it's the most demanding things asked in relationships that can be the very key to your spiritual transformation. There is the story of a famous author who fathered a mentally challenged son. The condition left the boy totally dependent on his parents to take care of almost all his physical functions. The father was a proud person and was humiliated and embarrassed by his son's condition. He resented the boy, calling him his "little monster."

When the boy was several years old, it became evident that the child had a gift for music despite his difficulties. This awakened something in the father. He realized that his son was not a "little monster" at all and that there was a soul inside trying to express itself. The father's attitude completely changed. He realized that the issue was not his son's disability but his own pride. He came to love the boy and dedicated himself to helping him in every way he could. It turned out that the boy grew up to become a famous pianist, more famous than his father. The son continued to need physical help for even the most basic things, like shaving, but his father was always there for him. This man showed a great spiritual transformation, from severe disappointment and ignorance to selfless love. His trial was a great opportunity to learn the spiritual lessons of love.

You're here to learn the lessons of life—and many times you learn them from others. Once you learn how to love others regardless of their imperfections, then you're showing your capacity to love the Divine. As the Bible says, "He that loveth not his brother whom he hath seen, how can he love God whom he hath not seen?" (1 John 4:20). You can't be very close to loving God if you're at war with others. All problems in relationships stem from a lack of love shown in one way or another. So many people say they love, but do they really?

Most of us know how important love is. We can understand the principles of Divine Love in the abstract, but sometimes it seems so hard to actually apply these principles in real-life situations. Wise souls have been professing spiritual love for centuries. Why is it so difficult to put into action? Why isn't the world a more loving place? Our nemesis is our own human ego—the petty ego, the puffed-up little "i" that keeps getting in the way of our natural love flow. Our human nature likes to hold on to its jealousies, angers, and hatreds, even though these are the very bonds that hold us back and make us suffer. In our petty self, we can't see beyond the immediate narrow field of whatever is happening in our lives. We're afraid to venture out beyond the familiar. Even though it's our nature to love, we get in the way of our own expression of that love when we allow the imperfections of our human ego to take control of our lives.

Love is an essential element to your aura. One of the first things I look for in reading auras is how the love energy is moving. This reveals how connected to the Divine the person is. The primary energy to look for is deep rose pink. This can show in a variety of ways in the aura depending on the type of love and how strongly it's being expressed. Rose pink light can be seen in the chakras or sometimes as a band of pink light around the perimeter of the aura, which shows a loving nature.

Most of us have some deep rose pink in our auras, indicating that we have some of that spiritual love already and are expressing it in some way. We may not recognize it as spiritual, but it is. What generally happens, though, is that we taint this love with our own selfish wants. Someone may genuinely love someone, but at the same time be very selfish in that love. The deep rose pink will be in the aura but mixed with some cocoa brown, which expresses the selfishness. Or they may be possessive in love, which mixes the pink with avocado green. There can be lust in love, which adds vitiated red to the pink.

Much more rare to see is the high, divine, selfless love. With this celestial love, a light pale pink and violet will accompany the deep rose pink and is seen above the head. This is the love that expresses when people think of someone else's interests above their own. This high pink energy usually comes and goes in most people. It's very hard to sustain such an energy unless you're living a life of selfless service.

The avenue of your world affairs in the Hermetic center that deals with human relationships is, appropriately, the pink ray. This ray connects you to Divine Love and opens your feeling nature. Without this ray, it would be very difficult to have healthy relationships. This loving ray can express itself in all aspects of life: love of people, art, music, animals, nature, etc. Like the other rays of your human Earth affairs, this ray cannot be destroyed or disappear no matter what you do, but it can become weakened if you are set on closing your heart. The deepest place in your aura that love registers is in your Hermetic center, because this is where desires are born—in the soul.

You can work with the love ray directly to increase your spiritual capacity for love. Begin working with the deep rose pink at all levels of your being. See it going into the four main centers, especially your heart center, and into your soul levels. You can follow the meditative prayer in chapter 6 on spiritual love or use the following meditative prayer.

MEDITATIVE PRAYER TO INCREASE DIVINE LOVE FLOW

"Down-ray the deep rose pink of spiritual love into all levels
of my consciousness, igniting my spiritual centers with this
Divine Light and especially touching into my Hermetic center
and soul levels to release any old hurts and soul wounds,
and to uplift me into the divine ecstasy of Thy infinite love
and everlasting embrace."

AURIC INTERACTIONS

When you interact with someone, not only is there an exchange of words, ideas, and feelings, there's an exchange of spiritual energy. This exchange is normal and natural.

We all know how exhilarating a positive exchange with someone else can be or how debilitating and disturbing a negative exchange can be.

Many people unintentionally take exchange to an extreme and depend on the energy of another rather than turning to the divine source. You want to have exhilarating exchanges with others, but not to the point of moving out of your divine center and becoming dependent on another's energy. One of the things you are doing when working with spiritual energy is learning to draw on your own divine source for spiritual power and nourishment and love. This connection with the Divine helps you be less dependent on others, which in turn has the effect of enhancing your relationships. It keeps your auric interactions moving on a positive, high level.

While various facets of the aura can intermingle, most auric energy interactions occur within the energy centers themselves. Since these centers are receiving and transmitting stations, it makes sense that they play a key role in the exchange of energy. Here is an example of how auras interact.

Two People Fighting

In this scenario, Person A has started an argument with Person B. (See Illustration 11.1.) Vitiated red energy of anger shoots from the emotional center of Person A to Person B. If B accepts this negative energy, which has happened in this case, then it will immediately hit B in the emotional center. Person B has now become incensed and reacts with anger to Person A, sending a vitiated red energy back to A's emotional center, thereby accelerating the argument. At this point, the fight can turn into a screaming match as the energies escalate. As angry thoughts and barbed words fly back and forth, energy moves from the emotional to the mental centers, destabilizing the thinking levels and further inflaming the destructive exchange. This is a fairly typical example of a full-blown fight.

Refusing an Angry Outburst

In this example, Person A is still directing anger at Person B, but this time B is completely refusing the negative energy. (See Illustration 11.2.) As a result, that negative energy does not enter the energy field of Person B. Instead, it simply dissipates. Not only does this keep B's aura clean, it also stops the escalation that would result

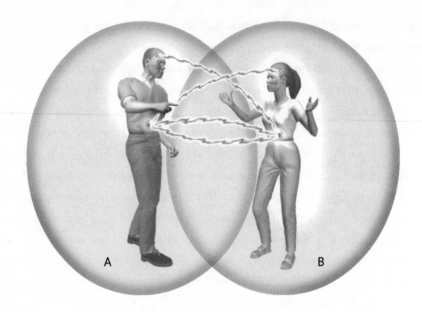

ILLUSTRATION 11.1-*Two People Fighting*

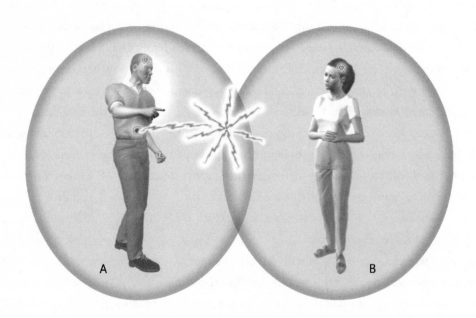

ILLUSTRATION 11.2-*Refusing an Angry Outburst*

if B were to give in to A's negative influence. In this example, B has put on a mantle of spiritual protection, so the energy does not penetrate the auric shell. Yet, even without protection, if B were still adamant about refusing to react, A's negative energy would not get much farther into her aura.

FAMILY

Let's now look at how to apply the light in specific types of relationships. We'll begin with family. We all know the importance of family and its relation to our well-being. The family unit is the backbone of society and one of our main support systems in life. Family experiences usually set the tone for our feelings and beliefs about ourselves, others, and life in general. Family is where we start building our relationships with people. It's where we learn how to give and take, and how to love. The importance of a strong family life cannot be overstated. When we have a good family experience, we carry that stability and confidence throughout life. It's a powerful foundation we can build on. Conversely, growing up in a dysfunctional family can create difficulties in future relationships if we don't take the time to bring the energy into a more positive flow and rise above that experience.

Helping to heal family traumas has been a recurring theme in my spiritual counseling work. I remember one case that was especially touching. There was a boy whose parents were killed in a car accident. He had no other living relatives and was put in an orphanage. A couple soon adopted him, and they tried to do everything for the child. The boy was heartbroken and would often cry through the night for his biological parents. He would express his frustration and anger to his adoptive mother, saying things like, "I don't like you. I don't want you. I want my mommy back." The woman did the best she could, but as time went on, things didn't get any better. The boy became more intolerant and difficult. The adoptive father was away a great deal on business trips, so it fell to the woman to care for the child. She didn't know how to handle him and wondered if she had done the right thing in adopting him. She loved him, but in her frustration at his lack of cooperation she made several mistakes, including slapping him a few times, which compounded the problem.

She came to me for counseling and began to work with the light to try to turn things around. First she turned to the love ray, to instill more patience and love in herself, so that her natural love could flow more freely. At the same time, frustration and anger that had caused her to mishandle so many situations needed to be released. She also brought in the silver ray to guide her in understanding and dealing with the boy better. Then she worked with the pink ray, sending it to him to help him heal from the loss of his parents and to show that she really loved him. She also used emerald green and gold for balance and strength to manage his difficult behavior. This went on for several months until, finally, the boy started warming up to her. They began to go out and do things together, which had never happened before, and a very warm and loving relationship began to grow.

Many times, your most intense conflicts occur within your own family. This may seem a paradox: if the family unit is such a critical part of your development and character, then why does it so often turn out to be a major source of discord? Many dynamics come into play, but generally your biggest joys and tests in human relationships will be with members of your own family. The family experience can touch into the deepest recesses of the human soul. Karma plays a huge part in family dynamics. You can't always control the circumstances that are coming your way, but you *can* control the effects of those experiences so they don't haunt or limit you. Working with spiritual energy can have a very positive effect on any type of family dynamic, helping to strengthen ties and resolve conflicts. The best time to call on the light for help is as you are going through any difficult periods. If the family discord is past but the effects are still there, the light can cleanse the aura of any old traumas and memories.

Parent to Child

In understanding parent-child relationships it's important to recognize that it was no accident that determined the family you were born into or the family you have built. In the spiritual dimension, you have agreed to this family situation as part of your soul's experience. It doesn't matter whether you were born into wealth or poverty, good parents or bad parents, or even raised as an orphan with no parental support at all. This is all part of the greater plan of life.

There's an old saying, "Give me the first seven years of a person's life and you can have the rest." In the first seven years, key character traits and tendencies are established. How that person is brought up, and the kinds of stimuli and experiences the person is exposed to, will shape his or her character from that time on.

Some would argue that our character is completely developed in our early years because the soul is a blank slate, so to speak. Our upbringing is everything, as there is no predisposition. The metaphysical point of view does not agree with this. Despite the strong influence of upbringing and environment, spiritually speaking, a child has a life independent of these factors. We had a life prior to physical existence and we have a life after as well. This Earth life is a stage in our spiritual development. Because of this we are in eventual control of any family influence.

From the spiritual point of view, the first seven years do indeed have a unique place in a soul's development. It takes seven years for key auric energies to establish themselves within the consciousness. When the child is very young, the aura and consciousness are very adaptable and fluid. This is necessary because the soul is learning so many new things, it needs to acclimate to its environment quickly. So in these early years the child is especially impressionable. By the time a child is seven, the auric energy is set, and the person begins a new phase in its unfolding development. This means that in the first seven years, the auric flow is very pliable. If there has been a disturbance, it can be more easily fixed. After age seven, of course, it can still be done but now it requires more effort. So those first seven years are critical.

This means that the most crucial time for parents to nurture and love their child is in the early formative years. Love is important all the time, but it's especially important then. Nurturing means sacrifice, time, dedication, and energy. It means learning how to care for the child. When a child is born, the first people it meets are its parents. The child's natural instinct is to look up to the parents.

As a parent, it is important to recognize that your child is a full, complete soul with free will and a destiny all its own. From the spiritual perspective, up to age sixteen, parents have a karmic responsibility to care for their child, and this includes making certain decisions on behalf of the child. But parents need to do their best to honor the unique character traits in the child and not try to simply mold the child in their own image. While parents and children can build deep friendships, even later in life when the child is an adult and on his or her own, in the formative years, the parents' first job is to be the parent and a friend second. Even if the child is difficult to deal with at times, it's the parents' job to bring out the best in the child and do everything they can to help in the child's maturity.

Sometimes parents can raise their child right and still there are problems. This is because the soul within the child is still an individual with its own tendencies and desires. It's a delicate balance here at times. Parents may look at the child and think it's so cute and helpless, but connected to that child is a full adult soul slowly establishing itself. Although parents are responsible for the child's upbringing, they are not responsible for that child's evolution. The soul within the child is responsible for its own spiritual development.

Child to Parent

One of the key jobs of the child is to honor the parent. It's a divine agreement and even if the child does not agree with everything the parent does, it's the child's job to follow the parent's guidance as far as possible. When the child is an adult, of course, the child assumes responsibility for his or her own life. The parent has to be careful not to still try to dictate the affairs of the child or make decisions for the child once he or she is grown. The child continues to honor the parent, but the spiritual dynamics change.

Some are very strong and pass through family adversity, while others are haunted by childhood traumas, which can stay with them for the rest of their lives. The thing to see is that you have the ability to pass through and rise above any conditions in your life. God always gives you the spiritual courage to pass through any trial. Abraham Lincoln grew up so poor he was not even taught how to read. He taught himself by moonlight. So whatever handicap or trying situation you're faced with, you can remedy it, or make things much better. If you had a difficult childhood, you can release that energy and create the life you dream of. You now have spiritual tools to heal those conditions. It's part of your destiny to work your way out of those limitations.

Siblings

Brothers and sisters can be your best friends throughout life, or they can be irritating, a cause of friction, or even indifferent, drifting away to become strangers. The usual underlying cause of friction between siblings is rivalry or jealousy. One child may feel he or she got the short end of the stick. Perhaps a parent has a favorite child and the other child resents it. It's a mistake that parents often make, usually without even knowing it. Or it could be that one child has an outstanding talent and is getting more attention because of it, which may excite jealousy in a brother or sister. As we know, these rivalries can be carried over into adulthood.

The Light and Family

If you are having problems with a family member, pull out all the stops to help turn things around. You want to be particularly careful not to simply blame the other person or persons for what's going on. Search your heart to see what your contribution might be to the present dilemma. Then use the light to help keep yourself above the turmoil going on around you. This will help not only you, but all the family members involved, so they can begin to see things from a spiritual perspective. As in any type of relationship, sometimes the other person will respond to the light, sometimes not. The main focus should be on building your own light rays to face what you are going through with courage and fortitude. You will most likely have to use a combination of energy techniques, including a mental/emotional clearing, forgiveness, and perhaps divine guidance. Your situation is not going unnoticed by the Divine. The Higher Self understands the challenges you are facing and is doing everything to help. The spiritual life is far more understanding and attuned to the sufferings of humanity than we give it credit for. It does everything it can to help alleviate that suffering.

In addition to whichever rays you feel you need to use for the particular situation you are in, I also recommend that you include these meditative prayers to help lighten the load of your family difficulties. Again, you need to be patient with these dilemmas. Their roots are deep, and it takes time and persistent effort for things to be worked out.

MEDITATIVE PRAYER TO HELP ALLEVIATE FAMILY DISCORD

"Down-ray the pure white light into all levels of my being,

releasing me of any animosities connected with (*name person*).

I ask that the purity and power of this divine white light

go to (*name person*) and me, touching deep within our souls

and lifting our spirits and awareness of our oneness with

God. I place this entire situation on the altar of God, releasing

all lower vibrations and any heavy burdens or pressure."

Take your time with this prayer to really feel the white light touching deeply into your auric field. If you find you still have difficulty finding the strength to face the situation, add the following prayer. In this particular light work, you are bringing down two energies at the same time.

MEDITATIVE PRAYER FOR SOUL UPLIFTMENT

"Down-ray the gold and emerald green rays into all levels of

my consciousness and especially my soul levels, to give me

the courage and strength to resolve this family situation in

Thy Divine Light and Love."

Keep the light and protection strongly around you after doing this work.

Spiritual Connection of Parent and Child

In addition to the normal family dynamics, a very special auric connection exists between parent and child. This spiritual connection can be seen at the emotional level. It appears as a ray of gold light connecting each parent with the child at the emotional center. It's referred to as the umbilical connection because it almost looks like the physical umbilical cord between fetus and mother. Yet in this case, the spiritual umbilical connection exists with both father and mother. This umbilical connection is there because the child needs a great influx of spiritual nourishment while growing up. You can clairvoyantly see energy being transmitted through the cord. I have seen beautiful pink and violet energies flowing from the parent to the child.

This connection stays with the child and parent until the death of the parent. Once the child is grown, the connection is not as strong as in childhood, but it's still very much there. This tells us that the parent and child relationship is one of the more unique human relationships we will have in life, again another reason to honor it. This umbilical connection exists with the biological parents only. Even biological parents who have nothing to do with their child's upbringing will still have the connection, but it will be very weak. It means that the child has to build this emotional support in other ways.

If parents do not treat their child well, they may transmit energy that is not of a high vibration. You as the child can refuse this energy, but it does require effort. Here is a meditative prayer to help clear out that vibration. If needed, do a separate prayer for each parent.

Meditative Prayer to Cleanse and Uplift the Spiritual Umbilical Connection

"Down-ray the pure white light into my emotional center, filling it with Thy pure divine essence. Out-ray through my spiritual umbilical connection with my (*name parent*), releasing all destructive energies directed toward me intentionally or unintentionally. I ask for special protection with the white light and gold light to be placed at my emotional center to keep me uplifted and in my own divine center."

FRIENDS

True friends are among our greatest blessings. The only reason for people to be friends is natural affinity and desire to be together. There's no formal commitment. The bond of friendship is forged out of love. It's built on loyalty, honesty, and trust. In the aura, it's often seen as a beautiful exchange of lemon yellow energy at the mental level, because friends share common interests, and a pink exchange of energy at the Hermetic level, expressing the love and comradeship friends feel for each other. One of the greatest forms of friendship is the spiritual brotherhood that's formed by two people walking the path of light together.

The key to friendship is simple: "To have a friend, be a friend." If you feel lonely and desire real friendship, don't bemoan your fate and feel sorry for yourself. Go out and express friendship! Make yourself available. Eventually people of the same affinities as you will be attracted to you. One of the most beautiful things about working with the Divine Light is that you naturally attract people to you. As your aura brightens, people find themselves drawn to you, and some wonderful friendships can be formed.

Don't push things. You can't make someone like you; it has to happen naturally. Use the deep rose pink ray to create a more loving auric energy that helps to attract new friends. The following is a meditative prayer to help attract new people to you.

MEDITATIVE PRAYER TO ATTRACT NEW FRIENDS

"Down-ray the deep rose pink of spiritual love to all my centers,
especially my emotional center, generating more love
in my consciousness and strongly opening my path to
attract new friends and to strengthen the bonds of friendship
I already have. I ask this in Divine Light and Love for the
good of all concerned."

PROFESSIONAL

Professional relationships have their own unique energetic dynamics. The point of professional relationships is to work together toward a common goal. Since career is very connected to your purpose in life, the people you work with are sharing in that cooperative purpose. Remember, your professional aspirations are never about just you. For the spiritual energy to be balanced and productive, everyone has to be effectively playing their part, like the movement of a fine Swiss timepiece. It doesn't matter if you are the president of the company or working in the mail room, each is making his or her important contribution and needs to be honored and respected. While there may be differences of opinions or approaches, cooperation and collaboration form the cornerstone to healthy and successful professional relationships.

When involved in a professional relationship, remember this affirmation:

"God is the employer and God is the employee."

Too many people cast their superiors in an adversarial role. This can make one fearful or resentful of that person's authority. Remember that by serving your employer to the best of your ability, you're serving God. It's reassuring to know that God is the only true boss. You may disagree with your boss, but you can't judge the situation because you don't know all that person is dealing with in that position. There are spiritual lessons in playing the role of boss or employee. If you don't like your station in life, then work to change it. Yet honor where you are by doing your best in the situation you are in.

If you are an employer it's important to honor the Divine in those who are working for you. Employees are not your underlings to do with as you please. You are in a position of responsibility and you must honor that position by seeing your leadership role as an act of divine service. Your first job is to inspire those working for you. Encourage their inner creative nature to express itself. Recognize the divine part they are playing. Many people in positions of power are insecure. Although they may not show it, many are not confident in the position they are in and try to mask that by being aggressive or unreasonable. Remember, it is God who put you in the leadership role. Serve God by serving your employees and watch how the relationships blossom.

The same spiritual principles apply to coworkers. There may be jealousies and competition among fellow workers for recognition and promotions, and this can create a lot of stress. Look at your work associates in the same compassionate spiritual light. They, too, have the divine spark in them and are in a spiritual growth process. Look for ways to collaborate more effectively, even if they are not always showing you the same courtesy. Take the magnanimous position.

When it comes to professional relationships, two essential power rays to work with are the deep rose pink and the emerald green to create greater love and harmony. The silver ray is a good energy to work with when there is difficulty in communication. If there's already been confrontation, do the forgiveness work and try for a fresh start. If the relationship has become adversarial, follow the meditative prayer given in the next section, below, for restoring harmony to relationships.

MEDITATIVE PRAYER FOR COOPERATION IN THE WORKPLACE

"Down-ray the deep rose pink ray of spiritual love to touch into
my Hermetic center and out-ray to fill with Divine Love and
compassion for everyone I work with. May I see them
as the divine spark that they are. I ask that this uplifting
love ray bless everyone I work with so there is
mutual cooperation and respect."

Then follow up with the emerald green ray.

MEDITATIVE PRAYER FOR HARMONY IN THE WORKPLACE

"Down-ray the emerald green ray of spiritual balance and
harmony to touch into my Hermetic center and out-ray to
my worldly affairs, quickening my workplace with this divine
harmony. May all whom I come in contact with feel and
respond to the divine impulse of this holy light. I ask this in
Divine Light and Love for the good of all concerned."

ADVERSARIES

Our "enemies" present our biggest tests. How you handle adversarial relationships is one of the clearest indicators of your true character. There is a wonderful story about Mother Teresa when she was first setting up her hospital for the destitute. She had encountered a great deal of resistance from a local Hindu priest. He did everything he could to stop her work, because she was not Indian and not a Hindu. Mother Teresa did not react to his diatribes. Even when the priest became deathly ill—and was ostracized by his own faithful—he continued to despise Mother Teresa. However, no one would help him during his time of trial and need—no one, that is, but Mother Teresa. When she heard that he was dying, she immediately took him in and treated him with the same love and affection that she showed to all the sick and dying. He could not believe that this woman could shower so much kindness upon someone who had hated her so. He eventually died, but not without asking her forgiveness. News of what she'd done traveled, because all knew how much trouble the priest had caused her. It was this particular incident that put Mother Teresa on the road to international fame.

If you are faced with animosity, the following exercise is very helpful in disconnecting the tangle of energies involved. It may or may not remove the person from your life entirely, but it will definitely help to release the destructive connections that most likely exist between you.

In this particular meditation, raise your consciousness and see yourself in a bubble of pink and white light. Feel it enveloping you and uplifting all levels of your being. See the golden bubble of protection strongly around you. Then, using the following prayer, ask the light to release you and the other person from any negative energetic exchanges.

MEDITATIVE PRAYER TO RELEASE ADVERSARIAL RELATIONSHIPS

"I ask the Divine Light of God to go to (*name person*) and
myself, releasing us mental to mental, emotional to emotional,
physical to physical, astral to astral, and soul to soul.
Free me and free (*name person*) in this Divine Light and
Love. I ask it all in Thy holy name."

Repeat this exercise as you need to. Notice on how many levels this meditation is working. The irony of an adversarial relationship is the strange attachment that exists between people who may hate each other. Strongly negative feelings can attach you to the other person just as strongly as love. Elie Wiesel observed that the opposite of love is not hate, but indifference. You must detach from hate if you really want to be free of another person's influence. In addition, keep your balance strong when dealing with such a person.

ROMANCE AND MARRIAGE

Now we focus the light on one of the most volatile and dynamic of all human relations—the romantic interaction. There have been so many questions, debates, so-called rules, and conflicting opinions about the true nature of romantic involvement and sexual relations that many people are cynical and disillusioned about the whole process of dating. This has been reflected in unrealistic expectations, high divorce rates, broken families, and a host of mental and emotional miseries.

The male-female relationship is a sacred one. Physical evolution divided the sexes into male and female as a manifestation of its spiritual counterpart—the dynamic and magnetic nature of life. The dynamic-magnetic polarity is the very essence of all manifested life. It's the give and take, the ebb and flow of life. This duality of active life may be seen at all levels of creation. Even God manifests as the Dynamic Father principle and as the Magnetic Holy Mother principle. It is the cosmic union of these two forces of life that give birth to our human soul.

The key feature of the dynamic nature is *mind*. God the Father is Divine Mind in action. He is the giving out, the initial step, inner strength, divine will, and wisdom. The key quality of the magnetic nature is *heart*. God the Holy Mother is love. She is compassion, love, beauty, unity, nurturing, and desire. All created life interplays between these two poles, producing cosmic balance and the spiritual rhythms of life. Both aspects of God are of equal importance. When we appear to be putting God the Father principle before the Mother, it's only in the sense that there needs to be an action before there can be a reaction.

This brings us to the second principle of the male-female relationship: within each of us exists this polarity of dynamic and magnetic activity. This means that our soul is neither male nor female, but contains *both* divine attributes of the dynamic-magnetic life. When we incarnate in physical form, we polarize either our dynamic or our magnetic nature, depending on the sex we become. This doesn't mean the other isn't there. By being born male, we are meant to express the dynamic principle of our being. Yet we must balance that dynamic with our magnetic nature. If we are born female, we are meant to express our magnetic nature and balance it with our dynamic flow. The spiritual goal is to balance the two flows, so that we can express both spiritual qualities regardless of our gender.

There's a divine reason you are born the sex that you are. It was not a mistake or chance occurrence. The first step in creating greater harmony with the opposite sex is to be comfortable and in harmony with your own sex. If you are male, enjoy your maleness. If you are female, enjoy your femaleness. There's nothing wrong with expressing characteristics of your sex as long as you keep things in perspective.

Problems can arise when one gender tries to dominate or manipulate the other gender. You must never use gender advantages over another person, but rather as a complement and counterpart. As part of your spiritual growth, you're meant to learn how to live in peace and joy with the opposite sex. It's one of the greatest blessings of physical life. A couple that loves, honors, and stands up for each other is an on-going work of spiritual beauty. Romantic love helps to advance souls on the path to God.

These dynamic-magnetic flows express themselves very clearly in the aura. The right side of the aura brings in the dynamic flows of light and the left side attracts the magnetic flows. (See Illustration 11.3.) This polarity is critical to a balanced aura. The right side tends to express gold, red, and other dynamic energies while the left side will have pink, violet, and other magnetic energies. Some energies can be both dynamic *and* magnetic, such as the green and blue rays. In addition, the Higher Self will down-breathe beautiful dynamic or magnetic rays to either the right or left side of the aura, depending on the particular need.

If the aura is unbalanced in its dynamic-magnetic flow, the energy will favor one side over the other. An overly magnetic soul will not have the dynamic radiation needed on the right side, and an overly dynamic person will generally not have the magnetic radiation needed on the left side. If you are loving and kind but have no backbone, you must develop your dynamic side while continuing to be kind and loving. In the same way, if you are a go-getter to the point of stepping on other

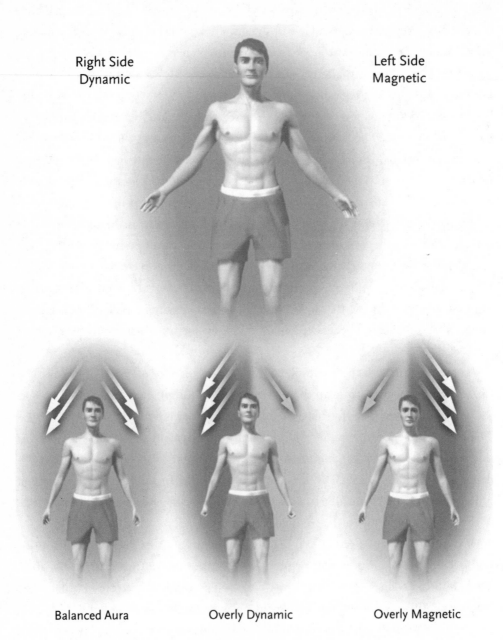

ILLUSTRATION 11.3-*Polarity in the Aura*

people's toes, you must learn to be more giving and kind, but still be that go-getter.

Dating

The key element in dating is *compatibility*. People can date for all sorts of reasons, but to create healthy romantic exchanges, you want to find someone you're compatible with. The aura is very good at showing the compatibility of couples. When two people are compatible, there is a beautiful exchange of energy on the Hermetic and emotional levels. Usually there will be pink, showing the love flow. Orange reveals the enthusiasm and excitement that the couple have for each other. There will also be a violet energy exchange, showing that there is a peace and serenity with the other soul. They intuitively trust each other and are very comfortable with each other. When I see this kind of energy exchange, I know these people would most likely make a fine couple. If the two are incompatible, there will usually be an exchange of gray energy. It will emanate from the Hermetic center, showing that there is distress or worry going on.

If you're having difficulty finding someone who's compatible, you can work with the light to help attract someone suitable. First you want to get an idea of what it is you're looking for. Rather than contemplating specific physical traits, look for qualities such as a sense of humor, trustworthiness, kindness, a giving nature, and so on. In the same way, evaluate the qualities you have to offer another person. People often focus so much on what they want in another person that they don't look at what they themselves have to offer. There has to be give and take. Practicing visualizations is very effective here.

If you feel you have done all these things and still have not found someone, then perhaps look to identify any possible negative thinking that may be getting in the way of attracting what you want. For example, you may say you want a marriage partner, but deep down, perhaps you're not ready to give up the pleasures and care-free quality of single life. Or you may want someone very sincerely but feel you're undeserving of a worthy companion. All these issues are things you must confront and deal with before you can attract the person you desire.

There are several ways to work with the light to attract the right person to you.

Clarity is a good place to start. If you're in confusion, you will often draw the wrong person to you. So, if you're having trouble attracting a truly compatible person, first do a spiritual cleansing with the orange-red flame to release any wrong pictures and patterns you may have developed.

Then, work with the pure white light and ask that it touch into your Higher Self Point to help set the energy in motion to draw the right person to you.

Meditative Prayer to Attract the Right Romantic/Marital Partner

"Down-ray the pure white light to quicken all levels of my consciousness. I ask that it especially touch into my Higher Self Point of Spiritual Knowing to give me a clear picture of the person who is right for me."

Follow up this work with the silver ray to quicken the recognition in your mental body of the image being given to you. In this instance, the silver ray will also help to better stabilize that image.

Meditative Prayer to Quicken the Mental Body

"Down-ray the silver ray of divine intelligence into my mental body to quicken me in the recognition of the image of my rightful mate, given to me by my Higher Self."

I would also add the blue-white fire, as it can help sustain the energy until that person can become a reality for you.

Meditative Prayer to Sustain the Rightful Image

"Down-ray the blue-white fire of eternal life to touch into all levels of my consciousness and especially charge and recharge my mental body to hold and sustain the image of my rightful romantic partner."

With these three rays, you have greatly quickened your mental levels to get your mind focused in the right direction. This way, when the right person does come along, you will recognize him or her. Once you have worked on the mental levels, follow up with the wisdom light. Now it's time to start setting the energy in motion to manifest your rightful partner.

MEDITATIVE PRAYER TO ATTRACT A ROMANTIC/MARITAL PARTNER

"Down-ray the golden ray of wisdom light to my Hermetic
center and out-ray in my human Earth affairs to
attract the right person to me."

Be patient when it comes to romance. You can't force the right person to appear in your life. In the same way, don't be lazy and expect the dream person to just suddenly appear. You have to put yourself out there and make yourself available. As the saying goes, sometimes you have to kiss a few frogs before you find your prince (or princess!).

Then crown your work with the deep rose pink ray of spiritual love. Above all, love is the power that draws people together. It is the indispensable element in any relationship. It helps balance the dynamic-magnetic flow. Ask the love ray to touch into all levels of your consciousness, but especially your emotional levels so that you are open and will be accepting of the person coming into your life.

MEDITATIVE PRAYER WITH THE LOVE RAY IN THE EMOTIONS

"Down-ray the deep rose pink ray of spiritual love to all levels
of my being and into my emotional body. Let this light
bathe all levels of my emotional nature, so I am coming
from a place of love and kindness. And let this love ray
open my heart and emotions, so I am accepting of the
rightful person entering my life."

SEX AND SPIRITUAL ENERGY

Sex has a very definite effect on our lives and our auras. Of course, we all know that sex serves the critical function of perpetuating the species and that it's part of the attraction that brings people together. We also know that every human entering puberty experiences sexual feelings and that we all have these urges and sensations within us regardless of how we express them. The question in metaphysics is not *whether* our sexuality should be a part of our spiritual life, but rather *how* our sexuality should be a part of our spiritual life.

In the aura, sexual energy emanates from the root chakra. The root chakra operates a little differently from the other centers when it comes to how its energy moves. In the four main centers that we have been working with, energy is in a constant state of receiving and transmitting. The root chakra does not function this way. The root chakra already has within it a special reservoir of power. The spiritual power within this center has been placed there as part of our spiritual design to serve a very specific function. This function is something we've been doing for eons in various forms. It's something that's an intimate part of our life and character. The energy of the root chakra gives us the power to *create*. It's not the actual creation, inspiration, or act, but the power, drive, and spiritual force necessary to put the creative energies into action and carry them to fruition.

The root chakra energy has been given to you as part of your spiritual heritage. How you use this creative energy determines its effectiveness in your life. This energy flows in one of three ways:

1. *Generation*
2. *Degeneration*
3. *Regeneration*

Generation uses the root chakra energy for creating offspring. This root energy is necessary for the conception of children. Without it, conception could not take place because in addition to the physical union of egg and sperm, there is a spiritual connection that occurs as well. The power to procreate cannot be underestimated. The ability to reproduce is one of the most holy traits you possess, whether you choose to bear children or not.

Normal sexual activity without the goal of having children may also fall under the category of generation. This is because it still mirrors the procreative process even if the act doesn't result in the conception of a child. In this form, the procreative energy becomes purely sexual because the root chakra energy is used primarily for pleasure and intimacy. The energy is not quite as bright as in the act of procreation, but it's still an elevating energy if the sexual activity is done out of genuine love and affection. This sexual interaction is part of the bonding and strengthening process that can bring two people closer together.

Degeneration is the wasting of root chakra energy through the intentional or unintentional misuse of that creative force. We misuse the root chakra energy through heavy excesses and distortions of sex. When we indulge in these practices, we may find them momentarily enjoyable, but they're serving no useful purpose. Perversions and deviate acts can result in degeneration of root chakra energy. We have to be very careful, because degeneration is a form of devolution. If individuals are determined and persistent in acting out degrading sex, it's going to distance themselves more and more from their spiritual nature. In this situation, the root energy doesn't dissipate, but it becomes dirtied and defiled.

Regeneration means using the root chakra energy for purely creative endeavors. We see this in people who refrain from sex before a big event and artists who abstain during creative periods. You need this power for all creative and productive endeavors. Without it, you could not create, whether it's to design a building, sing a song, or paint a picture. It's the power behind great artists, inventors, musicians, etc. It gives us the energy, stamina, and drive necessary to create something new and original.

You can also direct root chakra energy for purely spiritual purposes. One of the greatest creative acts is your own metamorphosis from human consciousness to the realization of a fully matured divine being. This creative act will require a strong regenerative flow of the root chakra energy. Here's where the concept of celibacy comes in. For those who are aiming to reach the pinnacle of spiritual development, there is an eventual need for sexual abstention, so that the spiritual power can be completely directed to the spiritual goal. Such a sacrifice, however, is not necessary until a soul reaches the advanced stages of spiritual development, and even then there are exceptions. To take a vow of celibacy before one has properly developed can create problems. You can end up repressing normal desires, which is not healthy. The point is, you don't have to stop having sex to develop spiritually, but you do have to control your sexual activity.

When the root energy is in the generative mode, the energy in the aura beams upward from the root center. (See Illustration 11.4A.) It usually extends to the level of the emotional center in a carnation red color. If the person is trying to conceive children, the color will be a very bright red with white light around it. It's a vital, beautiful energy to see. If the person is simply in a romantic relationship, there will be only the red energy moving upward, and it won't be as bright. If the person is a little too intoxicated by sex, the energy will still move upward, but the red can be dirtied and dulled to maroon red. On the other hand, if the person is in a strong degenerative mode, the root energy now moves in a downward motion, sometimes reaching below the feet—indicative of a devolving consciousness. (See Illustration 11.4D.) The energy is deep, vitiated red.

What's beautiful to see is the light moving in a regenerative flow. If the person is in a high creative mode, the root energy can move all the way up to the mental body, giving it tremendous energy and power. (See Illustration 11.4B.) This helps to regenerate and replenish the brain cells and can make you look and feel young. It's one of the reasons so many productive and creative people have youthful vitality and stamina. If you find yourself confused, or uninspired, one of the best ways to get on target is to start (or resume) being productive and creative. It renews and revivifies the whole landscape of your thinking. In the case of the spiritual master who has directed all his or her energy to spiritual purposes, the root energy will move up beyond the head and into the Higher Self Point. (See Illustration 11.4C.)

Most of our problems with sex come from a misunderstanding and misuse of this energy. Instead of using the creative power of sex to its fullest potential, we limit its power, squandering its vitality to no particular end. We do this mainly out of ignorance. If you are unhappy in your sex life, first look to see if you are placing too much emphasis on sex. The truth is, when the sexual energy is balanced, it will not

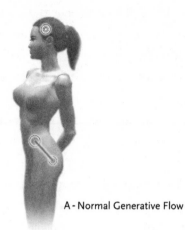

A - Normal Generative Flow

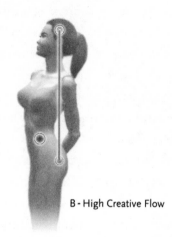

B - High Creative Flow

C - Spiritual Mastery Flow

D - Degenerative Flow

ILLUSTRATION 11.4-*Root Chakra Energy*

be such a preoccupation. Sex will feel like a natural part of life. Oversexed people are almost always expressing an unbalanced energy. These people end up feeling dissatisfied, even after they've had their sexual conquests, because the energy's not balanced. People who have balanced the sexual energy with all other aspects of life enjoy sex, but it's not an issue with them. The truth is, as you climb the spiritual ladder, there will be less and less desire for sex because more of your root energy will be flowing into creative and spiritual avenues. Working with the Divine Light in this center will help to clear and cleanse misused energies and get the whole flow moving the way it should.

Most important, it will help to elevate and spiritualize the root center. The following prayer may be used before sex to put the Divine Light into the act of making love to raise its vibration. Ideally, it's best if both partners say this prayer together.

Meditative Prayer to Uplift the Sex Act

"Down-ray the pure white light into my root chakra and
sexual organs to uplift and elevate this sexual act into an
expression of Thy light and love."

Regardless of where you are, you want to begin the process of spiritualizing and rarefying the sexual vibration. By getting a handle on this part of your nature, you're harnessing one of the most potent forces in you. I recommend using the orange-red flame to help cleanse and clear any dark energies.

Meditative Prayer to Purify the Root Chakra

"Down-ray the orange-red flame of purification into my root
chakra to purify all depleted and defiled sexual energies.
Cleanse all black and gray atoms and impurities, taking them
to the mineral kingdom to be dissolved in the light."

Although you can't extinguish the power of the root chakra no matter how you may misuse it, you can deplete its potency. The blue-white fire can help to quicken the regenerating process, so it's still necessary to use this energy following the purification.

MEDITATIVE PRAYER TO REPLENISH THE ROOT CHAKRA

"Down-ray the blue-white fire into my root chakra to
charge and recharge all depleted and exhausted areas with
new spiritual energy and vitality."

You can also use the emerald green to balance the flow in your root chakra, which will help to get the energy moving in the direction it needs to. In closing, my advice is to use the sex act sparingly. When you do have sex, do it with good intentions. Care for and love the person you're being intimate with. The physical act of love is the closest two auras can get. Not only do you affect your root chakra flow, you draw energy from the other person's aura. So you want to be careful that your partner is coming from a place of love. Respect this sacred energy God has given you, and it will serve you better than you can imagine.

The Sacrament of Marriage

Marriage is designed to assist human souls in their spiritual evolution. It's part of the spiritual plan. Regardless if the goal is to bear children, through love, respect, fidelity, and sacrifice, the couple learns to serve God. One reflects the other: loyalty in marriage demonstrates loyalty to God.

Many intelligent people question the need for marriage, especially when there is no intention of having children. They ask why, if two people love each other, is it essential for them to marry? Spiritually, marriage is not just about two people in love. It's about two people and God. We can't take God out of the equation. When we sign that marriage license, we're signing part of ourselves as well. We're making a commitment. We can't escape that it's like any legal document. When a student graduates from school, he or she gets a degree. When a medical student becomes a doctor, he or she is bestowed the honor of M.D. and obtains a license to practice. The same is true of marriage. So, the challenge of marriage is not in the design but in our ability to live up to that design.

When you marry, you're giving part of yourself—part of your human self. The Divine always remains its own, but each of us does give of our human self. Many people are afraid of this sacrifice. They fear that it will stifle their creativity, that they will lose their identity in this union called marriage. Look at the stereotype of married life as "the old ball and chain." Those who have gone through a stifling or harsh marital experience will often say, "No more!" Their fears are understandable, but they are just that—fears. The truth is, you are in the process of surrendering your human self to your divine self. That's the whole point of spiritual evolution. Day by day, you are dropping a little of your old self to pick up your true self. Any opportunity to drop some of the human opens you up to more of the Divine. If you do right by the marriage, you're not restricting yourself at all. Quite the contrary. You're opening your creative flow to new heights and expanding your identity to new dimensions. On top of that, you're forming a support system that's unbeatable. And the auric exchange between strong marriage partners is a great enhancement to life.

Marriage born of true love brings a wonderful blessing from the Higher Self. Not only is there a physical and legal marriage—there is a spiritual marriage as well. Spiritual marriage can be seen in the aura as a thread of pink light connecting the spouses at the emerald hub within the Hermetic center. This thread is the spiritual blessing of the Divine, and it's created when there is true love and earnest commitment between a man and woman. Such spiritual connection is essential because it keeps the love flow going. It unites at the Hermetic center because that is where this commitment is made in the human Earth affairs. However, it does not affect the soul levels. Even in marriage, each partner is still on his or her own evolutionary ladder. The marriage becomes part of the learning experience but each is still a spiritual individual. This spiritual bond is created only in the sacrament of marriage. The marriage can take place civilly, in a church, or wherever, but must take place legally. And it must be done out of love. If you date someone, live with someone you love dearly, even have children with that person out of wedlock, you may have a beautiful exchange of energy, but this special, sacramental bond will be lacking. It's a spiritual blessing that stays with the couple throughout married life until death or divorce.

There are just as many ways to work with the light in marriage as there are spiritual traits to develop—harmony, fidelity, loyalty, understanding, gentleness, patience, adaptability, commitment . . . the list goes on. If there's a problem in your marriage, you must do everything in your power to remedy it. Call on all your divine tools, everything in your possession, to turn things around.

MEDITATIVE PRAYER FOR SPIRITUAL HARMONY WITHIN COUPLES

"Down-ray the emerald green ray of balance and the deep
rose pink ray of spiritual love into all levels of my consciousness,
restoring and reestablishing mind-body-soul harmony
between (*name person*) and me. May (*name person*) also
receive this mind-body-soul harmony at all levels of consciousness
and may this light strengthen our marital bond in
the fires of Thy light and everlasting love for the good
of all concerned."

TO FORGIVE IS DIVINE

Forgiveness is essential in healing any relationship. In your relationships, you're bound to step on each other's toes at one point or another. You're not perfected yet, so you're inevitably going to make mistakes. As a result, there'll be times when you'll need to ask forgiveness, or be forgiving. Forgiveness is an essential skill to develop in your spiritual unfoldment.

It's not always easy for people to ask for forgiveness or to forgive. The human ego gets involved and wants to hold on to its anger, grudges, and so on. On the one hand, you may not recognize or want to recognize that you have done anything wrong to warrant asking someone's forgiveness. On the other hand, it may be doubly hard for you to forgive others for wrongs done, especially if they are serious. There are people who have gone to their graves without forgiving the people who injured them.

Perhaps what makes the act of forgiveness so difficult is the mistaken notion that if you forgive someone, you're letting him or her off the hook. In truth, when you forgive someone you're letting *yourself* off the hook. There's freedom in forgiveness. When you forgive, you're cleansing yourself of your own negative reactive energy associated to the wrong done to you, perceived or real. The other person will still have to work out his or her own negative actions, but you are freeing yourself of any connection to that energy, and that is a very liberating experience.

There's a well-known story of a woman who endured the Nazi concentration camps of World War II. She survived the experience but had been misused by one jailer in particular. The woman became very religious, which helped release many of the horrible memories she carried. She did her best to practice forgiveness and live a godly life. Years later, she was at a public function when she spotted the guard who had abused her. Upon seeing him, the memories of the abuse returned and her initial reaction was to walk over and kill him right then and there. Fortunately, her religious convictions took hold of her. She realized that this was her opportunity to apply all the spiritual principles she had learned over the years. With all the strength she had, she walked over to the astonished man (who recognized her) and told him point-blank that she forgave him for all the things he had done to her. She said it sincerely and with conviction. To her amazement, after truly forgiving him, the first thing she felt was relief. For the first time since the whole ordeal, she felt a deep sense of peace and that this was past her. She had truly let it go from her life.

Did her actions free this man from his offenses? Of course not. He still had a great deal of work to do to redeem his soul for all his misdeeds. But she was now free of him, and, in the process, she had helped him along his road to redemption. There is enormous power in the act of forgiveness.

If you commit an offense to someone, you need to ask forgiveness, and do it quickly. This needs to be done in deed as well as in word. There is no need to condemn yourself. Just take action to correct whatever it is you did. Take responsibility for your actions. Remember, there is no sin past redemption. God always gives us a second chance. One of the greatest stories of God's forgiveness is the life of Saul, who became known as Saint Paul. Saul, as we know, was a persecutor of the early Christians. Locked into his own religious traditions, he felt that the budding Christian faith was a threat to his system of belief. He was persistent and cruel in his systematic attacks on the early Christians, killing many. Yet this very man, after his spiritual awakening on the road to Damascus, became one of Christianity's greatest exponents. Through his redemption, God imbued him with great spiritual power and authority. No one is immune to times of weakness. There's a saying that even the angels have to be reprimanded every once in a great while!

The Forgiveness Principles

In working with forgiveness, keep in mind these three fundamental principles. They will take you a long way toward success in your forgiveness work.

1. *Forgive quickly.* Try to forgive or ask forgiveness as soon after the incident as possible. If anger or resentment has time to seep into the consciousness and aura, it gains momentum and is harder to eliminate.

2. *Forgive and forget.* Someone may have done a hundred good things, but what do many often remember about him or her the most? It's that one rotten thing he or she did. That's human nature. Learn to forgive and forget. If you say you forgive, but constantly dredge up mistakes from the past, you haven't really forgiven. You must forgive from your heart and *truly mean it* to let it go.

3. *Forgive "seventy times seven" times.* Many times mistakes will be repeated. If you're in the process of learning an important life lesson, but it still hasn't quite "sunk in," you're going to repeatedly make the same mistake, sometimes hurting the same person, until that lesson is completely understood. This is why it is said you must forgive not once, not seven times, but "seventy times seven" times. There can be no limit to forgiveness. You must continue to be supportive of your forgiveness. You can't say, "I'll forgive you this time, but if you do it again, I'll never forgive you." That's the same as *not* forgiving.

The Forgiveness Prayer

In this prayer, included are both forgiving and asking forgiveness. This reciprocal activity is important because from the human point of view, it's hard to be sensitive to the full range and interplay of energies that created a wrongful action. It might be very obvious that someone did wrong to you and that you need to forgive that person. Yet, there may also have been something *you* did that contributed to this person's acting the way he or she did. By returning the forgiving act, you're ensuring your spiritual release.

Once again, the key energy to work with is the deep rose pink ray. Meditate with this energy before doing your actual forgiveness work to bring more love and compassion to yourself. Feel the uplifting quality of this energy. If the wrong was serious, include meditating with the pure white light as well to redeem the defiled energies.

Get into your Higher Self Point and begin the forgiveness prayer. In this case, you're not working with a particular light ray, although you can use the love ray if you want. You're working primarily with your Higher Self.

FORGIVENESS PRAYER

"I ask forgiveness for anything I may have done that
injured you in word, thought, act, or deed, knowingly
and unknowingly.
"And I forgive you for anything that you may have done
to me that injured me in word, thought, act, or deed,
knowingly and unknowingly.
"I ask that all these negative energies be dissolved in the
holy fires of eternal love, freeing us completely in God's
Divine Light and everlasting peace."

Notice the words "knowingly and unknowingly." Many times you can hurt people or are hurt by others unknowingly. Since you're not always fully conscious of your motives and actions, you need to include the unconsciousness factor. Fortunately, one of the magnificent things about working with spiritual energy is that it gently brings more of your unconscious thoughts, words, and actions to conscious light, so that you can do something about them.

In addition to your forgiveness prayers and light work, as the situation warrants it, confront the person face-to-face. You can repeat this prayer as often as you feel the need. If you wish to forgive or ask forgiveness of someone who has passed on, you can still use this prayer. Remember, the soul of that person is still very much alive, and your prayer and light reach them wherever they are.

CHAPTER XII

Divine Direction and Guidance

· ·

Sometimes we get stuck in life's activities. Like a lesson in school we just can't seem to master, there are some situations we're confronted with that we simply don't know how to handle. You may have a career decision to make or a personal issue that you need to address, and clarity as to the best course of action is eluding you. It is these times you can call on the Divine Light to request help from an extraordinary aspect of the spiritual life—rightful direction and divine guidance.

Direction and guidance are complementary but different spiritual tools. Rightful direction means knowing the right road to take that will keep you in alignment with your higher purpose. Perhaps you're trying to find your career path, deciding if you are going the marry the person you are dating, or contemplating whether to have children. Maybe you simply want to change your life in some way but are unclear about where to start. In all these situations, you can greatly benefit from working with rightful direction.

Right direction is connected with your destiny here on Earth. Each of us is ideally suited to accomplish certain things in life. Intuitively you already know what that purpose is, but, as can too easily happen, you may become distracted and confused to the point that you lose your way. By tuning into right direction, you're tuning into the energy of your spiritual purpose, the part you are playing in the divine plan of life.

Divine guidance brings in a different aspect of the divine life. It helps you navigate through life's twists and turns once you know your direction. For example, say you have decided to pursue a career in business. Divine guidance will help steer you through those waters to be successful in your aspirations. So call on right direction when you are trying to find your way, and work with divine guidance to help steer you once you are on your chosen path to keep you on the right path despite any bumps or obstacles.

An essential part of your spiritual growth entails learning how to work with spiritual energy to help guide and direct your life. The key is to actively call on the light for help, and then to use the inspiration given. You are inspired every day by the Divine but may not always pay attention to the signals. Many times the inspiration coming in may not be what you expect or wish it to be even though it's in your best interests.

A common misunderstanding when it comes to guidance and direction is relying on the Divine to do all the spiritual work for you. Too many people say things like, "God, tell me what to do and I'll do it." Remember, the light is not meant to bypass the normal growth process. To really connect with divine guidance and direction you need to be in the process of self-discovery. The light won't "tell you" what to do. It will illuminate so you can see for yourself what to do. As the conduit of consciousness, the Divine Light uplifts your consciousness so you can see more through the eyes of spirit.

Many people when they come for an aura consultation want me to essentially tell them what to do. They figure that with clairvoyant insight all I have to do is say "Do this or that" and the problem is solved. But that's not how it works. Certainly, I share my clairvoyant insights, but no one can or should make a decision for another soul. We have to do our own growing. Each of us needs to discover life's answers for ourselves if they are to have meaning. Ironically, the times where direction was given very clearly as a tool of encouragement, the person most often didn't follow through on the inspiration. Why? Because there was no self-discovery. The inspiration didn't come from them. As you work with guidance and direction, it can sometimes take time to make that discovery. But that time is well spent. Don't be discouraged. Keep calling on the light for help and you will make those genuine moments of divine awareness.

In the aura, there are several spiritual energies connected to direction and guidance.

If gold is strongly seen in the aura, it shows a decisive person who is outgoing and willing to take chances. Such people have learned from their experiences and become the wiser for it. They are usually clear in their direction. When silver is strongly seen in the aura, especially if it is seen in the heart chakra, this indicates a quick, perceptive person who is following through on the guidance and direction that is being given. White light seen in the aura indicates high spiritual power, a visionary person. This soul is very in tune with the Divine. He or she does not get caught up in petty things or distractions and can see the greater perspective.

The skills of being divinely directed and guided can be strengthened only through use. You have to develop your character to be in alignment with your higher purpose. To effectively connect with divine guidance and direction, cultivate a receptive, dynamic nature. Be a person who is willing to take a risk on something that you intuitively know is worthwhile. Even if mistakes and failures happen, take personal responsibility and learn from those mistakes.

As always, meditation is the master key to tuning into the Higher Self. Go into the silence, the oneness of life. Tune into your own higher nature to hear what the mystics call "the still, small voice within." With practice and sincere intention, you can build an intimate relationship with the Higher Self that will bless all facets of your life.

BECOMING RECEPTIVE TO INSPIRATION

Your Higher Self Point plays a crucial role in connecting you with guidance and direction. In addition to acting as intermediary for the spiritual light, the Higher Self is the emissary for inspiration from the Divine. The Higher Self sees the bigger picture of your Earth life, and part of its job is to help steer you in your life's journey. As inspiration flows from the Divine, it makes a strong connection with your Higher Self, which then "translates" this inspiration into a form you can understand and use.

To receive guidance or direction, it helps to be clear about what you need help with. When you're in the throes of an important decision, you can lose sight of the real issue. So take a moment to reflect on what you want the light to do for you, and formulate that thought into a sentence or question.

Once you've been able to more clearly define the problem or dilemma, let it go from your conscious mind. Free your thoughts and emotions and leave room for the light to inspire you. You want to switch your conscious brain/mind thinking to a receiving mode rather than a sending mode. In this receiving mode, your conscious mind listens to the spirit. Of course, do your part in evaluating a situation or in making a choice, but when ready to open to the Divine, let the concern go. Put it on "the altar of God." Too many try to solve a problem by being immersed in the problem. The answer comes by being immersed in the Divine, where the divine solution appears.

Begin your work by relaxing. In this relaxing there is a trust, a knowing, that you are putting things into God's hands. With this trust comes a belief in the unlimited capacity and readiness of the Higher Power to help you. As the biblical saying goes, "Ask, believing." There is great power in belief. In believing, you know there is an answer even if you can't see that answer yet. You're not challenging God. You're opening to God. You're saying, "God, I know You know the answer. I open myself up to receiving that answer." There has to be open-mindedness and open-heartedness on your part for this whole process to work. If you're assuming a doubting or challenging attitude, essentially telling God to "prove it," all you're doing is blocking the very flow you're trying to open.

Letting go of your problems can be more difficult than it seems. Chances are, a perplexing concern may be still "hanging in there" simply because you yourself have been holding on to it, and not letting your higher nature work with you. Your answer could be staring you right in the face, with you refusing to see it. The issue is not the spirit connecting with you, but you connecting with the spirit.

Some people resist the idea of being helped altogether. They want to do it on their own. Of course, there will be times when you must pass through a trial on your own, no matter how you may pray and call on the light. However, in most cases, you are meant to make your decision in cooperation with your higher nature. That's the whole point. You're supposed to be building a bridge between your higher and lower nature. How can you do that unless you learn to make contact with the Higher Self through repeated practice?

In the aura, if a person is confused and cannot see clearly, there can be gray and creamy mustard energies, especially around the head area. Often people in a confused state will be restless, which can make the energy field disoriented as well. With such an aura, it's not surprising that the person is having difficulties and not able to make decisions. There can be lethargy in the mental body if the problem has been active for a while. If you feel confused, begin your meditation by working with the orange-red flame and the blue-white fire in the mental and emotional areas. They will help to cut loose that confusion and indecision and create a clearer receiving station for the divine ideas to make their impression.

When you go to the Higher Self for guidance, make sure you are going without conditions. When receiving inspiration from the Divine you need to be ready for *any* answer that might come through. The truth is, many times the very guidance you receive may not always be what you feel like doing at the moment. But it's what's in your best interests. There was a lady in a workshop I did on guidance who commented, "I thought if you don't feel like doing something, then you're not supposed to do it!" How wrong! Certainly pay attention to your emotions, but they do not necessarily know your higher purpose. They can be too steeped in immediate concerns. You need to get out of the emotions of the moment and reach up to the Higher Self Point where the real answers are. In that clarity of consciousness, truth will come through.

When someone has received the inspirational light, I'll often see a white glow around the head area, showing the guidance at work. This is a temporary situation while the light is doing its job. There will also be active emanations of violet and light pinks, showing that the Higher Self is trying to quiet the soul so it can be receptive to the inspiration given.

CONNECTING WITH YOUR SOURCE OF INSPIRATION

Three key energies to call upon for guidance are gold, silver, and white light. Gold is wonderful for inspiring decisive action. If you're ambivalent or allow others to confuse and influence your decisions, the gold can bring in a dynamic power to straighten things out. The gold is the energy I personally call upon the most when making important decisions. The gold gives the power to put inspiration into action.

The silver is excellent for clarity and insight. When things seem obscure, the silver ray can bring in perception and comprehension. And the white light is excellent for illumination and revelation. It can lift you out of present concerns so you are freer and in a more elevated state of mind.

In calling for guidance and direction, raise your consciousness to your Higher Self Point, and take extra time to really feel the divine presence. Feel that you are truly on holy ground. In this presence, there is only love, light, and wisdom. Then when you begin down-raying the Divine Light, you will be asking that the light down-ray to the Higher Self only. Hold your attention in your Higher Self Point as you are making your connection with the light and asking your spiritual question. On its own, the light will touch into your aura as needed, but again, you want to stay in as high a level of consciousness as you can while asking for help. By keeping your attention on the Higher Self Point, you're making a more direct contact with your source of inspiration. The actual idea or inspiration will come through with the light. The Higher Self will quicken this divine idea, so you can recognize and understand its meaning. Begin by calling on the gold light with the following meditative prayer.

Meditative Prayer for Divine Guidance and Direction with the Gold Light

"Down-ray the golden ray of wisdom light to my Higher Self Point of Spiritual Knowing, bringing forth the pearl of Thy direction and guidance to reveal that which I need to know, and that which I need to know now, concerning (*name situation*). I ask this according to Divine Light and Love for the good of all concerned."

Feel the light beaming down into your Higher Self Point, activating it. Once you feel the connection has been made, ask your question. After you ask, be still and see if any thoughts come through for you. Keep your mind as receptive as you can. The inspiration might come as an image or idea. Generally, you'll know you've hit on something because you'll feel exhilaration. Regardless of what does or does not come through, conclude with the following expression of gratitude.

"I thank Thee that this is so, and I hold to
the knowing that my answer is forthcoming."

This prayer will help to establish your connection with the answer to your question, so that at the right time it can reveal itself to you. If you feel that something is being communicated to you but that the answer is still not clear, work with the silver ray to quicken your powers of discernment and comprehension. Again, let it work at your Higher Self Point.

MEDITATIVE PRAYER FOR DIVINE GUIDANCE WITH THE SILVER RAY

"Down-ray the silver ray of divine intelligence to my Higher
Self Point to quicken my awareness of this Divine Light and
inspiration Thou hast given me. I ask to be released from all
blocks or resistance to my full reception and
comprehension of Thy guidance."

ACCEPT AND USE THE GUIDANCE GIVEN

If your answer does not come through during your meditation, it may yet come to you at any time, according to your receptivity and the timing of the need. The answer could manifest during contemplation or even in the midst of an animated conversation. Someone might say something that sparks an idea. You may not even recognize it as inspiration, but it is.

Many people have asked, "How do I know that the thoughts I may be getting are truly divine inspirations, rather than just my own thinking?" The truth is, you won't fully know until you put that inspiration into action. If it was your own thinking and not the Higher Self's, you will know and be the better for it, having learned from experience. Next time you go to the Higher Self, you'll be that much more astute. If the inspiration was from the Higher Self and you are following through, then you'll know that, too, and will strengthen the connection to the Higher Self.

The Higher Self knows what you're doing and is going to make every effort to make that connection work. There will undoubtedly be some trial and error in this process as you strengthen your connection to the Divine. The voice of the Divine has a quality all its own. And with practice, persistence, and patience, you learn to recognize the divine voice.

Divine guidance isn't a servant. It's not going to help you win the sixth race at Santa Anita. Its sole purpose is to guide you in your spiritual evolution. Sure, it helps with everyday life situations, but its focus is guidance in activities directly relevant to your growth and purpose in life. Guidance is not about demanding things of God; it's about putting your life into God's hands. If you're stepping into this process with the best of intentions, most ambivalence will clear up.

Often, spiritual guidance will most likely reach you through some type of prompting. There will be something that will urge you a certain way. Now that you're on the lookout for spiritual guidance, you'll be more attuned to its prompting. You may be fortunate and make a strong connection right away in the form of an epiphany or spiritual revelation. Eventually you could build the connection with your Higher Self to the point where you are in full conscious awareness, continuously receiving guidance. Many spiritual initiates, avatars, and saints work from this high spiritual level and eventually you will build your connection to the direct level of communion.

Most people connect with spiritual inspiration through what is commonly called intuition. Intuition and divine guidance walk hand in hand. So many people tell me they had a feeling they shouldn't have done this or that, but then went right ahead and did it anyway. They didn't trust their own intuition. They permitted another part of themselves to speak for them. You must *listen* to what is said to you—and act on it. Again, divine guidance doesn't mollycoddle: the answer you get may not be the one you're expecting. And it may not be to your liking. Yet, it will be what's best for you and what you need at the moment.

Don't sweat what comes through. If it feels like you're on target, try it. God would never inspire you to do something hurtful or dangerous. If you get such thoughts, you can be very sure they're not from God. So when you get inspiration that feels right, try it out and see what happens. By seeing your ideas in action, you'll know right away if your receptivity to divine inspiration is on target. If it doesn't work out, you'll learn how to better recognize when Divine Light is communicating with you. Be flexible. Even divine guidance is not set in stone. Life is fluid and things change. But if you're in the divine flow, you'll have no problems that can't be solved.

In following through on guidance and direction, I've found it effective to ask the light to come down and touch directly into the Hermetic center. Since the Hermetic center is where you project your energy into action and outer manifestation, by asking the light to work on the Hermetic level, you're making a conscious effort to connect with this active energy and move it strongly on the Earth plane level. The gold and white light work equally well in this situation.

Meditative Prayer for Manifesting Direction and Guidance with the Gold Light

"Down-ray the golden ray of wisdom light to my Hermetic
center, bringing me clear thinking and decisive action concerning
(*name situation*), all in accordance with Thy divine
will and right direction. I ask for the holy power to
manifest Thy divine will and all that is for my
highest good."

You can complete your work with the white light.

Meditative Prayer for Upliftment with the White Light

"Down-ray the pure white light into my Hermetic center
and all levels of my being, lifting my consciousness and illuminating
me to see with Thy spirit eyes, that I may choose
the right path for me and follow through and complete
all that I am meant to accomplish."

SPIRITUAL ILLUMINATION

Perhaps you have a problem but can't pinpoint what it is exactly. The nature of the problem may elude you altogether. Spiritual illumination can give you the vision to better understand the nature of the decision to be made. Spiritual illumination is seeing with spirit eyes. Call on spiritual illumination when you want to gain a greater understanding or comprehension of something in general, not necessarily for specific guidance or direction—although it is excellent for this, too. You may not have a clear understanding of why there are certain problems in your life. Spiritual illumination can reveal a greater perspective, which can then give insight about what to do. The key energy to work with here is the pure white light.

MEDITATIVE PRAYER FOR SPIRITUAL ILLUMINATION

"Down-ray the pure white light into my Higher Self Point,

lifting me up into Thy divine consciousness that I may see

with Thy spirit eyes, illuminating and revealing what I need

to work on in my life."

After you've made your connection, become still and receptive. There's no question to pose here because you've simply asked to see what you need to work on. So be quiet, and let God speak to you. You may get an answer right away or it may be revealed to you later.

CHAPTER XIII

The Aura and Spiritual Evolution

A most beautiful benefit of working with spiritual energy is that it helps to bring all facets of your life into unity and wholeness. As you ask the light to help strengthen relationships, guide you with career issues, and address personal character traits, you are improving the quality of your life and spiritualizing your aura. As this happens, the soul starts to see the greater possibilities of life. It starts to realize there is a definite spiritual path to walk upon. It realizes it has a divine potential, an inner prompting urging it to the higher life. We call this process of unfolding the soul's divine potential our spiritual evolution.

Can you work with the Divine Light directly to help in your personal spiritual development? Of course; the light is doing that already. Your "Earth life" and "spiritual life" are part of the same divine life. Everything going on in your life is an opportunity to learn and grow spiritually. Yet as you fill your life with more divine power, you will be fanning the desire to live a more spiritual life. In the beginning when working with the light, you are using that power to help your present activities and all you are doing. But as you expand the power in your aura, you will find yourself starting to adapt your activities to more closely mirror your unfolding spiritual life.

While the Divine Light cannot suddenly bring you to spiritual maturity and enlightenment, it can help you condition your consciousness to facilitate your spiritual evolution. Unfolding your spiritual potential is a gradual process where the soul unfolds its greater powers. There are many stages in this unfoldment, as there is in any growing process. Meditating with Divine Light can help you navigate through these stages of developing your soul's potential.

HOW EVOLUTION EXPRESSES ITSELF IN THE AURA

The aura reveals where individuals are in their spiritual evolution and if they are living up to their potential. As we have seen, as you develop your aura, it brightens. Eventually it will even change shape to reflect its enlightened status. We are all eventually going to develop the enlightened aura. With this aura, all facets of the consciousness will come together and express a new level of the divine life.

In the journey to enlightenment, the aura will go through many stages of development. In fact, evolution reflects itself in every aspect of the aura. The brightness of the aura, its shape and expansiveness, its intensity, the configuration of energies, its clarity, the organization of energy flow—all reflect varying levels of spiritual development. Yet within this spiritual anatomy, certain areas of the aura particularly reflect specific facets of spiritual development. It shows if you are dealing with an evolved soul and if that person is expressing his or her potential.

One of those areas is the spiritual division (see chapter 2). These beautiful arcing bands of light are directly indicative of the spiritual status of the individual. Quite simply, the brighter this division, the more developed the soul. These bands of light represent accumulated Divine Light earned throughout a soul's evolution. We all have a spiritual division but some people have spent more time building their spiritual power than others.

Interestingly, I will often see a person with a very bright spiritual division, meaning this is a developed soul, but is not accessing that divine power. This reveals that this soul has a wonderful spiritual potential but is not in touch with that potential. He or she needs to delve deeper into the spiritual life. Such a person may not even be walking the spiritual path yet, but has the potential to do very well once dedicated to the task. While you cannot work with this division directly to access its power, as you develop other parts of your consciousness, the bands of light in this division brighten. Eventually you will naturally start drawing from this part of you. Souls that are accessing their spiritual division are tapping into an extraordinary part of their being. They are demonstrating that they are truly living the spiritual life.

The Higher Self Point is another indicator of spiritual development. Even though it is already in a divine state of consciousness, it is still expanding and developing even more. Every time you bring light to the Higher Self, not only are you blessing your aura, the Higher Self expands in light. The more developed the soul, the brighter and more expansive the Higher Self Point will be. When the Higher Self Point is developed, its light rays are very expansive and luminous. Sometimes I will see a perpetual flow of light coming down from the Higher Self to the aura, indicating that the person is deeply into the spiritual life and is in very close contact with the Higher Self. It shows someone who has trained and cultivated his or her ego to let go of petty appetites and serve the greater good.

Similar to the spiritual division, sometimes you can see a highly developed Higher Self Point but the person's aura does not reflect that high spiritual status. Too often, we ignore the promptings of the Higher Self and while we do not diminish the power of the Higher Self when we do this, we can diminish the power that can be received from there. Yet even if we lose light through ignorance or misuse, that does not affect our Higher Self. It remains in its pure state of consciousness. This is our saving grace. It means that even when we make missteps in life, our Higher Self always tries to steer us back on track. There is no soul past redemption once it turns itself back to the Divine Light.

Another aspect of the aura that shows the spiritual status of the individual is the Hermetic center. As you have learned, the Hermetic center is the nucleus of your outer world activity. It is the seat of the soul. Here is where the soul is gathering up the many experiences of life to learn and grow. As it builds up power, the whole aura brightens, especially the Hermetic center. Intense radiations of light move out of this center as the soul matures. There are many colors and facets to this soul light. As we learn the many lessons of life, gradually we build up the power in the soul energy in the Hermetic center.

Then of course there is the mental center. To elevate the soul, the mind must be elevated. In a spiritually illumined soul, the bands of luminous light surrounding the upper part of the head are particularly strong. The mental chakra is dazzling with light. In the mental division are enlightened thought forms gracefully active and moving. Rays of the white light of spiritual illumination can be seen down-raying from the higher realms connecting the conscious mind of the individual to the infinite mind of God. This person is in a steady flow of divine inspiration and has great clarity and spiritual understanding.

One other aspect of the aura I would like to look at in connection to spiritual evolution is the crown chakra. Much study has been done on this vital center. Although you don't work with it in the same way as the four centers when doing the light work, this chakra is helping you to rise up to your higher nature. It helps you to be more consciously aware of the spiritual processes of life. Once this conscious awareness process begins, this chakra changes its configuration and begins radiating fantastic flows of light. It's easy to understand why mystics through the ages have been fascinated with this chakra. A developed crown chakra is an unmistakable sign that this soul is expressing its spiritual potential. It must be noted that as the soul grows, all the chakras become more luminous and exciting. Sometimes I will see pyramid-shaped forms in the chakra when it is in a high state of consciousness.

MEDITATIONS TO ACCENTUATE EVOLUTION

There is no single meditation that will bring you to enlightenment, just as there is no single exercise that can turn a child into an adult. Evolution is a process. Yet there are things you can do to condition your consciousness to make more room for the Divine in your life.

The following meditations are very helpful to support your unfolding spiritual life. A good energy to start with is the orange-red flame of purification to help cut loose resistance from the lower nature.

MEDITATIVE PRAYER TO RELEASE RESISTANCE FROM THE LOWER NATURE

"Down-ray the orange-red flame of purification to cleanse my
consciousness of any and all resistance to the Divine Light and
to the promptings of the spirit. I ask that this light especially go

to the emotional center to release any reluctance or hesitation at
accepting higher, divine life. May all my centers and all parts of
my aura be bathed in this holy purifying light, casting all black and gray
atoms to the mineral kingdom to be dissolved in the light."

Take time to feel the light doing its job. If you recognize a specific area of resistance, focus the light in that area. But don't force things. When the apple is ripe, it will fall from the tree. Sometimes we are not quite ready to let go of something, and that's okay. The soul has its own rhythm and tempo of growth. Be patient yet persistence with yourself. If you are noticing a particular area of resistance is strong, you can conduct the purifying exercise with the white light instead of the orange-red flame.

Then follow up with the blue-white fire. Here you want to really feel the new life force uplifting and inspiring you.

Meditative Prayer to Refresh the Soul with the Blue-White Fire

"Down-ray the blue-white fire of eternal life to all four spiritual
centers and all facets of my being to charge and recharge the aura
with new life force. I ask this holy power to refresh my soul in its
spiritual journey and give it strength to accomplish its highest
potential. I am breathing in the holy breath of God."

Take a few deep breaths as you say the last sentence, repeating it a couple of times so you feel the spiritual flow of this life-giving light.

Once you feel established in these powers, bring in a very special energy that is directly connected to your spiritual growth—the apple green ray. It is what is called a "pearl luster" energy because the hues are like the opalescence of the inside of a seashell. Pearl luster energies are generally more delicate and lighter in shade than some of the other rays but they can be even more powerful. This is because they bring in the high ethereal vibrations of light.

The apple green is actually a combination of energies. It brings in the emerald green ray of balance and the golden ray of wisdom light. As already noted, when this energy is seen in the aura it means this person is making advances in his or her spiritual development. Working with this ray brings in one of the best energies to help condition the consciousness to feel comfortable with the process of spiritual evolution.

MEDITATIVE PRAYER WITH THE APPLE GREEN RAY OF SPIRITUAL GROWTH AND RENEWAL

"Down-ray the apple green ray of spiritual growth and renewal to open up my spiritual life and highest divine potential. Let this light flow through all levels of my consciousness, especially into my soul levels, to attract new experiences that are for my highest good. I ask that this light help me to shape my life to reflect the divine life, to be willing to explore and try new things. I ask that the apple green ray uplift my soul, releasing anything that is burdening me or holding me back. May I always keep looking upward and hold to the highest ideal of what I can be."

As this energy is so ethereal, it may take a couple of meditations to get into its divine rhythm. To help with this energy, you can also work with another pearl luster energy—the powder blue of inspiration. The powder blue ray is the ray to call on for new creative ideas. It is one of my favorite energy rays. It's especially effective if you are artistic or inventive. In your evolution, it can open you up to a more enlightened way of thinking.

MEDITATIVE PRAYER WITH THE POWDER BLUE RAY OF DIVINE INSPIRATION

"Down-ray the powder blue ray of inspiration to all levels of my consciousness, especially my mental center, to open my mind to elevated levels of thinking and ideas so that I may more clearly envision my highest ideals and divine potential. With this holy power may I be given the vision to live up to who I am and what I can be."

Once again, take time to let this energy set in and remain open to pictures or ideas that you may be given. Complete your meditation with the lemon yellow ray to strengthen the mental center and your intellectual powers to help you in your spiritual journey.

MEDITATIVE PRAYER WITH THE LEMON YELLOW RAY FOR GREATER FOCUS ON THE SPIRITUAL PATH

"Down-ray the lemon yellow ray to my mental center and all levels
of my consciousness to increase my concentration to stay focused
on my spiritual path, releasing any confusion or distractions so my
full attention is on my spiritual growth. I ask that this light increase
my intellectual powers so that I use common sense and good
judgment as I seek to fulfill my spiritual potential and
unravel the mysteries of life."

Once you finish your meditation, in a separate session, follow through with the Divine Light in any other areas of concern that might be holding you back from fully pursuing your spiritual goals, such as financial, professional, personal, relationship, or health situations. Working with the light separately in these areas will give you more confidence in your spiritual pursuits.

MAKING ROOM FOR THE DIVINE IN YOUR LIFE

A common complaint I hear when teaching the Higher Self meditation is "I don't have time to meditate." Certainly many of us live a fast-paced lifestyle. But it's up to you to prioritize your time so that the most important things take precedence. You can't do everything. When people say they don't have time to meditate, it means they have not really made their spiritual aspirations their priority. There may be interest or curiosity but not yet a driving passion. Some try to bring their meditation into their active life by calling in Divine Light while they drive or exercise. While calling on the light during activity is a good thing (as long as you are not distracted), this is not meditation. In meditation, you are in the meditative pose.

Your body and mind are in a still, receptive place. For the time you are in meditation, the world does not exist. This is your one-on-one time with God. What can be more important than that? Make your spiritual work your priority and watch how the rest of your life falls into place.

Spiritual growth is a gradual process. To be really effective, your spiritual work needs to become a lifestyle choice. Steady application conditions you for the higher life. As with anything, as you organize your life to accommodate your blossoming spirituality, the Divine in you unfolds.

The bright orange ray of motivation is excellent to work with to better organize your time, activities, and responsibilities. This ray is different from the orange-red flame, which is used for purification. If you've been discouraged or need more enthusiasm and ambition, this is the energy to work with.

MEDITATIVE PRAYER WITH THE BRIGHT ORANGE RAY FOR MOTIVATION AND ORGANIZATION

"Down-ray the bright orange ray of motivation and enthusiasm into
all my spiritual centers, and especially my Hermetic center, to increase
my drive to succeed in my spiritual quest. Let this energy out-ray
from the heart center to all my world affairs to help organize
my activities, including my job, relationships, and finances,
so that I may dedicate more time to my spiritual goals and more
fully express my inner spiritual desires. I ask this power ray to
increase my motivation and excitement for the spiritual work."

Feel the wonderful stimulating quality of this ray. I then recommend following up with the pure white light to help increase your overall desire to reach your spiritual potential. It takes not only a desire, but a *burning* desire, to reach your highest self. Some recognize the value of the spiritual work, but their desire is not as strong as it could be. Fortunately desire can be fanned. Take the desire you have and build on that. The white light is wonderful to work with, as well as the pink ray, to help cultivate a genuine desire for the higher life.

MEDITATIVE PRAYER WITH THE PURE WHITE LIGHT TO HELP BUILD DIVINE DESIRE

"Down-ray the pure white light to my Hermetic center to stimulate
my soul desire to make my spiritual ascent my priority. Help me
to feel my spirit self, my oneness with God, and the
creative process of life."

The emerald green ray is excellent to work with next if you feel your attention is divided and that you are doing too many things at one time or if something in your life is unbalanced and absorbing too much of your time and energy.

MEDITATIVE PRAYER WITH THE EMERALD GREEN RAY TO HARMONIZE SPIRITUAL PURSUITS

"Down-ray the emerald green ray to my Hermetic center to
bring my life into divine order so that all facets of my life
are the expression of my spiritual life. I ask to release any
counterclockwise activity and to bring all parts
of my life into harmony."

BEING OF SERVICE

The spiritual path is never about just you. While it is essential to work on yourself to build up your auric power and spiritual expression, part of that expression is meant to reach out to others. We are not islands unto ourselves, even if it feels like that at times. We are all interconnected. So what you do affects the greater whole. You are ultimately responsible for only your own soul's evolution, yet a wonderful benefit of working with Divine Light is that by improving yourself, you are changing the world.

As part of your light work and spiritual development, dedicate some of your time, energy, and resources to helping others. It doesn't matter so much what you do, whether you volunteer at a hospital or soup kitchen or you reach out to help family and friends in need, but give of yourself. This act of service needs to be selfless, without thought of personal remuneration. Give for the joy of giving. Don't count your contributions. Some of the more generous and gracious donors and philanthropists in the world do not broadcast their work; they just do it.

If you find that in your spiritual work you are getting a little self-absorbed, work with the deep rose pink ray of spiritual love to open your heart. Then simply follow through on some type of humanitarian act. Get outside of yourself and you will notice you are even closer in rhythm with the Divine Light.

MEDITATIVE PRAYER WITH THE DEEP ROSE PINK RAY TO AWAKEN SELFLESS SERVICE

"Down-ray the deep rose pink ray of spiritual love into all facets
of my aura and consciousness to open my heart, mind, and emotions
to be more loving and generous with my time, talents, and
resources. I ask that this loving power bring me courage and
confidence to reach out and help others in joy and gratitude,
without condition or judgment, and without thought of personal
gain. I recognize that in giving of myself, it is the Divine in me
acknowledging the Divine in whomever I am privileged to help."

WORKING WITH THE COLOR DIVISION AND THE INNER AURA

Without question, the greatest challenge to reaching your spiritual potential is not any outside situation or condition, it's you! No matter how we may desire the higher life, the lower nature most often resists the process until it is brought under control. As you work on your character traits, you perfect your soul attributes and are more willing to let your spiritual nature unfold. All facets of the aura help build character. Yet two aspects of the auric anatomy play a direct role in energetically supporting character building—the color division and the inner aura.

The color division is an unusual part of the auric composition. (See color Illustration 2.2E.) The brilliant, swirling sparkles of light that are the elements of this division directly reflect how strongly you have been building your character. If you have been working on your character weaknesses and expressing your character strengths, these pinpoints of light can greatly brighten. Since there are so many of these pinpoints of light, a developed color division creates a dominant expression in the aura. It supports and encourages the person to continue to develop and express those character traits. In the same way, if you avoid or ignore working on yourself, if you hide your talents and good qualities, or if you outright cultivate disturbing or destructive habits, the points of light darken and diminish. And a darkened color division can support and encourage more destructive behavior.

As you develop your character qualities at different times in your life, certain character traits will stand out the most. These energies will become dominant in the color division for the time you are expressing them. For example, if you are good with people and in the process of interacting with others in a productive way, the pink light will be pronounced in this division. If you show a particular gift for healing and are helping others in this capacity, the rich blue sparkles of light will be outstanding in this division. If you are a person who craves peace and exudes that quality to others, the purple light will be strong.

While you have to be in the act of building your character to enlighten the color division, you can ask the Divine Light to strengthen this area of the aura so you are more motivated to be the best person you know how to be.

MEDITATIVE PRAYER WITH THE GOLDEN RAY TO
STRENGTHEN THE COLOR DIVISION OF THE AURA

"Down-ray the golden ray of wisdom light to my Higher Self Point
of Spiritual Knowing, and from there direct this dynamic light
to my color division. I ask that this light strengthen my
color division and my dedication to improving and expressing the
diversity of my character. I honor my unique soul and character
traits and strive to lead a good life of high ideals."

In addition to the color division, the inner aura plays a major role in character development. The inner aura is truly a mystical part of your nature. It's called the inner aura because in essence it looks like an aura within the aura and stays close to the body. In contrast to the "outer" aura, which is the aura we have been working with in this book, the inner aura has a very different pace of development and changes slowly over time. So you won't work with the inner aura in the same way you work with other aspects of the energy field.

This aura is very connected to the soul expression and the life lessons the soul is going through. How is a life lesson different from experiences you deal with on a daily basis? As used in this book, a life lesson refers to a recurring theme in your life connected to your soul character. Each of us in this lifetime has certain qualities and traits that repeatedly express themselves. You may have a recurring theme in your life regarding patience. Maybe this is a lesson you have a constant battle with. You may be too impulsive and miss opportunities. Slowly over time, you learn patience, but it may take a good part of your life to do so. Or maybe a recurring lesson is tolerance. Maybe you find yourself being inflexible with people who do not share the same beliefs as yourself. And again it may take the majority of your life to build a more tolerant nature. On the other hand, say you show a wonderful determination. You don't let things deter you from what you wish to accomplish. Yet you find yourself faced with adversity where you have to repeatedly express that determination. All these experiences and character expressions build power in the aura and especially the inner aura. Once a life lesson is truly learned, the inner aura becomes luminous, reflecting that strengthened character trait. And it also indicates that the person has made great strides in his or her spiritual development.

So this type of character building is called a life lesson because it usually takes a lifetime to learn! It doesn't mean we are stupid or slow for something to take a lifetime to learn. Just the opposite. Life lessons are part of the big picture of who we are as souls and our expression as part of the eternal process of life. Mastering a life lesson is one of the most important things we can do in life and it will carry us far in our spiritual journey.

Before doing this meditation on strengthening the inner aura, take time to review what you feel is a life lesson for you. What is a recurring theme in your life when it comes to your character? And how successful or unsuccessful have you been in strengthening this part of you? Strengthening the inner aura is clearly something that will take patience, understanding, and commitment. You are going to get out of this what you put into it.

The purple ray is wonderful to work with in the inner aura to still your consciousness so you can better tune into where you are in this part of your life. You can also work with the gentler violet ray or the deep rose pink ray. Many times we don't pay attention to our actions; we don't take enough time to improve ourselves. And if it's a life lesson, we can get discouraged if we don't see the improvements we desire soon enough. Yet one of the most elevating things is the cultivation and mastery of a life lesson. It truly helps us to see the big picture of life, to walk to the rhythm of the Divine, and to better appreciate the spiritual forces at work in our own consciousness and the breadth of the spiritual path we are walking on.

MEDITATIVE PRAYER WITH THE PURPLE RAY OF PEACE TO BLESS THE INNER AURA

"Down-ray the purple ray of peace to my Hermetic center and out-ray to my inner aura to bless this part of my consciousness so that I may be still to hear my soul speak. Through this peace, let my spirit speak to my soul so that I may better understand and appreciate my soul's life lesson and see my soul's qualities for what they are. I recognize my soul is a divine spark of life, and it is undergoing a process of evolution to more fully express the powers within it. May God bless me with patience, love, and understanding to master and fully express this lesson of my life."

OVERCOMING ADVERSITY

There's an expression, "Our soul is forged in fire." No one gets through life without facing tests and challenges in some form; that's part of why we're here. Sometimes when we are going through difficult times, we mistakenly think that this is the time we are spiritually growing the least. Yet if we are holding true to ourselves and doing the best job we can, we can actually be making some of the greatest spiritual strides. Often our biggest challenge in pursuing the spiritual life arises not when things are difficult but when things are going well. It is in these times we may relax and fail to keep pursuing our spiritual aspirations.

All the spiritual energy rays can help you through difficult times. But since this chapter is focused on the aura and spiritual development, certain energy rays are particularly helpful if you are finding it difficult to pursue your spiritual goals.

One of the most power spiritual energies to work with to help you overcome adversity and build spiritual fortitude is the indigo ray of spirit. This energy brings in strength to the spirit. If you feel like you don't have what it takes to live up to your potential, or that you don't feel you have the strength to follow through on something that is being asked of you that is in your best interests, this power ray can help. When this energy is seen in the aura, it indicates a high, advanced soul. I don't see this ray often in people.

You don't need to receive much of the power to feel its strong transformative effect. The indigo is a very deep blue, sometimes with purple in it. In addition to any energy ray you feel can help, here is a meditative prayer with the indigo ray. Visualize the light coming down as a pearl of light rather than a beam.

MEDITATIVE PRAYER WITH THE INDIGO PEARL TO STRENGTHEN THE SOUL

"I ask that if it be Thy will to down-ray the indigo ray of spirit as a
beautiful pearl of light to my Hermetic center to bless my soul.
May I be given the strength of spirit to overcome any test or trial
and to realize that with God anything can be accomplished. With the
holy power give me the strength to fully complete my spiritual
journey and reach the spiritual summit. I express my love
and gratitude for everything in my life and all that the
Divine blesses me with."

One other exercise I would like to offer to help in overcoming challenging and discouraging situations is to ask the Divine Light to go below your feet. The lower part of your aura is where you are working out a lot of old issues. They may not always be as active in your life as in other times, but they are still there. But the lower part of the aura is also where you build your spiritual platform of power, where you create your foundation of Divine Light, so sending light to below the feet is very helpful.

Some interesting energies can be seen below the feet, including the purple light as described in the mixed aura in chapter 2. (See color Illustration 2.5.) When purple waves of energy are seen below the feet, it shows you have been dealing with matters of life and have "overcome them." If the person is really doing well dealing with a very difficult challenge, there can be a strong sphere of gold light just above the purple, demonstrating that the person has really overcome a particularly challenging situation. Sometimes if no purple light is there, it means it is a quiet time and there are no pressing issues. Or if the purple is not there it can mean that there are challenges but the person is not doing a good enough job in dealing with them. Remember, the test of your spiritual mettle is not what's happening to you, it's how you're dealing with the challenges of life. So depending on what is going on, this energy can come and go.

In this meditative prayer, ask that the emerald green light go to the area of your aura below your feet to give you a strong spiritual foundation for all your activities and spiritual growth.

Meditative Prayer with the Emerald Green Ray to Strengthen the Auric Power Below the Feet

"I ask to down-ray the emerald green ray of balance and harmony
to below my feet to form a strong foundation to fortify the auric
power there. I ask this divine power to keep me steady and
strong wherever I go and whatever I do."

WALKING THE PATH OF LIGHT

You can't force evolution. It has to unfold naturally. At a certain point the soul becomes aware of its true potential. This is what's called the spiritual awakening.

When the soul awakens it's an exhilarating feeling. There's an excitement beyond description—a feeling that anything can be accomplished and a willingness to do anything to reach that potential.

What can you expect while walking this path of light? First recognize this is a holy path and treat it with reverence. It's the path that will lead you back to your Eternal Home and eventually to God. Every step of the way is sacred. This is why you enter with a clean heart and pure motives.

The blessings of traveling on this path of light are beyond description. The Divine Light is dazzling. Once you are awakened to the greater possibilities, a whole new world opens up. With each conscious step, you will draw one step closer to unraveling the mysteries of life, one step closer to perfecting yourself. You will reach the point where your outer life will be the reflection of your inner divine life. No longer will you live solely by your wits but through the awareness and connection to the greater whole. You will become the embodiment of all you aspire to be. You won't need to search for love because you will embody love. You will not need to worry about money because you will be the embodiment of abundance and supply. You will eventually embody all the attributes of light, love, and wisdom.

Some think that when they start their spiritual journey they have to drop everything and live like a recluse. There have been many stories to support this idea. For some the path of renunciation is their spiritual road. But for many others the goal is to reorganize their life to reflect the Divine. The spiritual path is not an escape from life, but the fulfillment. It's an enhancement of all life's processes. The best place to start on the path is right where you are. Start at home. Start on your path by being a better wife or husband, by being better at your job, and so on.

There's a story about Mother Teresa that beautifully reflects this principle. A very rich woman admired Mother Teresa greatly and wanted to join her work of serving the poorest of the poor. Mother Teresa, seeing she was not quite ready for such a life, dissuaded her from joining. The woman was perplexed and saddened, asking what could she do. Mother Teresa looked at the dress she was wearing and asked how much it cost. The woman told her a large sum. Then Mother Teresa said, "Next time you go to buy a dress like that, give the money to the poor instead." So begin from where you are and with what is comfortable, but begin.

Working with spiritual energy will help you see things in their true light. You will engage more in activities that help your spiritual growth and start dropping away activities and things that are not helpful to your spiritual growth. The Divine Light helps you see others in their true light. This will help you build true and lasting friendships but also help you let go of relationships that are not looking out for your best interests. You may discover that you're in the wrong job and start looking for a new and better one.

The Divine Light will begin to show you in your true light. You'll see more clearly your own strengths and weaknesses. The parts of your life that are already strong will amplify and you'll find yourself appreciating those positive qualities more. The fruits of your spiritual life will begin to embody themselves in your daily life. You'll find yourself looking at your own character traits and gradually forgive and let go of self-destructive habits that hold you back.

CHAPTER XIV

The Light in All Aspects of Your Life

· ·

You now have a strong working knowledge of the Divine Light. You have the tools to call on your Higher Self to access the Divine Light and many examples of how to implement that energy in your active life. In this chapter, we will explore techniques you can use in conjunction with the Higher Self meditation that will amplify the light process to an even greater extent.

LIVING IN A SEA OF ENERGY

All life is teeming with spiritual energy. Even what appears to be empty space is filled with spiritual activity. Because you live in this sea of energy, you're constantly intermingling with other energy flows. Think of how many people you interact with on a daily basis. Each one of these people has his or her own auric field, which may be enlightened or devolved or mixed. So in developing your aura, you need to be aware not only of your own vibration, but of how you are interacting with other vibrations. To maintain your spiritual equilibrium, strive to maintain a healthy interaction with the world around you.

PROTECTION

To stay in your own auric flow, start by keeping your spiritual protection strongly around you. People who are unaware of the interaction of auric energies always ask me, "Protection from what?" I begin to explain all the ways you can open up to negative energy. Fortunately, the aura has protective energies built into it that buffer unwanted negative energy. Yet adding spiritual protection is extremely valuable.

Golden Sphere with Orange-Red Flame

This protective exercise is very similar to the golden bubble of protection you use when going into meditation. The difference is that you surround the circumference of your golden bubble with the orange-red flame to dissolve any negative energy that might be trying to push in. All positive flows continue normally.

In the same manner as in step 2 of your Higher Self meditation, stand up and hold your arms out, envisioning yourself surrounded by a golden bubble of light about arm's length from your body. Sense and feel this sphere of golden light as vividly as you can. Envision seven flows of this living light enfolding you in a protective sheath. Once the gold light is established, envision the orange-red flame surrounding the golden sphere and making the bubble look like a fireball of living light. Envision the protective light surrounding you while saying the following prayer.

GOLDEN PROTECTION WITH THE ORANGE-RED FLAME

"Encircle me now in a golden bubble of protective light. I
ask that seven flows of this light surround me, keeping me
in perfect protection. And I ask that Thou place the orange-red
flame around the circumference of this protection, dissolving
any negative energies that might try to
penetrate this bubble."

I recommend surrounding yourself with protection before you leave your house, and reinforce it as needed throughout the day. This protection is especially important if you're going into a crowd of people, whether at a party, business meeting, concert, movie, or any gathering. Protecting yourself will quickly become second nature to you and is one of the most important spiritual tools you possess. As you work with the protective light, it will become stronger.

CLOSING THE PSYCHIC DOOR

One of the first exercises I give students for building their spiritual protection is called "closing the psychic door." The psychic door is an interesting part of your spiritual anatomy. It's a spiritual filtration system connected to your subconscious mind. The subconscious is the seat of memory. It records every experience verbatim. Your subconscious mind is particularly susceptible to outside influences. It is like an incredibly sensitive recording device that picks up everything that's happening around you. As a result, and without your intending it, the subconscious mind can take in negative mental currents.

To protect the subconscious, the aura has built into it a filtration system. Its purpose is to shut out outside destructive thought currents, allowing only positive thought currents to enter. However, this door can swing open through stress, destructive behavior, disturbances, and emotional outbursts. Once this "door" is open, you're open to *any thought moving in the periphery of the subconscious*—the good, the bad, and the ugly. This door can become an Achilles' heel if you're not careful. It's not at all uncommon to have the psychic door open, yet it's easy to close.

The psychic door is located just behind the right ear and looks like a blue flap when it is open. It's important to make sure this door is kept closed at all times, permitting only good thoughts to enter. Having a stiff neck, or feeling that someone is a "pain in the neck," can be a sign that your door may be open. The actual spiritual mechanism by which this door is closed is too involved to describe in these pages, but by following this simplified procedure, you'll get the job done.

Place your right index and third fingers behind your right ear over the psychic door and envision a golden gingerbread man (I like to have fun with this!) in the center of your head. See his right hand extending out shooting light rays and shutting the door from the inside. (See Illustration 14.1.) Then envision that door being sealed with three impenetrable golden white locks. As you are doing this, recite the following prayer in an affirmative, strong tone.

ILLUSTRATION 14.1-*Closing the Psychic Door*

Closing the Psychic Door

"I command my psychic door to be sealed and locked with
three impenetrable golden white locks, and I refuse to permit
anything negative to enter therein."

Envision the door sealing shut like the locks on a bank vault. Once you have successfully performed this exercise, your door is closed. Later, if something has upset you and you feel the door may have become open again, just repeat the exercise.

THE ENERGY WE LEAVE BEHIND

Albert Schweitzer once said that whatever we do in life, we should "leave the footprints of love behind us." We've all felt the ripple effect of our actions. How many times have you entered a home for the first time and felt either comfortable or strangely repelled? This can be even before you meet the person living there. Why do you feel this? Because the house has been "charged up" with that person's vibrations. Churches and temples demonstrate this principle very noticeably with their chanting, glowing candles, incense, holy water, etc. These places have accumulated the spiritual vibrations of these inspiring expressions, not to mention the years of prayers, so people can't help but feel spiritually uplifted just by being there.

This works at both ends of the spectrum. There is a story about a bridge in London that's particularly famous for people committing suicide by jumping off it. This in itself isn't so unusual. What makes this bridge so unusual is that a very high percentage of these people jumped from the same exact spot. Of course, they were unaware they were doing this, but they usually gravitated to the same place. Why would they do this? Because that certain area had been charged up with the vibrational energy of suicide, and people in this frame of mind were intuitively drawn to that energy.

This auric effect works at all levels of interaction, including chairs you sit in, places you visit, the clothing you wear, and everything you interact with. I had a dear friend who bought an ancient chair dating from the Ming dynasty that a high official was supposed to have sat in. She was proud of this purchase and placed it prominently in her home. Yet, for some reason, having it in her house made her feel very uncomfortable. She told herself she was just being irrational. As the days passed, her uneasiness only grew. She invited me to see if I could tune into anything that would explain her unsettling feeling. The chair was jet-black and somewhat plain for a piece of furniture designed for such a regal purpose. The moment I got close to it, my stomach did several flip-flops, which told me something was very wrong. I clairvoyantly looked at the chair and saw black light around it. I knew right then and there that the chair had been connected with terrible things. Then I got the pictures that the person or persons who had sat in this chair had been responsible for many cruel acts, and those vibrations were still embedded in the chair. My friend did some research and discovered that the official associated with the chair had been responsible for executions and barbaric acts. We purified the chair, but she decided to sell it anyway.

As you work with the light, you will get into the feeling and knowing of where and when you need to send the light. My first recommendation in working with energies around you is to send the light ahead of you to places you'll be going to and people you'll be meeting. In my morning meditations, I add the following prayer, asking the light to walk ahead of me to prepare every person and place I will be dealing with that day. If I know specifically who or what they are, I name them. This sends a signal to the Higher Self to begin the energy process.

Meditative Prayer to Send the Light Ahead of You

"I ask the Divine Light to walk ahead of me to prepare the
way as I go to (*name place or places*). Let it touch into (*name
people you'll be in contact with*) and purify them of any black
and gray atoms, dissolving them in the mineral kingdom in
the light and bringing in new life force and divine energy."

You can name any other energy you feel is appropriate as well, such as love or peace. This prayer will help to dissipate any negative energy you may encounter. You can also purify things as you go along. If you get a letter that may not be so good, you can ask the light to go into it before you read it. If you're going to make a difficult phone call that might be distressing, ask the light to touch into the person you'll be calling and into the call itself to help keep things moving on a positive level. Even when you go to a movie theater, you'll want to purify the seat you're in so as not to pick up the spiritual atoms of the person before you.

The purification for cleansing objects is also very simple. If you can hold the object in your hands, hold it in your left hand with your right hand on top. If not, ask the light to go to the object. Ask your Higher Self to cleanse whatever you feel needs it with a prayer like the following.

Meditative Prayer for Object Cleansing

"Down-ray the orange-red flame into my right hand and into
(*name object*), purifying it of any black and gray atoms and

> dissolving them in the mineral kingdom. Then bring in the
> blue-white fire to establish new life energy within this
> *(name object)*."

It may take several minutes for the energy to start working. You can ask that the cleansing be done for you either in meditation or right as the need arises. By the way, material cleanliness has nothing to do with this process. An object can be immaculate and germ free while also being spiritually dirty.

I also recommend when you are out and about to ask the Divine Light to purify seats you are sitting in at restaurants, theaters, and other public places. You don't need to raise your consciousness to do this or go through the six steps to meditate with light. Just ask the orange-red flame of purification to cleanse the seat you are sitting in and your job is done. By doing this, you are keeping the consistency of the Divine Light working with you even outside your meditation time.

In general, watch your energy flow as it relates to your environment. Do you notice times when you are getting hit by negative energy? Are there certain places or people that seem to disagree with you on a consistent basis? Are you able to brush these vibrations off easily or are you easily affected? Are there places you frequent that you are better off staying away from?

Remember, your goal is to maintain your spiritual equilibrium regardless of what is going on around you. Your meditation time is a sacred time to connect with the light, but you must also maintain that presence of light as you go about your daily activities. It is as you live these principles of light that you are evolving.

CHILDREN AND MEDITATION

I am often asked if children can do the light work. It's exciting to see with more people interested in the aura and spiritual energy that they wish their children to be a part of that experience. Sometimes, it's the child expressing an interest in spiritual topics.

Children have an aura just like adults do and they earn spiritual light. We must remember that there is a full soul in every child's developing body, so children are going through the same process of evolution as everyone else. Yet there are some differences and considerations here.

First, while it's an adult soul in that little body, the spiritual power of the child is still developing. As we explored previously, the aura energy is not "set" until age seven, which means that until that time, the consciousness is very pliable and impressionable. This is needed because of all the child must absorb and learn. Then there is another auric milestone at age twelve. This is when the soul receives its Higher Self Point. Up to that time, the child has the other chakra points, which are also getting stronger, but not that radiant Higher Self Point above the head. Until age twelve, children receive Divine Light and assistance in other ways. They get a lot of support from what we know of as the guardian angels and another group of celestial beings called "sisters in light." These divine beings, understanding that the children are developing their full awareness, do a lot of the receiving and transmitting of light until they mature.

It is not recommended for a child to practice the Higher Self meditation until he or she is twelve. After that it's a wonderful and life-enhancing experience and hopefully one the child will want to practice. Up to the age of twelve, what a child can do is practice reflective meditation (see chapter 16). Reflective meditation will bring in spiritual energy. It's a fun process and gets a child's creativity and imagination involved.

Introducing children to meditation at a young age is becoming more common at home and even at school, where some school systems are offering a "quiet time" for their students with wonderful positive results.

If you notice your children are curious or interested in the light work you are doing, you can gently introduce them to the idea that all of us have this beautiful colorful aura around us. It tells us who we are and what is going on with us. This is God's light in us. And every day God blesses us with Divine Light to help us. They can simply close their eyes and ask God to bless them with Divine Light.

You can introduce your children to the idea that every time they do something good and help someone, say a kind word, learn something new, or strengthen their own character, they brighten their aura. Teach them that God's light is in everyone, even if others don't believe in God or are doing things that are not so good. Remind them that not everyone understands meditation and prayer, especially when it comes to spiritual light. They may think what you are doing is silly. That is okay, as they can believe what they wish. Let them be where they are. But you have to be true to yourself. It's often better not to talk about the light work you are doing.

When teaching your children about working with Divine Light, make it fun. For example, if they are scared, they can envision a golden bubble and feel God's protection surrounding them. Let them know they must still show the same caution and common sense as usual, but this is an added help, like having a secret friend in their corner.

If your children are nervous, they can envision themselves running through a field of purple flowers and feeling very peaceful. If they need more confidence, they can see themselves in a golden waterfall feeling strong and mighty, able to do anything.

When they are feeling sad about something, they can envision pink hearts floating down from above and going inside their bodies, filling them with a loving, warm pink light that makes them feel happy and joyful.

If they are tired, they can see themselves in a garden of bright red roses, which will send them their beauty, strength, and vitality, making them feel peppy.

For times when your children are sick, in addition to seeking the medical care to get them well, tell them to see themselves floating in a pool of deep rich blue water. This water is like living healing light. As they are floating in this water, they feel healthy and well.

To help them study, they can see silver diamond points of light showering them, the sparkles of light making them feel more alert and clearheaded. Or they can see themselves in a bubble of lemon yellow light and feel focused and motivated to learn.

If discouraged, they can envision themselves eating a celestial orange. As they do, bright orange light fills their bodies and makes them feel encouraged and motivated.

When your children finish with these types of reflective meditations, they should take a moment to feel grounded, alert, and awake.

As an alternative to visualizing Divine Light, you can play games with your children to think about qualities. They can close their eyes and image themselves very happy, joyful, kind, caring, adventurous, smart, humorous, strong, and so on. The variations are endless. By doing this, they will attract these spiritual attributes to their auras.

Of course, you do this in addition to all the good parental advice you would instill in your child, the good ethics and morality. It's also important to teach a spiritually minded child to pray—which is the complement to meditation. Prayer is a reaching out to the Divine; meditation is a receiving from the Divine. Reflective meditation wonderfully complements any religious practice or is effective alone simply for its own intrinsic value.

Introducing children to the tools of reflective meditation at a young age—again, if they are interested—will elevate their aura, help them in their lives, and prepare them for when they are older. It can be a wonderful way to bring in healthy spiritual principles at a young age.

PURIFYING YOUR HOME

An important place to concentrate your purification work is in your own home. Your home is your sanctuary and obviously an important place to keep spiritually strong. People coming to your home or living in your home can unintentionally generate negative energy and that energy needs to be cleared. Otherwise, you could pick up that negative energy without even knowing it. The purification needs to go to your door, computer, TV, mobile device, mailbox, telephone, and especially the bed you sleep in. Many people burn incense to cleanse their home. There are religious traditions of asking a priest or holy person to come and bless your house. These are all wonderful practices and should be done periodically.

To cleanse your home with the light, it helps to work with candles. A wonderful exercise is to burn three orange candles in a triangle formation in the center of the house. Put a bowl of water in the middle. This will act as a "demagnetizing" bowl to draw the black and gray atoms being released. Burn the candles for twenty minutes. (Votive candles work well. Safety first. Never leave a candle unattended or in reach of young children or animals.) Ask the orange-red flame to sweep through your home, dissolving any negative energies and dissolving the black and gray atoms in the mineral kingdom.

After the twenty minutes, blow out the candles, then throw out the water and replace it with new water. Place three blue candles in a triangle formation and light them. Ask the blue-white fire to sweep through the home, charging and recharging your home with new life force. Again leave the candles lit for approximately twenty minutes. Extinguish the candles, throw out the water, and you are done. The following meditative prayer can be used to help start the cleansing process.

MEDITATIVE PRAYER TO PURIFY YOUR HOME

"Down-ray the orange-red flame into the center of this
house, and then out-ray throughout the house,
including all rooms, grounds, and property. Take all
black and gray atoms at least ten feet into the mineral
kingdom and dissolve them in the light. Upon completion
of this purification, down-ray the blue-white fire to charge
and recharge all aspects of this home, retaining this energy
and bringing this house into the highest vibration possible."

If you need to focus the light in a particular room, place the candles in that room and do a cleansing for just that room. If you live in an apartment building, see the light radiating throughout your own unit and also dissolving any negative energies from adjoining units. I have found that burning sage and taking that sage to all rooms of the house effects a wonderful cleansing as well. If you do this, ask the light to go into the sage itself to amplify the cleansing process. I would repeat this exercise every day until you feel it's well established.

Follow up your spiritual housecleaning with a prayer of protection. The prayer itself is a power that builds up over time, helping to keep negative energies out, while also uplifting visitors who come in.

"Down-ray the golden ray of Thy divine protection to surround
this home in seven flows of this light, strongly protecting
everything herein and everyone who enters. In Thy
holy name I ask this."

SENDING DIVINE LIGHT TO OTHERS IN NEED

Although this book is focused on working with spiritual energy for yourself, you will discover that the more you work with the light, the more you will become aware of how much others need the Divine Light. You can always offer to teach them the techniques of the Higher Self meditation. Yet, many times you will find it best simply to pray for others to be blessed with Divine Light.

There is an art to being a channel of light for others. This requires training beyond the scope of this book, yet I want to offer a simple technique for sending light to others. The method of sending light to others is called absentee healing, which means the person receiving the light is not physically present with you.

The most important thing to remember in prayer for others is that you are the channel of light, but you don't want to "give" your own light to someone else in need. You want to be a channel for the light, Higher Self to Higher Self. Second, you don't want to take it upon yourself to direct the light to specific areas of another person's consciousness, such as specific chakras, auric divisions, etc. You may do this for yourself, but it's different for others. When sending light to others, all you are doing is permitting the Higher Self to use you as a base of Divine Light. How the light works with them is entirely in the hands of the Higher Self.

To be a channel of Divine Light for someone else, start by sitting in a chair and envision the golden light of protection surrounding you. Feel very protected and safe. Get in the meditative state and raise your consciousness as you normally would. Envision the person you wish to send the light to. Then ask the Divine to down-ray to your Higher Self Point the energy ray you feel that person needs. For example, if you wish to send love to someone, first see the love ray down-raying to your Higher

Self Point. Then ask permission of the Higher Self Point of the person you are working with to send the light to him or her. Hold in silence for a moment. Then ask the Higher Self to use your Higher Self Point to send this love ray to that person's Higher Self Point. Hold for a few moments as this is being done "according to divine law and love for the good of all concerned." As mentioned, don't go into details of where the light is going. That is not your job. You don't want to get personal about this. All this is happening Higher Self to Higher Self. That way you are the channel and not pulling on your own energy field. And by doing it this way you are not imposing your own will on the spiritual realm; you're simply being of selfless service to another in need.

Once you feel the connection is made, you are finished or you can repeat this exercise with one or two other power rays at most. Don't overdo this! I would also not do this for more than a couple of people in a single day. When you get into the rhythm of this, it is a powerful tool and it's a beautiful, loving process to watch. When you are completely finished with your work, ask the orange-red flame of purification to shower you to release any negative energy you might have unintentionally picked up. Reinforce your protection once again and you are finished!

LEADING A GROUP MEDITATION

A wonderful way to work with Divine Light is in a group meditation. This is what I do in all my classes. You can invite a group of like-minded individuals to join you in your light meditations. In this work, you are not being the channel of light for another person. Rather, you are leading the meditation and the others are receiving the light from their own Higher Self. This is a great way to introduce the light work to other people so they can experience the light for themselves.

In a group meditation, you would verbally bring the light down as you would for yourself but include the people present in the room with you. So instead of starting the meditation by saying, "I raise my consciousness into Thy consciousness . . ." you would say, "We raise our consciousness into Thy consciousness . . ."

Then when you start bringing down the light, you would include the others by saying something like, "Down-ray the Divine Light to our Higher Self Point and to all our spiritual energy centers . . ." Everyone would be following your lead as the light comes down, yet will be experiencing the energy in their own way.

Group meditation is powerful because when everyone is in harmony with the meditation, the effect of the light can be even stronger than when you meditate on your own. I encourage people to start their own informal meditation group, as it can be such a support in their Divine Light work and help many others.

CHAPTER XV

Fashion and Color

. . . .

While in high school, I was doing my best to lead a "normal life." Metaphysics was little understood then and, from experience, I found it best not to tell people of my clairvoyant gifts. Yet these talents were blossoming in miraculous ways, and I was receiving regular inspiration from the spiritual realms. My understanding of how to work with spiritual energy deepened, including developing an understanding of the role the aura played in health.

It was during this time that I discovered the colors I wore in my clothing made an impact on the aura. As the fifth of six children, with two older sisters, and growing up in the Depression era, I wore hand-me-downs throughout my childhood. Until I got older I really didn't have much of a say in what I wore. But as I was learning more about the aura, I saw that there was a correlation between the spiritual color energies, with their various interpretations, and physical colors of similar hues and saturation. For example, wearing something bright red had the effect of attracting the auric energies of vitality. Wearing pink could draw in more of the loving spiritual energies. This wasn't in every instance, but even if it didn't bring in the exact color correlation, it still had this aura-enhancing effect.

In the same way, wearing dark colors that reflected the unenlightened energies tended to detract from the aura. Wearing dark browns, blacks, and grays often had a dampening effect on the aura, depending on the situation. I started dressing in brighter colors and in a way that better reflected the colors of my aura and it had a definite positive effect.

In this chapter, I would like to complement your light work by offering suggestions as to colors to dress in for various situations that would strengthen and enhance your aura. You may ask, "How does physical color make a difference if the aura is not physical?" First, I am not talking about fashion in the sense of colors that match skin tones or seasons of the year. I'm also not speaking of chromotherapy. This is the fascinating study of the healing effects of physical light and colors on the human body, a practice that goes back to ancient times. In exploring the effects that colors in the physical spectrum have on consciousness and the aura, we are stepping into the psychological and metaphysical arena.

The spiritual effect of color is based on the similar principles of reflective meditation and visualizing the spiritual energies you are calling on. One of the secrets of consciousness is that "you are where you place your attention." In your light meditations, by placing your attention on the color of the energy ray you are requesting, you are helping to draw that energy to you. The color acts as a door to the consciousness of the energy. For example, by vividly visualizing pink, that can have the effect of helping to tune you into the actual spiritual power of the love ray. You don't need to be clairvoyant to effectively visualize color.

This spiritual effect of color also calls into play another aspect of our being—the unconscious. The unconscious (not to be confused with the subconscious mind, which is the seat of memory) is a primal part of us that deals with aspects of mind that are not readily accessible to the conscious mind. This is the mind that expresses unrecognized desires, wants, fear, hopes, and dreams. It is the aspect of mind that can be irrational, wild, and unpredictable. This mind expresses itself in sometimes unexpected ways and can be accessed through the dream state, through symbols and mythic imagery, as well as certain meditative states.

Since by definition the unconscious mind is processing and interpreting information below the conscious level, there can be more freedom with its expression. This is why in a dream anything can happen and even the most bizarre happenings can seem normal and acceptable until we awaken back to our conscious mind. When we visualize or wear a physical color, it interplays with the unconscious mind. Your unconscious awareness of color has the effect of attracting that corresponding spiritual energy to you. One beauty of wearing color as a tool to spiritually strengthen your aura is you don't have to think about it. The positive effects are working for you automatically.

In the aura, the effects of the colors you wear can be clairvoyantly seen. They usually affect the mental and Hermetic centers. When you wear bright colors that reflect the enlightened energies of the aura, beautiful radiations come out of the mental and/ or Hermetic center. These radiations are somewhat delicate and to the untrained clairvoyant eye can be mistaken for mental active emanation. But in fact they represent the consciousness reacting to the environment. This helps to uplift the aura.

In the same way, when you wear dark, unenlightened colors, this can have the effect of detracting from the auric power. This is most often seen in the Hermetic center. While wearing dark colors doesn't usually attract that type of energy (although it can if the intention is strong), what it can do is weaken some of the Hermetic rays, which can detract from most effectively expressing yourself spiritually. It can create a discouraging, draining effect on the consciousness.

In the spirit world, color is very important. The spiritual dimensions of life are full of color and majesty. Angelic beings wear robes of living colors that have great impact on the work they do. You are recognized by your light rays just as you are by your form and appearance. You are a light being, so why not surround yourself with color?

When it comes to wearing clothing of certain colors to enhance your aura, there are two ways to go. You can wear colors that reflect the enlightened aspects of your consciousness. For example, if you feel loving, wearing pink will enhance that feeling. Or you can go the other way and wear a color reflecting an energy you feel you need. So if you are feeling lonely or sad, wearing pink in this instance can help pick up your spirits.

We all have colors that we like to wear and that seem to "agree" with us. Sometimes they fall in the enlightened range, sometimes not. If you notice you wear a lot of the darker shades, it's time to start adding color. It's also a good idea to add variety to your wardrobe. If you see you wear mostly blues and greens, for example, bring in some other colors. As in life, variety is good and creates excitement.

WEARING BLUE

Blue is a wonderful color to wear in many situations. The rich sapphire blue is an excellent color to wear when you need healing, as it can help attract the healing energies to you and help keep your mind focused on health. The bright peacock blue (also called the electric blue) is the color to wear when you are engaged in creative activities. I was lecturing at a children's acting camp once. These were really smart kids and many of them were already working in the motion picture industry. I was amazed at how receptive they were to the idea of the aura. After I told them that electric blue was the color of talent in the aura, the teacher of the camp told me that the next day, half the kids came in wearing bright blue!

The deep royal blue is good to wear when you need more strength and determination, such as at your job. Wearing this color can help keep you steady, especially if others are trying to pull you in different directions. It's a good color to wear when in a leadership role. The royal blue is excellent when interacting with friends and family, as it brings out your devotion and loyalty.

Wearing light, powder blue is excellent when engaged in creative pursuits and trying to feel more inspired. It can help you gain fresh insight and outlook on things. If the blue goes more to a sea blue, this has a calming, soothing effect on the consciousness. It's good to wear when you want to relax.

The indigo is an interesting color to wear. It's not always easy to find a true indigo color in clothing. Many physical shades that are called indigo are really a blue-black, sometimes mixed in with other dark colors. This is not really indigo; it's more of what is called the "moody blue," which is a depressing energy in the aura. The true indigo color could be a very deep blue or blue-purple. This is a good color to wear if you're going through a difficult situation. It's helpful when starting a new project and trying to break through challenges and apparent obstacles.

WEARING RED

As you might imagine, red is a stimulating color. All the brighter shades of red work well. Wearing this color vitalizes the energy field. If you are doing something athletic and physically strenuous, this is an excellent color to wear. In the same way, if you are tired or fatigued, wearing this color can help pick up your energy levels. Wearing red clothing can build up your stamina when engaged in activities that require sustained effort over time. If you have come out of an illness and still don't feel like you have your full strength back, this is an excellent color to wear.

It also has the effect of stimulating other people. If you are with a group of people doing an activity together, wearing red can help. It's helpful when other people have to be active with you. Red is the color of passion, so it is a good energy color to wear in romantic situations to help create excitement. Be careful not to wear red when you need to sleep or relax, as it can be overstimulating.

WEARING PINK

Pink is generally thought of as a woman's color, yet from the point of view of the aura, it's one of the most uplifting colors to wear for both men and women. This color will help bring out your loving nature, especially if you are shy or hold back too much from expressing your feelings to others. If you are lonely or feel uncared for, wearing something pink can help you feel more nurtured and cared for. It's one of the best colors to wear when engaging in relationships with others. Even wearing this in the workplace can help encourage better cooperation among coworkers.

Of course it is the color to wear when in a romantic relationship or if you wish to attract a romantic partner. In a similar way, it's excellent to wear in interacting with friends and family and it can help attract new people into your life. This is a wonderful color to wear if you are in a depression and wish to pick up your spirits. It can bring you into a more joyful state of mind, more hopeful and optimistic.

WEARING GREEN

Bright greens are often associated with nature and renewal, depending on the shade. This is an important color to wear in a variety of situations. It is a stabilizing and centering color. If you are feeling too busy doing all sorts of things, or feeling you are out of rhythm in your life, wearing bright emerald green can bring you into divine balance and upliftment.

Like the pink, green is excellent for relationships. If you don't feel comfortable wearing pink, you can wear a nice bright shade of green to encourage healthy, harmonious relationships. It encourages cooperation. If there have been disagreements or if you find yourself in the middle of a dispute between two people, wearing green can help to resolve those situations and find the common ground. Wearing the deeper shade of kelly green can help stimulate financial abundance. This is similar to the color turquoise. Yet, whereas turquoise is abundance in any aspect of life, kelly green is especially good in money matters. Green can also be a healing and relaxing color to wear.

WEARING ORANGE

Not many people wear this color and that's too bad because it has a lot of benefits from the point of view of the aura. Like the red tones, orange is a very enlivening and uplifting color to wear. If you are very athletic, wearing both the orange and the red will get you as stimulated as you can get from the color of clothes you wear. The two are a great combination. Wearing orange can help you get motivated to start or finish a project you are working on, especially if you have been procrastinating. It brings out your ambitious nature to be successful at what you do. If you're feeling discouraged, wear something orange to pick up your spirits. It's a very good color to wear when you are in the midst of reorganizing your office or home. Similar to the red, orange is a very lively, active color. Think of it as a sunshine color.

WEARING WHITE

Wearing white generates some of the most diverse effects in the aura. Depending how you wear this color it can have a neutral effect—neither supportive nor detractive. But when you wear it with spiritual intention, it serves many wonderful functions.

White is one of the most uplifting colors to wear. Think of it like being lifted up in a white cloud out of cares and worries. As with the energy in the aura, white can help you see things from the higher perspective, especially if you feel you've been too enmeshed in your concerns. White brings in holiness and purity. When you want to feel closer to the Divine, closer to God, wear this color. It helps bring in a redemptive quality as well. If you've done something that was not so good, wearing white can help you get out of that state of mind so you are more motivated to correct whatever was done. It brings in the energy of idealism to live to one's highest standards. It helps to stimulate the connection with your higher nature. It's excellent to wear if you have been feeling compromised, violated, slandered, or misrepresented, so you don't absorb those energies.

There is a wonderful unifying effect to wearing white. However, be careful of wearing white in situations where others are not in so good a place spiritually, as it can make them feel uncomfortable. There can be a restful quality to this color as well. It's good to wear white if you are having trouble sleeping.

WEARING YELLOW

Since it is difficult to find gold clothing without going to metallic colors, bright yellow can be used for the spiritual qualities of both yellow and gold. Yellow is a stimulating color, similar to the reds and oranges. It's an excellent color to wear when teaching or learning new things. If you are studying for a test, this is a wonderful color to wear to help stay focused. If you feel "scattered" in your thinking and feeling, wearing this color can help you feel centered and together. If you notice you have a very short attention span, losing interest too quickly, wearing yellow will help focus the consciousness.

Yellow, like the gold, is a dynamic, outgoing energy. If you are feeling fearful, or if you are procrastinating or hesitating about something, wearing this color will help you get out of that frame of mind and be more outgoing and willing to take chances. This is a good color to wear for more willpower when feeling wishy-washy. It's excellent for decision making—anything that requires dynamic activity. Combining yellow with other dynamic colors will help you be even more outgoing.

WEARING PURPLE

Purple is a magnificent color to wear. When seen in the aura to a marked degree, it indicates an advanced soul. No wonder purple has been associated with regality. It centers you and helps to keep you in the divine oneness. It's the color to wear when you need deep rest and relaxation. If you are nervous or anxious about something, this energy will calm you down; it is powerful yet restful. It's excellent when the nervous system has been overworked. If you've been putting in a lot of extra hours at work, wearing purple can soothe and relax the nervous system. Purple is the color to wear when overcoming grief, such as following the death of a loved one. If you are having trouble sleeping, try wearing something purple to help get you in the mood to sleep.

WEARING MIXED COLORS

It is interesting that in the electromagnetic spectrum, the colors of visible light are continuous from one wavelength to the next. Reds are in the area of longer wavelengths, then, moving through the spectrum, you work your way to the purples, which are shorter, or "higher," wavelengths. But when it comes to the human eye, there are three basic receptors that pick up certain wavelengths of light then combine those impulses to produce our perception of physical color. Mirroring this process, there are the primary colors, which can be additive (as in adding different colors of light to produce other colors) or subtractive (as in mixing primary colors of paint to produce secondary colors). Mixing primary colors can produce a great variety of color choices.

In the spiritual spectrum of Divine Light, spiritual energies that are a combination of more than one color do share certain similarities to physical light but there are unique differences. Remember, Divine Light is a conduit of consciousness, so energy rays that bring in more than one color dynamic are not simply a combination of two or more colors. There is a unique consciousness or divine attribute placed in that light that is all its own.

For example, the apple green ray of spiritual growth is a combination of the emerald green ray of balance and the golden ray of wisdom. Yet the apple green ray is not simply balanced wisdom; it's a unique attribute all its own.

The following colors reflect spiritual energies that have this blending of power but also their own unique attributes. They are excellent to wear to help create more dynamic energy in the aura.

Turquoise

This blue-green color is excellent to wear when you wish to attract prosperity in all forms. It may be a prosperity of material needs, ideas, friendship, opportunities, health, or any number of things. I recommend wearing turquoise jewelry to further cultivate a climate of abundance. If you have been worried about supply, or others around you are in a poverty consciousness, wearing turquoise can help keep you in your own center of divine wealth.

Apple Green

This color helps with creating a feeling of new beginnings, a fresh start. Wearing this color is very good when starting a new project or wanting to feel more connected to your spiritual self. Similar to the sea blue, it has a calming effect on the aura.

Coral

This is an unusual energy, not often seen in the aura. It brings in the deep rose pink and the bright orange, with more pink than orange. This is an excellent color to wear when you are trying to bring people together in a common activity. It helps to engage people, especially for activities of a personal nature. A group of people enjoying each other's company is one of the joys of life and wearing this color can help create that loving atmosphere.

Chartreuse

This spiritual energy brings in the emerald green and the lemon yellow ray. I often see this power ray in the Hermetic center. It is a type of balancing power. It's strong and has an energetic, bouncy quality. It helps make you more assertive and expressive. Wearing this color will help you be more outgoing. It's a good color to wear to a dance or social occasion where you are meeting people for the first time. It has an attractive quality and can help draw people to you. This color is an alternative to the emerald green when you are looking for more balance.

Tangerine

This is another color that is not worn often, but has a very uplifting effect in the aura. Similar to the coral, tangerine brings in the pink and orange energies. But in this case there is more orange than pink. This is an excellent color to wear when coming out of a depression or a difficult situation. It is an inspiring color to wear and promotes a feeling of well-being.

Amber

This color is especially popular with amber jewelry. Wearing this color has a very uplifting effect in the aura. It shares qualities with yellow and orange. If you feel blah, dull, or bored, wearing this color can lighten you up; it brings in dynamic power.

WEARING NEUTRAL COLORS

Some colors do not support or detract from the aura. You might say these are "safe" colors, spiritually speaking. Having these colors in your wardrobe is fine, especially if you are in a situation where wearing brighter colors is discouraged. These neutral colors include various light tans (as long as it does not go to the darker "mustard yellow") and very light grays.

Clear brown is an interesting color. (This is not the dark cocoa brown discussed in chapter 3.) Clear brown in the aura indicates an earthy person. It is not an unenlightened color but not exactly one of the enlightened colors, either. It's also not a neutral color because it has an effect in the aura. This color can be good to wear when you feel like you need spiritual grounding.

WEARING DARK COLORS

I remember speaking to a group of students at a fashion institute about the impact color has on the consciousness. These were ambitious students and they were fascinated by the idea of the aura and its colors. I went down a list of colors and their effects. When I got to the part about how wearing black can detract from the aura, there was a silence in the room. Most were wearing black and I don't think they wanted to hear that!

I get a lot of questions about wearing colors that reflect the unenlightened energies of the aura. I have to remind people that I'm not speaking as a fashion expert and not trying to offend anyone who likes wearing these colors. I'm speaking of the spiritual effects of color and can only express what I see and let each person come to his or her own conclusions. I have almost no dark colors in my wardrobe. People buying me gifts know that I simply won't wear something that falls into the darker ranges. I'm too sensitive to their vibration.

As we explored, dark, gloomy colors can detract from the aura. And all colors can reveal aspects about a person. I like to joke, "Don't buy a car from someone wearing avocado green—that person will try and cheat you!" I'm being humorous, but there is some truth in that often we wear colors that reflect our character. So, speaking metaphysically, you want to be wearing the brighter colors. Yet there are situations where you won't have a choice and there are situations where wearing dark colors can be spiritually appropriate.

Intention does make a difference. When wearing black as a minister or priest might wear it, it is a sign of respect and humbleness, as is the brown of the monk or renunciant. Dark colors can be viewed as conservative colors indicating someone who isn't boastful or self-centered. Many uniforms include dark colors, and the people wearing them have little choice. And of course if you are an actor, wearing gloomy colors may be perfect for the character you are playing.

Fortunately you can work with the Divine Light to counteract any negative effect dark colors might be having on your aura. The following is a meditative prayer to use when in a situation where you find yourself with little choice as to the colors you wear. It is recommended that when you are out of that situation or back at home, you change clothing to the brighter shades.

MEDITATIVE PRAYER TO BLESS CLOTHING WITH THE WHITE LIGHT

"Down-ray the pure white light to my spiritual energy centers and
all levels of my consciousness to counteract any negative effects
the clothing I wear might be having on my aura. I ask that this light
go to my unconscious to uplift me in Thy holy light. May my
clothes be filled with the white light to saturate them
with the divine vibrations."

Now, there are situations where wearing very dark colors can actually work for you. This would be where there is a lot of discord around you and essentially you want to detract those energies from yourself. And in some situations wearing bright clothing will make you stand out too much, especially if the people around you are not in a good place spiritually. In these cases, you want to cloak yourself so you do not become a spiritual target. It's a little like wearing spiritual armor. If you are in a job where difficult situations are going on beyond your control, or you are dealing with souls who are not in a strong vibration spiritually, wearing dark colors can be appropriate. When you do this, be discerning. Separate yourself from the colors you wear.

COLOR IN YOUR HOME AND AT WORK

The auric effect of color extends beyond clothing to colors in the home and workplace. Your surroundings affect your consciousness and thereby affect your aura. Creating beauty in your surroundings helps to enhance the aura. Disturbing surroundings can detract from the aura unless you take the time to counteract that effect, which you can do with the Divine Light. You are a being of great color and vitality. Strive to fill your world with color.

When designing color in your home, keep the spiritual understanding of color in mind. The gentle, soothing colors, such as violets, pinks, sea greens, and powder blues, can be very relaxing for your bedroom. The brighter colors, like reds, yellows, and oranges, might work well in your kitchen or dining room or family room. More neutral colors such as white might work well in the living room where people congregate with their many different energies. But even here color can work wonders to help bring people together. Yellow can be wonderful for an office or study room.

Your car and office are two other areas where you may have control. Depending on the kind of work you do, pick colors that reflect that type of profession. If you are an artist or doctor, you'll definitely want the blues somewhere in your office. If you are scientific, the yellows and white will be very good. If you are interacting with people a great deal, a hint of the greens will help bring people together. Combine them with other brighter colors that can encourage activity. A banker or financier would do well to have kelly green or turquoise in his or her profession surroundings.

Of course, these are all just suggestions. The possibilities are endless. As you work with your aura and colors, you will discover an incredible world and wonderful new spiritual support system.

CHAPTER XVI

Reflective Meditation

. . . .

Reflective meditation is a wonderful and simple way to work with the light. If the Higher Self meditation feels a little complicated at first, if you're having trouble concentrating during your meditation, or if you're simply not in the mood to go through the steps of down-raying light, reflective meditation is another way of drawing energy to you. It's wonderful for stilling the consciousness when you are looking for spiritual inspiration and guidance, or simply to feel your oneness with God.

In a reflective meditation you're focusing your attention on an image that's pleasing and uplifting. In your imaging, you visualize the color of the energy you want. By doing this, you're attracting the energy and vibration you're envisioning. For example, if you envision yourself running through a field of bright yellow flowers, you're putting your attention on the beauty and vibrancy of that yellow color. If you really connect with that image and really feel and sense those yellow flowers, this actually triggers the effect of drawing in the lemon yellow energy to you. The energy will not come with the same intensity as it would with your Higher Self meditation, but the connection will be made. This principle of attraction is nothing new. You experience this reflective power when you daydream and let your mind wander to a beautiful tropical island you would like to visit, or in contemplating the face of someone you love. These daydreams have a quality of automatically uplifting you because, for that moment, your consciousness is actually connecting with the person or thing you're contemplating. Reflective meditation is applying this principle.

Reflective meditation helps relax the conscious mind from stresses. By concentrating on mental images that are pleasing and soothing, you will quiet the mind. Once the mind is stilled, the spiritual energy can flow more freely, energizing the mental levels and making them more receptive to the higher flows of light.

You can use reflective meditation for any condition you would work on with your Higher Self meditation, but now you use specific imagery instead of downraying to attract the light you need. To begin your reflective meditation, find a quiet place to do your work as you would with the Higher Self meditation. Light a candle if you wish. You can play a little music if that helps to set the mood. Put your protective light around you and begin. In this case, the only preparation you need is to decide which energy you want to work with and what imagery you want to associate it with. Make the image something that really appeals to you and something you can envision vividly. Then close your eyes and mentally see yourself there. Take your time with this so you really step into the picture, feeling and sensing just what you're envisioning.

A simple use of this imagery is to see yourself receiving a showering of the light you desire. For example, if you're calling on the purple ray of spiritual peace, see this color showering your entire body as if you were in a waterfall. Let it touch into every part of your being, soaking in through the pores of your skin, relaxing and uplifting you in this peace. You can follow the same exercise with each energy you feel you need.

You can use scenes to generate the energy you want. If you're depressed, visualize yourself in a waterfall, and feel orange-red water rushing down over you, releasing you from those dark atoms. Once that's established, envision scintillating sprays of shimmering blue-white water caressing your entire being with beautiful, energetic life force, lifting you out of depression and soul sadness. Enter a pool of emerald green water and feel the balance and harmony of this brilliant green water surrounding you. Try to envision the colors being as rich and as pure as you can. If it is difficult for you to visualize such scenes, let your feeling and sensing take over as you go through your reflective meditation.

If you wish to endow your mental body with more powers of concentration and studiousness, you can take a stroll through a meadow of bright yellow tulips, breathing in and filling yourself with their vibrant yellowness as you become one with its power. Continue to stay in this field until you actually feel energized. If you are lonely and feel unloved, sit on a hill and merge with a deep rose pink cloud and just float, dropping away all the cares of the day. Feel yourself in this beautiful pink cloud, resting in the arms of love. Or run through a field of pink roses and feel the beautiful essence of that pink swirling around you and filling you, until you feel the spiritual love established. There are infinite variations. Through practice, you will find the imagery that works best for you. Let your imagination really take over. Reflective meditation adds wonderful variety to your meditations.

GUIDED IMAGERY

With guided imagery, there is nothing to do but experience. The reflective meditation should be experienced as though you were actually there, and you should encourage your feelings to come through. The best way to follow the scenes depicted here is to record the words and follow along as you play it back.

Forest Setting

Picture yourself at a mountain campsite. It is the start of a rosy-fingered dawn, and the singing of birds is just awakening you. Inside your sleeping bag, you're snug, warm, and cozy. You feel a hint of cool, crisp mountain air brushing your cheeks, inviting you to leave your tent and explore the beautiful forest around you.

You slip quietly out of your sleeping bag, put on your boots, pick up a towel, and step out of your tent. You then breathe in deeply the pine scent of the forest, feeling the life-giving breath filling your lungs and igniting every cell in your body. You stretch your body and lift your eyes, following the line of emerald green pines all the way up to the rosy skies of dawn. You see a path leading away from your campsite and into the forest; you want to find out where it goes. The rich red-brown earth is soft and supports your steps with gentle strength as you proceed along the path. You step on pine needles and hear them snap beneath your feet. You feel the tingle of the cool morning air around your nose and cheeks. You hear a gentle breeze rustling through the leaves. You sense the powerful life force flowing freely all around you, from the rich earth to the tops of the majestic trees. The trees tower over you, enveloping you in their eternal strength and stillness. You are at one with the tranquility of the forest's deep verdant green.

You proceed along the path and discover a clearing, which opens to a gentle cascading waterfall that feeds into a clear shallow pool, the source of a mountain stream. The pool reflects and shows the sky above. Clear blue, with streaks of pink and dancing golden sunbeams sparkling on the water. The sun is warm and the shimmering pool invites you to bathe in its pure, fresh waters. You remove your clothing and wade into the cool, invigorating water, feeling warm golden light as the sun streams down all over your body. You look down to the bottom of the pool and see brightly colored pebbles. They glisten and sparkle like precious gems and jewels, and all at once you feel wealthy, as if you had discovered secret treasures. You stand beneath the waterfall, and, as it washes away all impurities from your being, you feel clean, and renewed as never before.

You leave the pool and the very cells of your skin tingle, clean and alive in the cool air. You dry yourself with your towel, dress, and proceed away from the waterfall, mounting ever higher up the path. The breeze greets your nose with a fragrance so sweet, you feel compelled to learn what awaits you farther along the path. You climb steadily, and suddenly the path opens onto a vast green meadow filled with dazzling wildflowers in full bloom: oranges, reds, violets, pinks, whites, purples, yellows—all swaying joyously in the breeze. You run through the meadow, the brilliant green grass and flowers brushing against your legs, and you feel the warm sun shining down on you. The meadow sweeps upward, and you arrive at the crest of a peak. Your eyes behold panoramic vistas of rich green valleys, majestic purple mountains, and a turquoise sky, resplendent with white and rose pink clouds.

One of these rose pink clouds drifts near you, and you are enfolded in its billowy, loving pink softness. You drift away with this cloud, up into the sky, peacefully, higher and higher. The sun's rays warm and bathe you in the very essence of this deep rose pink light and love. This love and light flow in a rich pink through your mind, your entire nervous system, your entire physical body, and all around you on every side. This love enfolds you. You're feeling its healing power coursing through you, and opening you up to receive greater love, greater peace, and greater joy than you have ever known before.

The cloud now carries you gently back past the meadow, past the waterfall. The cloud then becomes a pink parachute. This pink parachute gently carries you back down to Earth. Gently, gently, it carries you as you slowly drift down to the campsite where your adventure began. You breathe deeply of the morning air once again, and you hold to the feeling, the sensing, and the knowing of what you have experienced in the very heart of your being, knowing that you are renewed. You are at peace, and you will keep that deep peace, tranquility, and serenity with you throughout the coming week.

Island Monastery

You are on a boat going to a tropical island. The water is a clear blue with shades of brilliant emerald green. You disembark and walk across a sparkling white sandy beach. The sand feels like velvet. As you walk, you see a beautiful flower garden and walk into it. The flowers are in beautiful hues and geometric shapes, vibrating their colors to you, enfolding you in their splendor. There are many beautiful birds and animals in the garden. They know you're there and are happy to see you. Beautiful fruit trees also send their vibrations to you. You are attracted to a particular tree that has a profusion of fruit you've never seen before. You pick one of the fruits and bring it to your lips. It's the most delicious morsel you've ever tasted! You are energized by its very flavor. You now move through the garden and realize that you are walking on a brilliant golden path that goes straight up a mountainside. You seem to be gliding effortlessly as you walk the golden path, climbing up the mountain.

Off in the distance, you see a monastery. You climb effortlessly toward it. As you approach, you hear bells chiming—beautiful tones—and you sense an atmosphere of power and light. You approach the monastery and go through the outer gate. This is like no monastery you've ever seen. It's large, with several white buildings, and filled with radiant gardens and fountains. There are brilliant colors everywhere. A monk greets you, dressed in golden robes. No words are spoken, yet there is a sense of love between you and the monk, and you understand each other perfectly. You see the grounds, and buildings of many rooms. The monk lets you wander through the halls on your own. You walk into one of the rooms and see paintings and sacred manuscripts. In a courtyard are enticing, multicolored fountains. You take your clothes off and step lightly into one of the fountains. The water seems to be made of pure light, moving in indescribable symmetrical formations. You are in awe of the beauty.

You step out of the fountain feeling refreshed and put on a magnificent white robe that has been placed on a bench just for you. You then see a circular glass building. You wonder how you'll get in. You don't see a door. The monk appears next to you and places his hand on a panel of glass; the glass slides open and you enter. The monk vanishes again. You walk to the center of this huge circular room. There is a circle of violet living light and a golden chair within that circle. You sit in the chair and feel the energies of the room. Your thoughts and feelings keep rising higher and higher. You look around and admire a magnificent golden dome above you. And as you're looking, a beautiful flow of light from the dome encompasses your entire being, establishing that flow of spiritual light deep within you. The light flows in different colors and seems to be exactly what you need. Then the light stops flowing from the dome. The violet circle that you are sitting in starts rising up all around you, a flame of life-energizing light surrounding your entire being and reaching all the way up to the golden dome. You stay in that flow for a few moments but feel like you could stay there forever. The flame subsides, and you leave the glass building. The monk guides you out of the monastery and down the mountainside. You end up at the boat that brought you to this beautiful place. You say good-bye to the monk, get in the boat, and sail away feeling completely refreshed and revitalized.

Plantation Setting

See yourself wearing a beautiful pink robe, sandals, and belt. You are walking along a gorgeous pathway of pure white light. On both sides of you are nothing but flowers. On the right side are warm colors of pink, red, orange, and yellow; on the left are cooler shades of green, blue, and violet. As you come up the path, you are met by a beautiful white horse. You mount that horse and immediately feel its tremendous spirit, life, and strength. It seems to know exactly where it is going and begins galloping in a flowing rhythm. You feel the breeze blowing through your hair and you feel a thrilling sense of freedom. The horse takes you through a green meadow and, as you ride, it gets greener and greener.

The horse takes you to a pillared mansion that looks like it belongs on a Southern plantation. You get off the horse and go up the steps into the mansion. No one is around. You think to yourself that this is one of the most beautiful homes you have ever seen. You walk inside, and the interior is even more beautiful. You're immediately drawn to a spiral staircase. You ascend to the second floor, which has a long corridor. There are six rooms to the right and six rooms to the left. You go to the first door on the right and enter. The room is huge, lavishly furnished with Louis XIV furniture. The bedspread is a beautiful light blue with little yellow flowers embroidered around its edges. You go to a magnificent bay window, and by that window is an ornamental golden chair, which faces a wall. On that wall is a very large painting.

You sit and study the painting. Your eyes are at once drawn to its focal point—a beautiful emerald green stream. It's very refreshing to look at. Alongside it are trees and little animals scurrying among the rocks. The sun seems to be directly overhead, in its full glory, rays streaming down. As you're looking at all the different things in the painting, suddenly the stream begins to move and become alive. You can feel the rays of the sun and you become one with that light. As you feel that flow enveloping and lifting you, you suddenly find that you have entered the picture and are walking by the water. You pick a spot that calls to you and sit by a rock, looking at the stream.

As you're sitting there, a beautiful ray of white light beams down on you, touching into the very center of your being. You drink deeply of this light, feeling yourself becoming more and more elevated. Then every home you have ever lived in starts flashing through your mind. You feel this light touching into every one of those homes, releasing any unhappy experiences or memories and establishing the radiance of this light in each of them. You feel thankful for what the light is doing. Then you feel another flow of this light touching into every vibration and every person who has ever lived with you in those homes, enfolding them in this light and lifting their spirits. Then the light fades. You feel like a new person. You get up and start walking by the stream, again sensing the sun sending you strength and love. All at once you're back in the bedroom, sitting in the golden chair. Through the window you can see the horse waiting for you. You bid farewell to the room, descend the spiral staircase, pass through the entrance, and get back on the horse. It takes you back to the path of white light where you first began your journey. Once again, you feel completely refreshed and revitalized.

CHAPTER XVII

Affirmations and Visualizations

. . . .

*A*ffirmations and visualizations are two very effective spiritual practices that we can employ to accentuate our spiritual energy work. I have found that not only do these work well by themselves, but used in conjunction with the light, their effect is enormously amplified.

AFFIRMATIONS

The late nineteenth and beginning of the twentieth century saw the blossoming of a spiritual movement called New Thought or, as William James called it, "the Religion of Healthy-Mindedness." The philosophy behind this movement is that our thinking has a direct impact on the quality of our lives, and that by changing our thinking, we can change any aspect of our life. Although we understand this philosophy much better today, at the time it was first introduced such thinking was revolutionary. The famous aphorism "Mind over matter" grew out of this movement. New Thought attempted to show the spiritual dimensions of our thinking, and how by using our mind in the proper way, we align ourselves with the divine scheme of life. Pioneers such as Norman Vincent Peale, Ernest Holmes, Charles Fillmore, and Thomas Troward were the forerunners of this movement, and several very successful religious organizations grew around it. Even today, New Thought is very much alive and continues to prosper and grow.

One of the most effective tools New Thought employs to facilitate mental change is the use of affirmations. The word "affirmation" comes from the Latin word meaning "to strengthen." The principle is that a strong declarative statement can have the effect of reversing a negative belief or attitude. For example, if you're constantly telling yourself "I'm worthless," and really believe it, you probably have created some corresponding negative condition in your life. By refusing that negative thought and replacing it with a sincere, positive affirmation such as "I am a precious child of God," you can create a positive change in your life. Affirmations follow the spiritual point of view that life works from the inside out. If you're already trying to focus on your positive qualities, affirmations can help to keep your consciousness set on your desired goals.

Designing Your Affirmations

You can have a lot of fun with affirmations. Here are a few guidelines for designing your own.

1. *Word your affirmations as if they were already a reality.*

   Your affirmations need to be stated as whole and complete and in the present time. For example, the affirmation "I am losing weight" isn't nearly as effective as "I am at my perfect weight." By seeing yourself already at the goal, you place the goal in the present, and that has the effect of drawing the condition to you.

   Use statements like "I am," as they keep you focused in the present. If you use tentative phrases such as "I will" or "I hope," there's not much conviction there, and your affirmations will have far less positive effect.

2. *Avoid the word "not."*

   The words "not" and "never" are negations, not affirmations. Your consciousness responds best to affirmations. Your affirmation must be a *positive* declaration. You want to affirm what you want— not what you don't want. Instead of saying "I am not sick," for example, you would say "I am in perfect health," or "I *accept* only perfect health," which are both affirmative statements.

3. *Feel what you say.*

You have to really mean what you say; otherwise, what's the point? If you are just saying the words, there is no substance to what you say. This needs to come from your heart. In designing affirmations, find the truth and meaning for you before using them.

THE LIGHT AND AFFIRMATIONS

If you were sitting at a table in a noisy, busy diner and in a quiet, meek voice asked the waitress or waiter for a cup of coffee, what do you suppose would happen? How fast would you get that cup of coffee? Would you even be heard amid all the noise and activity? You'd have to speak clearly and strongly to be heard in such an atmosphere. Affirmations work in a very similar way. If you repeat affirmations but put no power behind them, they will have little meaning. You'll become like a parrot, merely repeating words with little understanding of what you're saying. As a result, they will not carry the force of conviction needed to affect your consciousness.

If you want an affirmation to have impact, it must have power and conviction behind it. Your mental body is busy with many things, and you have to impress it strongly for it to respond to you. We're not talking decibels here; I mean *spiritual power* and sincerity. By putting the Divine Light into an affirmation, you give it far more power and authority. And perhaps most important of all, by using the light with your affirmation, you're infusing the words with some of the divine essence of what you're affirming.

You can call on the light to work with affirmations as a meditation in itself or use them before or after your normal light work. Either way, begin your Higher Self meditation as you normally would. If necessary, do a mental cleansing with the light first to get your mind as clear as possible. When you are in your Higher Self Point, bring down the pure white light to touch into your mental body, quickening it in the light. You can also ask the light to touch into your throat center as well.

MEDITATIVE PRAYER FOR AFFIRMATIONS

"Down-ray the pure white light into my Higher Self Point
and into my mental center to flow into my affirmations, giving
power and conviction to bring forth Thy divine results.
Let this light also touch into my throat center, quickening it
in this Thy light, so that the affirmations spoken move out
with spiritual tone into the vibrated ethers."

When you feel the light is established, start saying your affirmations. Repeat each one three times, feeling the light touching into every word you say. Declare your affirmation unequivocally. You don't have to force it or scream it out, but make it definite. Leave no room for your conscious or subconscious mind to misinterpret what you're saying. As you say the words, see the light moving out with the verbalized thought from your mental center. Hold to the knowing that that thought is now moving into the spiritual ethers, putting into motion and manifesting the affirmation in your life.

Examples of Affirmations

There are many fine examples of affirmations available today. It doesn't matter if you use your own or others', as long as they work for you. I use affirmations a great deal in my classes, because I find it's one of the quickest ways to unify a group of people and get them moving in a creative, positive way. Below are thirty affirmations I have used with great effect.

1. *I am perfect Health, Harmony, and Happiness.*
2. *I am perfect Power, Ability, and Success.*
3. *I am perfect Poise, Peace, and Plenty.*
4. *The kingdom of God, the glory of God, are here and now. I am forever a part of its being.*
5. *The perfect law of God is now operating in my affairs.*
6. *I am free of strain, stress, and fear in my life.*
7. *I am in the presence of radiant joy, of Divine Love, and of perfect power.*

8. *I know that I am drawing my good to me.*

9. *There is a silent power of attraction within me that is irresistible.*

10. *I am without worry about what happened yesterday. I know that today every-thing is made new.*

11. *I let go of all sense of limitation and I take the hand of God. My Father and I walk into the garden of Divine Love and everlasting light.*

12. *I give my full attention to the positive, creative, dynamic powers of God, right here, right now. I erase all illusions and beliefs that obstruction exists, and relax and establish divine order in me now.*

13. *The Divine Spirit of the Conquering Christ transcends all discord.*

14. *The Holy Presence of the Living God has full possession of this body temple and is in complete charge.*

15. *My mind, body, and soul respond only to perfection, beauty, wisdom, purity, and loving thoughts.*

16. *I give thanks that I am the ever-renewing, ever-unfolding expression of infi-nite life, love, health, and energy.*

17. *Divine Love and wisdom go before me, making my way easy and successful, for I am now guided, healed, prospered, and blessed.*

18. *My Father and I are One.*

19. *The light of love shines forth in me as new energy, new peace of mind, new power and dominion, new poise, new beauty, new prosperity, new harmony, and new good in every phase of my life.*

20. *Divine Love foresees everything and richly provides for me now.*

21. *The Spirit of God that dwells within me blesses my mind, heals my body, and prospers my way.*

22. *The divine child of God knows only total freedom and the unlimited life of the Eternal Being.*

23. *God is the creative principle of life, and I am one with all the creative intelli-gence and wisdom of the Father.*

24. *My life is guided by divine intelligence.*

25. *My creative flow is magnificent and perfectly expressed.*

26. *I am prosperous beyond my wildest dreams.*

27. *I am open to give love and to receive love.*
28. *My energy is boundless and I am filled with vitality.*
29. *I have excellent motivation to fill each day fully with harmonious thoughts, words, and deeds.*
30. *I release my past mistakes and the results of those mistakes.*

VISUALIZATIONS

The ability to visualize is one of the most important spiritual traits you possess. You cannot create anything tangible if you have not first visualized it in your mind's eye. When you strongly imagine something, you make an impression on the spiritual fabric of life. That impression has the effect of moving toward materialization. If you back up this visualization through application, it will eventually become a reality. Visualizations are actually God's attribute of divine sight acting in and through your mind. This power of creative visualization exists at all levels of activity, from the simplest creative acts to the greatest inventions or works of art. The universe itself was created from an envisioned, divine idea. So when you are consciously picturing in your mind a desire or a wish that you want fulfilled and projecting that image into life, you are using the most powerful tools of creative invention that exist.

Visualizations can accomplish wonderful things. There was a woman in one of my classes who was not particularly metaphysical, but she really caught on to the idea of visualizations. She was a real estate broker working for a prestigious agency. She somehow knew that by working with the light and visualizations, she could really build up her business. She began using the turquoise ray and visualized that she was closing deals and that lots of money was flowing in. She was so single-minded and diligent in her work that within a few months she had doubled her sales, becoming her company's top producer.

Planning Your Visualization

To be effective in your visualization, carefully plan out what you wish to visualize. The old saying "Be careful what you wish for because you just might get it" is especially true when it comes to visualizations. If you're not thorough in planning your visualization, you might create something you didn't exactly want, or neglect to create something you do want.

I worked with a woman who was visualizing a new job. She was very careful to construct exactly the kind of job she wanted, visualizing her salary, exact duties, and even the hours she wanted to put in. Then, after careful planning, she worked very hard to manifest the situation she designed. She eventually did get the job she wished for and the salary she wanted. But she'd left out one critical element that came back to haunt her—harmony in the workplace. She was so concerned about the nature of the work and the money, that she neglected to envision a congenial work environment. She ended up working in a place where there was friction from her boss and fellow workers. She eventually transferred to another division, where things went much better, but she learned about designing a well-rounded visualization.

God is always your partner in every constructive visualization you create. After all, it's God's vision you're calling on, God's power you're using, and God's spiritual fabric onto which you're impressing this visualization. An ancient spiritual teaching states

God is the Doer, the Doing, and the Deed.

A well-executed visualization is, in essence, tapping into the very creative principle of God and the divine plan for you. With this understanding, begin to plan your visualization. The first step is to determine a definite goal or desire to be fulfilled. What exactly is it that you wish? What do you want to bring forth? It should be constructive, honorable, and worthy of your time and effort. Are you looking for a new job or trying to find a romantic companion? Are you looking to buy a new car or house? Your visualization can be as simple or elaborate as you choose.

I recommend taking a week to plan your visualization. Write down all your ideas of what you want to create. By writing it down, you can look at it more objectively and see if that's what you really want. You can more easily add or take things away. You want to make sure your list includes everything you want. If you get stuck, work with divine guidance, asking, "Illuminate me if there is anything I've left out." Sometimes, the Higher Self will flash in something you haven't seen or thought of.

You may be picturing all the physical features of your visualization and forgetting the essentials, such as peace, love, and joy.

When you are writing down your ideas, do not actually do the visualization exercise yet. Once you have the ideas you want, organize your thoughts and state your plan in words as concisely and clearly as possible. Then you can begin the actual visualization. The following are some guidelines for planning your visualization.

1. *Be specific.*

The more specific you are, the better. For example, if you're looking to buy a new car, don't just visualize a car. See the specific make, model, and color if you can. If you're unsure of the exact thing you want, be very specific about the quality you want. Many times, specific qualities are more important than anything else. For example, if you're looking for a companion, you don't want to go into physical features as much as the qualities you're looking for in the person. Perhaps you want that person to be kind, funny, exciting, etc. This will help you get more clearly into the feeling of what you want.

2. *Be realistic.*

Anything's possible, but obviously the more outlandish your visualization, the harder it will be to realize. If your goals are doable, you're going to see results much faster, creating more excitement and drive. Just use common sense. However, there's nothing wrong with visualizing long-range goals. Just recognize this as a plan that will take greater energy and time to manifest.

3. *Watch your motive.*

Examine your motives for bringing such a creation into expression. You must approach your work constructively. If you're thinking selfishly, you're not going to connect with the God vision and you'll create problems for yourself and others. Your visualization must be a win-win situation for all involved. This is why in the meditative prayer you must include the phrase "according to divine law and love for the good of all concerned." By including that phrase, you are making sure you're putting things in God's hands.

4. *See yourself in the act of doing.*

Whatever you design, see it as something finished, complete, perfect, and in the present. If you're visualizing a new car, see yourself driving that car. If you're visualizing a mate, see yourself with that person, having fun, laughing, walking hand in hand. Or if you're visualizing a new job, see yourself already at that job. As with affirmations, you want your desiring to be active, in the present tense.

5. *Have complete faith.*

Before you start a visualization, it has to be with complete faith in the inevitability of success. If it's really part of God's design, how could it *not* come to pass? If you harbor fears, then you'll be projecting them, which is just the opposite of what you want. You'll be creating two antagonistic images and the result will be confusion.

6. *Don't put a time limit on it.*

This can be hard, especially when you're in desperate need. But once you do a visualization, you must let it go and grow in God's time. If you've done things right, the energy is in motion and will eventually materialize, but you can't dictate the exact route it must take, or even have a preference as to how and when it will come about. If, after a period of time, it still hasn't come to pass, you can reinforce the visualization, or reevaluate the situation.

7. *Keep your visualization to yourself.*

I've seen more beautiful plans knocked off course when people deflate and dilute the whole thing by talking about it. A visualization needs time to grow, and if you talk about it too much, you won't be giving time for the spiritual energy to accumulate, which will most likely neutralize the effectiveness of your visualization.

THE LIGHT AND VISUALIZATIONS

As with affirmations, putting the light into your visualization makes it much stronger. It also helps to keep your visualization constructive and in the light of God's will. The light accentuates God's power, acting within your consciousness to propel the picture you are projecting into your outer world.

Use the Higher Self meditation to bring down the pure white light to activate your visualization. You especially want the white light to touch into your brain cells so that they're receptive to the whole process.

Meditative Prayer for Visualizations

"Down-ray the pure white light into my mental body, charging and recharging all levels of my consciousness, especially quickening my brain cells. I ask the white light to give power and substance to the visualization I am now projecting into the vibrated ethers that it may manifest according to Thy divine law and love for the good of all concerned."

Once you feel your connection with the light, begin your visualization. Feel and sense that the white light is quickening and amplifying the power of whatever you're imagining and giving it life. See yourself actually doing whatever you wish to create. Act it out in your mind. Really *feel it* already happening for you. When your visualization is complete, hold to the knowing that your visualization is now in motion according to divine will. You can repeat the visualization periodically, but give time for the visualization to blossom. If you do something to disturb that knowing, simply repeat the visualization. If after a reasonable period of time it hasn't happened, then you can repeat the visualization, or reevaluate your plan.

CHAPTER XVIII

Parting Thoughts

• •

*I*t has been my privilege and pleasure to bring forth the knowledge contained in these pages. I hope I've instilled in you an enthusiasm to change your life and shown that you have a glorious and divine potential. You are more precious in God's eyes than you can imagine. It is said that if one person were missing from creation, the universe would be incomplete. You are indispensable in the grand plan of life no matter how vast that plan is. In this great adventure, your aura and the spiritual light are true friends you can always rely on, and they are the mainspring of your life's activities and endeavors.

Life cannot stay in the status quo. Activity and change are inevitable. The question is not whether life will change but *how* life will change. The answer to this question is entirely up to you. If you treat life laxly, you won't get much out of it and your progress will be slow. Be bold and take chances. As growth opportunities arise, take advantage of them as best you can.

You are the aura you radiate. When you leave this Earth and move into the hereafter, you're going to leave with the aura you've earned. If your life hasn't been the best, you're not going to suddenly come into a beautiful, saintly aura. You're going to be exactly who you are, so you need to start improving your aura right here and now. Aim to leave this life with a better aura than the one you entered with by continuously building your light through your good thoughts, words, and actions. The light you accumulate will give you a spiritual wealth beyond measure, a wealth that can never be taken from you.

Be alert. The world is a very active place today, and you need to keep your mind keen and razor sharp. Just as there are greater opportunities to grow than ever before, there are also more temptations and distractions that will only steer you away from your true destiny and delay your progress. Take advantage of your spiritual knowledge and awareness to live life according to the highest ideals you can imagine. Recognize that everything you do makes a difference to you and to everyone in the world, for better or for worse. It doesn't matter if your deeds go recognized or unrecognized by others. God sees your actions, and those actions are registered in your aura.

Make it a point to work on your aura every day, to connect with the light, and to infuse your every thought, act, word, and deed with this light. Remember that you carry the spiritual blueprint of yourself with you every minute of every day. Let that blueprint become an expression of Divine Love and wisdom, uplifting not only yourself, but all those who come in contact with you. It's a magnificent path of evolution that leads us upward to the heaven worlds, and eventually to God our Father, Holy Mother.

Quick Reference for Meditation

. . . .

THREE KEYS TO WORKING WITH SPIRITUAL ENERGY

KEY 1—*Decide what you want the light to do for you.*
KEY 2—*Draw the light into your aura.*
KEY 3—*Apply the light to effect the change you desire.*

SIX STEPS TO THE HIGHER SELF MEDITATION

1. *Relax*

    Before beginning any meditation, get into a relaxed state of
    mind. Take your shoes off and uncross your legs. This helps the
    energy to flow more freely.

2. *Establish Protection*

    Envision yourself in a bubble of golden light. Ask that it surround
    you in seven flows of this magnificent energy with the meditational
    prayer for protection.

    "Encircle me now in a golden bubble of protective light.
    I ask for seven flows of this light to surround me,
    keeping me in perfect protection."

3. Check Your Spiritual Centers

Make sure the four main centers are moving *clockwise* (as seen by an outsider facing you). Check your centers by placing your hands, right hand over left, over each center and feel if it's moving clockwise. If not, ask the white light to go to that center and move it clockwise.

4. Connect with Your Higher Self

While sitting upright in a comfortable chair, legs uncrossed, right hand on left over the emotional center, envision a golden sun twenty-four inches above your physical head (your Higher Self Point). Say the invocation:

> "Heavenly Father, Holy Mother God, I raise my consciousness
> into Thy consciousness where I become one with Thee.
> I ask to receive that which I need and that which
> I need to know now."

Feel yourself in a beautiful state of being as you place your attention in your Higher Self.

5. Down-Ray the Light

Ask that the light be down-rayed to you by making a verbal petition (meditative prayer). When you do this, envision the light going first to the Higher Self Point and then beaming down to your four main centers and aura. Three to five minutes for each ray is all you need.

6. Ground Yourself

When you are finished, give your thanks and take a moment to feel the light equalized throughout your aura. Feel you are grounded and centered before ending your meditation.

TEN SPIRITUAL ENERGIES TO WORK WITH

The Orange-Red Flame

Purification, cleansing. Releases black and gray atoms and dissolves them in the mineral kingdom.

The Blue-White Fire

Replenishment, new life force. Always bring it in after working with the orange-red flame. A wonderful healing ray.

The Golden Ray of Wisdom Light

Wisdom, courage, inner strength, self-confidence, faith, divine will, and protection. It brings in the dynamic power of God.

The Deep Rose Pink Ray

Spiritual love, compassion, trust, and understanding. It brings in the magnetic, nurturing power of God.

The Purple Ray

Deep peace. Wonderful for healing grief.

The Emerald Green Ray

Balance and harmony. Especially important to have in the Hermetic center.

The Silver Ray

Divine intelligence, perception. Especially important in the mental body and brain cells.

The Lemon Yellow Ray

Powers of concentration. Very effective when you are studying for a test or assimilating new material.

The Turquoise Ray

Prosperity, supply, and abundance.

The Pure White Light

Spiritual upliftment. It helps to equalize, align, center, and attune the consciousness to the divine impulse.

FOUR MAIN SPIRITUAL CENTERS

(All centers should be moving *clockwise*.)

Mental Center (Trinity Chalice)

Located in the middle of the forehead, this center is the nucleus of your conscious thinking. It's the point where you link up mind, body, and soul with spirit.

Throat Center (Eternal Ego)

Located in the middle of the throat, this center is where you express the power of your words. When you speak positively, your words move out in *spiritual tone*.

Hermetic Center (Heart Center)

Located in the middle of the chest, this center is the nucleus of all your worldly affairs, including persons, places, things, conditions, situations, and the conditions that constitute a situation.

Emotional Center (Spiritual Heart)

Located in the solar plexus behind the navel, this center is the nucleus of your emotional nature, positive or negative.

INDEX

· ·

Barbara Y. Martin is among the foremost clairvoyants and metaphysical teachers in the world. One of the first lecturers on the aura and the human energy field, she speaks across the United States and to a global audience through her highly successful online training classes. She is cofounder of the renowned Spiritual Arts Institute, where she has instructed thousands on working with spiritual energy. Martin is the award-winning coauthor of *Karma and Reincarnation*, *The Healing Power of Your Aura*, and *Communing with the Divine*.

Dimitri Moraitis is cofounder and Executive Director of Spiritual Arts Institute. An accomplished teacher and spiritual healer, he is coauthor of *Karma and Reincarnation*, *The Healing Power of Your Aura*, and *Communing with the Divine*. He teaches with Barbara Martin across the country and online.

Spiritual Arts Institute is an internationally recognized, premier metaphysical educational organization. If you're inspired to go further on your spiritual journey, we offer comprehensive, life-changing programs online and in person. Our mission is to help people reach their full spiritual potential.

Find out how we can serve you by contacting us at:

Spiritual Arts Institute
527 Encinitas Blvd.
Suite 206
Encinitas, CA 92024

Toll-free: 800-650-AURA (2827)
Email: info@spiritualarts.org
www.spiritualarts.org